# THE MATRIX TRILOGY
## CYBERPUNK RELOADED

edited by STACY GILLIS

 **WALLFLOWER PRESS** LONDON & NEW YORK

First published in Great Britain in 2005 by
**Wallflower Press**
6a Middleton Place, Langham Street, London W1W 7TE
www.wallflowerpress.co.uk

A catalogue for this book is available from the British Library.

ISBN 1-904764-32-0 (pbk)
ISBN 1-904764-33-9 (hbk)

Book design by Elsa Mathern

Printed by Thomson Press (India) Ltd.

# CONTENTS

# ACKNOWLEDGEMENTS

This collection emerged from my frustration – and the frustration of my students – at the lack of useful critical sources on such a seminal text – both in film history and in cybertheory – as *The Matrix*. For their enthusiasm for this project and our class discussions (including the ones about cyber-agriculture), I thank those students in my Cybertheory module at the University of Exeter.

I initially approached the contributors in this collection because I respect and admire their work. I can now say that they are also model colleagues, meeting all deadlines and responding with grace, alacrity and intellectual engagement to my comments – for this I thank them heartily.

Heartfelt thanks also to Yoram Allon of Wallflower Press who has known exactly when and what to suggest – he has been a dream editor.

A bout of gratitude is owed to Andrew who not only does not mind how many times I watch *The Matrix* but is also always happy to hear me out.

Finally, much love and thanks to my father, Rod, who first sat me down in front of a TRS-80 and who first watched *The Matrix* with me.

Stacy Gillis
Newcastle, UK
October 2005

# CONTRIBUTORS

**DIANE CARR** is a Research Fellow at the Institute of Education, University of London. Supported by the Eduserv Foundation, she is currently researching the relationship between computer games, motivation, gender and learning. She has published work on various computer games including *Sim City*, *Silent Hill* and *Anarchy Online* and is currently co-writing a volume entitled *Computer Games: Text, Narrative, Play*.

**CATHERINE CONSTABLE** is Senior Lecturer in Film Studies at Sheffield Hallam University. She has a PhD in Philosophy from the University of Warwick and her specialist field of research is philosophy and film. She is the author of *Thinking in Images: Film Theory, Feminist Philosophy and Marlene Dietrich* (2005) and has written articles on postmodernism and film. She is currently writing a book on Jean Baudrillard and the *Matrix* trilogy.

**ANNE CRANNY-FRANCIS** is Associate Professor and Head of the Department of Critical and Cultural Studies, Macquarie University. She has published widely on feminist fiction, media, cultural theory and literacy. Her most recent research is on information technology and includes *Multimedia: Texts and Contexts* (2005).

**THOMAS FOSTER** is Professor of English at the University of Washington. He guest-edited the special issue of the journal *Genders* (1993) on 'Cyberpunk: Technologies of Cultural Identity,' and has published numerous articles on technoculture topics in journals, including *Contemporary Literature*, *Modern Fiction Studies* and *PMLA*, as well as in book collections, including *Cybersexualities* (1999), *The Cybercultures Reader* (2000), and *Reload: Rethinking Women + Technoculture* (2002). He is the author of *The Souls of Cyberfolk: Posthumanism as Vernacular Theory* (2005) and he is currently working on a book entitled *Ethnicity and Technicity: Nature, Culture, and Race in the Cyberpunk Archive*.

**PAMELA CHURCH GIBSON** is Reader in Cultural and Historical Studies at the London College of Fashion. She has published extensively on film, fashion, fandom, history and heritage and has co-edited numerous books, including *The Oxford Guide to Film Studies* (1998) and *Fashion Cultures* (2001). She is currently working on a monograph concerned with cinema, cities and consumption in the post-war period.

**STACY GILLIS** is Lecturer in English at the University of Newcastle. She is the co-editor of *The Devil Himself: Villainy in Detective Fiction and Film* (2002) and *Third Wave Feminism: A Critical Exploration* (2004) and the co-author of *New Popular Feminisms* (2006). She has published articles on cybertheory, feminist theory, modernism and detective fiction in journals such as *Gothic Studies* and *Women's History Review* and in collections such as *Introducing Criticism at the 21st Century* (2002), *More Dirty Looks* (2004) and *Modernism and Mourning* (2006). Forthcoming work includes a monograph on World War One and detective fiction, and a collection on feminism, domesticity and popular culture.

**LISA NAKAMURA** is Assistant Professor of Communication Arts and Visual Culture Studies at the University of Wisconsin, Madison. She is co-editor of *Race in Cyberspace* (2000) and the author of *Cybertypes: Race, Ethnicity, and Identity on the Internet* (2002). She has published articles on cross-racial roleplaying in internet chatspaces, race, embodiment, and virtuality in the *The Matrix*, and political economies of race and cyberspace in publications such as *The Iowa Journal of Cultural Studies, Women's Review of Books, Unspun: Key Terms for Understanding the World Wide Web* (2000), *The Cybercultures Reader* (2000), *Reload: Rethinking Women + Cyberculture* (2002), *Domain Errors! Cyberfeminist Practices* (2002) and the *Visual Culture Reader 2.0* (2003). Her latest publication is a forthcoming volume entitled *Visual Cultures of the Internet*.

**DAN NORTH** is Lecturer in Film at the University of Exeter, specialising in contemporary British cinema, early film and technologies of illusion. He has published articles on special effects, magic theatre and early cinema, and is currently completing a history of virtual performance from mechanical automata to digital actors entitled *Performing Illusions: Special Effects and the Coming of the Virtual Actor* (forthcoming from Wallflower Press).

**KATE O'RIORDAN** is a researcher at the Centre for Social and Economic Aspects of Genomics (CESAGen) at Lancaster University, whilst on study leave from the University of Sussex. She has previously published work on gender and computer games in *Technospaces: Inside the New Media* (2001), medical imaging and female bodies in *Reload: Rethinking Women + Cyberculture* (2002), and identity, the internet, ethics and online community in the *International Journal of Sexuality and Gender Studies, Women and Everyday Uses of the Internet: Agency & Identity* (2002) and the *Journal of Ethics* *and Information Technology.* Her research interests are in the material and theoretical relations between bodies and technologies.

**ANDREW SHAIL** is Lecturer in Film at the University of Northumbria. The co-editor of *Menstruation: A Cultural History* (2005), he has also published on male feminism in *Third Wave Feminism* and on early British cinema history in the *Journal of Popular British Cinema.* His current work includes a monograph on the origins of the DC comics superhero.

**PAUL SHEEHAN** is a Research Fellow at Macquarie University. He is the author of *Modernism, Narrative and Humanism* (2002) and the editor of *Becoming Human: New Perspectives on the Inhuman Condition* (2003). He contributed a chapter on postmodernism and philosophy to *The Cambridge Companion to Postmodernism* (2004) and is currently working on a historical poetics of violence and aesthetics in literature and film.

**CLAUDIA SPRINGER** is an independent scholar living in Newton, Massachusetts. Previously she was was a Professor in the English Department and Film Studies Program at Rhode Island College for nineteen years. She is the author of *Electronic Eros: Bodies and Desire in the Postindustrial Age* (1996).

**AYLISH WOOD** is Lecturer in Film Studies at the University of Kent. Recent work includes articles in the journal *Screen, Technoscience in Contemporary American Film* (2002) and in *Action and Adventure in Cinema* (2004).

# INTRODUCTION
Stacy Gillis

I had the unique opportunity of sitting close to the ideal spectator of the film – namely, an idiot. A man in his late twenties seated to my right was so immersed in the film that he all the time disturbed other spectators with loud exclamations, like 'My God, wow, so there is no reality!' I definitely prefer such naïve immersion to the pseudosophisticated intellectualist readings that project into the film the refined philosophical or psychoanalytic conceptual distinctions.

– Slavoj Žižek (2001: 213)

When *The Matrix* was released in 1999 it did not achieve immediate blockbuster success and it was only the timely growth in the DVD market that brought the film its commercial success. Despite these not overwhelming beginnings, *The Matrix* has gone on to stake a claim as a must-see film. Its two sequels, *The Matrix Reloaded* (2003) and *The Matrix Revolutions* (2003), may have not had the same cultural and critical resonance as the first film but they were *the* box-office event of 2003, so much so that Warner Bros. designated 2003 'the Year of the Matrix'. The disappointment felt by some at the two sequels speaks to the way in which *The Matrix* had become, in the four years since its release, a vital point in the history of popular culture, film studies and cultural theory. The films have had more material published on and about them since the release of the first film than any other film in the same length of time. Joshua Clover notes this appeal:

It's a visual object, and much of its meaning must reside there. It's also a significant event in the history of film – its industry, its audience – and this too demands accounting. But, inescapably, it's a movie that alternately whispers and bellows its possession of Big Ideas; to ignore these cries would be as foolish as to accept them without question. (2004: 13)

An account of only a few of the mainstream publications – William Irwin's *The Matrix and Philosophy* (2002), Karen Haber's *Exploring The Matrix* (2003), Michel Marriot's *The Matrix Cultural Revolutions* (2003), Chris Seay and Greg Garrett's *The Gospel*

*Reloaded* (2003), Glenn Yeffeth's *Taking the Red Pill* (2003), Matthew Kapell and William G. Doty's *Jacking in to the Matrix Franchise* (2004) and Matt Lawrence's *Like a Splinter in your Mind* (2004) – give some indication of how the imaginary of the films has seized the popular imagination. Jonathon Romney notes that the sequels spun 'the original premise of *The Matrix* into a nexus of interlocking fictions which, taken together, lead the consumer down a choice of diverging narrative paths' (2003: 24). Similarly, it is apparent that the 'Big Ideas' to which Clover refers have been dissected in a diverging variety of publications.

The critical and popular interest in the *Matrix* films can only be partly ascribed to the fact that they are an intersection of early twenty-first-century debates about virtual reality and cyberspace. The fact that the official website for the films – http://whatisthematrix.warnerbros.com – contains a philosophy section indicates the ways in which the films have been marketed as speaking to contemporary debates about such topics as history, time, space, pastiche, memory, simulacra and authenticity, the interrogation of which can be loosely grouped under the umbrella term of postmodernism. Romney points out that 'in the most extravagant example yet of an attempt to extend a science fiction film's demographic target beyond the usual fan base, the *Matrix* films have been intensively sold as fertile ground for philosophers' (2003: 25). But in what ways might the films also speak to the concerns of the last two centuries, in their reflection upon the body, the city and technology, tensions which may be ascribed to the text that is science fiction, but which also mark much of the cultural production of the West since the Industrial Revolution? The *Matrix* films indicate the way in which science fiction gives voice to widely circulating concerns in a variety of texts: 'Science fiction in this sense is no longer anywhere, and it is everywhere, in the circulation of models, here and now, in the very principle of the surrounding simulation' (Baudrillard 1981: 126). While Jean Baudrillard is here referring generally to the ways in which simulation – a crucial element of his account of postmodernity – has generated (and been generated by) science fiction, one of the specific ways in which this manifests itself is the failure of science fiction and its concerns to be contained as a genre. In return, the films engage in dialogue with both popular culture and cultural theory, bringing together these two groups which may have been identified, within postmodernism, as speaking to one another but which, at times, are felt by their practitioners and by their observers to be speaking very different languages and very different pleasures, as Sean Cubitt describes:[1]

> There are pleasures in recognising *Alice in Wonderland*, Jean Baudrillard, or the cityscapes of Sydney, the signature wirework of Yuen Woo-Ping and the comic book art of Geoff Darrow. Some of these multiple pleasures compile together in complex harmonies, some are threads worked through the textile of the film. Each is in the process subordinated to the film and thence to its consumption on a global scale. (2004: 346)

The *Matrix* trilogy achieves this not only through its wealth of references for the scholar and the film fan, but also through the complexity of the narrative which is contained within the Hollywood film structure. The potency of the films thus lies in their ability to appeal to both the popular audience and the cultural theorists.

## CYBERPUNK(ED): BODY, CITY, TECHNOLOGY

The literary movement cyberpunk is considered by some to have died the moment the label was applied to a specific sort of new science fiction in the early 1980s, of which William Gibson's *Neuromancer* (1984) and Ridley Scott's *Blade Runner* (1982) are the most often cited examples. Some consider the genre to be moving into its third generation, with Gibson and Bruce Sterling at the forefront of the first generation, Neal Stephenson at the forefront of the second and the post-dotcom writers forming the third. For others, it was a transitory shift, as Scott Bukatman argues: 'As a literary movement, cyberpunk ended almost as soon as it began, but its impact continues to be felt across a range of media and cultural phenomena' (1997: 52). Reports of the death of cyberpunk, however, are greatly exaggerated. While Neil Easterbrook refers to the critical antipathy expressed towards science fiction as provoking 'Genre Wars' (2000: 510), something which Marleen S. Barr picks up on in her introduction to the *PMLA* special issue on science fiction (2004), the critical antipathy of the academy towards genre fiction does not apply to cyberpunk. It holds a rather anomalous space in these debates because of its punk qualities which appeal to the would-be academic rebel and because of the über-contemporary sexiness of its language and style. In this way it is clear that cyberpunk should be understood as an aesthetic rather than an institution of cultural production. That is, the name-object cyberpunk can be understood to not exist when used to refer to a text (for example, *Neuromancer* is a cyberpunk novel) – but the descriptor cyberpunked does. Fredric Jameson obliquely addresses this when he argues that

> cyberpunk determines an orgy of language and representation, an excess of representational consumption, as a way of talking yourself into it and making, more than a virtue, a genuine pleasure and *jouissance* out of necessity, turning resignation into excitement and the baleful persistence of the past and its prose into high and addiction. (1991: 321)

This is not to say that cyberpunked texts are more about style than substance but that, in engaging with disintegration, fragmentation and discontinuity in *specific* relation to issues surrounding the body, the city and technology, they are an aesthetic which allows us to give voice to concerns contained within both modernity and postmodernity.[2] While 'cyberpunk' has been traditionally understood as providing an epistemological language or emotional structure for late twentieth-century technological developments, 'cyberpunked' should be understood to refer to wider debates concerning the body, the city and contemporary technology, debates which do not necessarily take place only within the pages of science fiction.

Cyberpunk has been understood to articulate the tensions between human and machine, often through the abjection of the corporeal, apparently exemplified by the cyberspace cowboy Case in *Neuromancer*. Gibson famously wrote 'The body was meat. Case fell into the prison of his own flesh' (1984: 12). This is echoed by Agent Smith in *The Matrix*, when he says 'I can taste your stink'. But in assigning this attitude to the Agents the films switch from disowning the body – the subject of much cybertheory in the 1990s[3] – to celebrating the body. Although the hackers in the *Matrix* films may possess the ability to enter the Matrix and – certainly so in the case of Neo – to hack expertly through it, they choose bodies which largely correspond to their 'real' bodies. This virtual body or 'residual self-image' is *their* body, not *a* body or a consciousness. This celebration of the physical body is an elaboration upon the Enlightenment binary of human and machine. Veronica Hollinger argues that although cyberpunk seeks to interrogate the categories of human and machine – decentering 'the human body, the sacred icon of essential self' (1990: 33) – this critique collapses as a result of the conventions of the genre. Cyberpunk, for Hollinger, is concerned with 'the reinsertion of the human into the reality which its technology is in the process of shaping' (1990: 42). While the term 'posthuman' has gained increasing currency since the late 1990s, the perhaps too-quick bringing together of 'post' and 'human' often manages to obscure the unfinished debates surrounding the Enlightenment notion of the body. For example, while many refer to *Neuromancer* as a prime example of the exaltation of the mind in cyberspace over the body at the keyboard, this text which has been claimed as *the* cyberpunk(ed) text, actually articulates a number of tensions concerning the virtual body:

> 'How you doing, Dixie?'
> 'I'm dead, Case. Got enough time in on this Hosaka to figure that one.'
> 'How's it feel?'
> 'It doesn't.'
> 'Bother you?'
> 'What bothers me is, nothin' does ... This scam of yours, when it's over, you erase this goddam thing.' (Gibson 1984: 130)

Dixie so dislikes existing virtually – *without* a body at the keyboard – that he wants to be digitally erased. The kinetic and sensory pleasures of the body are a source of desire for Dixie, the obverse to Case's naïve rejection of the physical.[4] A cyberpunked text, then, would be one which is not necessarily bound by the conventions of genre, nor by theoretical configurations such as the posthuman. In this way, the tensions which mark *The Matrix* when labeled a 'cyberpunk' text are avoided as are the prescriptiveness of categories such as the posthuman.[5]

The city is one of the more resonant images of the urban in cyberpunked texts, with its noir atmosphere and pastiched architecture. Janet Staiger, in her essay on what she terms future noir, argues that one 'of the most immediate signifiers of the genre of science fiction is the representation of the known city in which readily distinguishable sections of today's landscape are present while other parts are rewritten' (1999: 97). The Sprawl in *Neuromancer*, the decaying metropolis in *Blade Runner*, the Burbclaves in Neal Stephenson's *Snow Crash* (1992) and the anonymous city in the *Matrix* films illustrate the ways in which notions of the contemporary cities are (uncannily) re-modelled in cyberpunked texts. Anne Marie Balsamo posits that the cyberpunk genre is concerned with capitalist structures of globalisation, configuring 'the space of the social as a landscape structured by the network of relations among multinational capitalist corporations' (1996: 137), a notion which is supported by Fredric Jameson's point that the generic structure of cyberpunk is an attempt to 'think the impossible totality of the contemporary world system' (1991: 38).[6] But these bases of cyberpunking must not be allowed to claim a genre. The cities of cyberpunked texts also articulate a relationship between the body and 'the public' which stretches back through literary history. As Charles Baudelaire wrote,

> For the perfect *flâneur*, for the passionate spectator, it is an immense joy to set up house in the heart of the multitude, amid the ebb and flow of movement, in the midst of the fugitive and the infinite. To be away from home and yet to feel oneself everywhere at home; to see the world, to be at the centre of the world, and yet to remain hidden from the world – such are a few of the slightest pleasures of those independent, passionate, impartial natures which the tongue can but clumsily define. (1995: 9)

The model of the *flâneur* is one which might be usefully deployed in speaking of what kind of bodies inhabit cyberspace, particularly in how these bodies engage with the information therein. Neo is a *flâneur*, always watching, always slightly detached but also only 'alive' – in that his 'function' as 'the One' is to hack the Matrix – when in the cyber-city which constitutes the Matrix. Looking beyond the generic conventions of cyberpunk to a cyberpunked aesthetic – one concerned with the body, the city and technology – enables the historical progression behind such texts as Baudelaire's 'The Painter of Modern Life' and Andy and Larry Wachowski's *The Matrix* to emerge.

Science fiction is not the expression of anxiety about technological change *per se*; rather, it is based on the prediction of technological change. Without the 'promise' of changes in technology, science fiction could not exist, whereas, crucially, 'through the language, iconography and narration of science fiction, the shock of the new is aestheticised and examined' (Bukatman 1997: 8). That is, science fiction stabilises the conception of modernity as a matter of novel shocks. The 'consensual hallucination' (1984: 12) of Gibson's cyberspace is merely one – albeit the most often quoted – example of this symbiosis, a symbiosis which marks any text concerned with technology and the technological. The *Matrix* trilogy both celebrates and criticises technological change, an ambivalence which could be claimed as being at the crux of postmodernity, through the medium of hardware, software and cyberspace. In her work on the cyber-thrillers of the 1990s, Claudia Springer points out that cyberspace in film functions to denote the dangerous and the unstable: 'cyberspace is constructed as an instigator of wild instability, and simultaneously as a therapeutic device used to restore conventional order' (1999a: 206). For example, Flynn, entering cyberspace in *TRON* (1982), initially finds himself instantly deletable but, subsequently, his new abilities lead to a previously impossible narrative resolution outside of cyberspace – that is, destroying the Master Control Program takes the corporation down from the inside. The *Matrix* films offer a notion of cyberspace in which the body and technology can be understood as not in opposition to one another, but in a continuum. There is nothing new in describing the body as hardware or software – or vice-versa – but the *Matrix* films suggest a relationship in which the one cannot be obviated by the other. Such narrative invocations as, for example, Shaolin kung-fu's belief in a continuum between mental and physical energies, symptomises the films' presentation of cyberspace as a place where the mind itself is meat: death in the Matrix is also death outside of the Matrix. Keeping images of technology ambiguous – as Tim Blackmore points out, 'we are told that thinking technologies are the enemy [yet] Morpheus' crew uses a great deal of high technology to fight the Matrix' (2004: 26)[7] – the *Matrix* trilogy continues to refer to beliefs in change ratifying the discourse of modernity as much as to refer to the discourse of postmodernity.

## 'THERE'S WAY TOO MUCH INFORMATION TO DECODE THE MATRIX'

The chapters in this collection are loosely divided into two sections – 'Media Intertexts and Contexts' and 'The Politics of Modernity and Postmodernity' – which are intended to act as guides to how the *Matrix* texts can be read and understood. The six chapters in the first section conceive of the *Matrix* texts as media forms, with topics such as the 'intertext' governing the production of 'high concept', the cinematic body and science fiction cinema, the relationship between gaming and cinema, the functions of special effects, the narrative function of the computer, and the history of noir. The seven chapters in the second section approach the *Matrix* texts as products of such historical matrices as race politics, discourses of movement technology, twentieth-century fashion, representational agendas of cyberspace, the visualities of race, postmodernity and social systems, and Western philosophies of the individual. The work of the contributors on the *Matrix* films constitutes part of the wider discussion of the event that is *The Matrix*. However, all the chapters are also firmly located within the above-discussed debates concerning the body, the city and technology. In this way, this volume should be of interest not only to historians of popular culture, film studies and cultural theory, but also to those who are interested in cyberpunk and contemporary science fiction more generally.

The narrative structure of the *Matrix* films is not particularly unique – whether it be the quest narrative of 'the One' or the notion that reality is a hallucination. One could say pretty much the same thing about the non-exclusivity of the narratives in *Alien* (1979), *Blade Runner* or *The Terminator* (1984), films which are now considered to be 'canonic touchstones not just for discussions of difference but also for those engaged in debates about "postmodernism" and the nature of "postmodern" aesthetics and representation' (Neale 2000: 103). The chapters in this collection suggest that *The Matrix* belongs in this category of films, of 'canonic touchstones' not just for film scholars but also cultural theorists. But should it? Whereas Slavoj Žižek feels that the ideal viewer of *The Matrix* is an idiot, Clover's volume on *The Matrix* for the British Film Institute's 'Modern Classics' series attempts to cut to the heart of the matter and to the tensions the films raises between popular culture and cultural theory:

> The anxiety isn't about the real, but about what our relationship to the real should be. Or, just as passionately per the predilections of postmodernism, what our relationship to the fake should be. Another way of initiating the same curiosity would be to ask why, exactly, superstar postmodernists like Slavoj Žižek come to devote themselves to speculating about a popular movie? (2004: 31)

But neither film scholars nor cultural theorists, although rarely popularly read themselves, need to be told to concern themselves with the popular. The *Matrix* franchise has made much of 'sensationally' making 'refined philosophical or psychoanalytic conceptual distinctions' (Žižek 2001: 213) popular but the ideas concerning the body, the city and technology which form and inform these films and their intertexts have always been embedded within the popular.

## NOTES

1   See Carl Freedman (2000) for more on the relationship between critical theory and science fiction.
2   Ziauddin Sardar makes the point that science fiction is predicated upon a particular understanding of science: 'science fiction employs the particular constellations of Western thought and history and projects these Western perspectives on a pan-galactic scale. Science fiction re-inscribes Earth history, as experienced and understood by the West, across space and time' (2002: 2).
3   See my 'Cybersex' (2004) for an account of these debates.
4   Just within Gibson's *oeuvre*, these tensions are further problematised by Bobby Newmark,

who is permanently in cyberspace although retaining a comatose physical body, in *Mona Lisa Overdrive* (1988) and by the virtual idoru in *Idoru* (1996).

5  For example, Laura Bartlett and Thomas Byers argue that while '*The Matrix* is in many ways a cinematic example of the cyberpunk genre, it is as much an affront as a homage to that movement … *The Matrix* places posthuman subjects at the centre of its action and flirts with a theoretical postmodenism only to reject the posthumanist configuration of subjectivity in favour of resurrecting a neo-Romantic version of the liberal-humanist subject' (2003: 30). For more on the debates surrounding the posthuman in the 1990s, see N. Katherine Hayles (1999).

6  For more on this see Joshua Clover (2004: 71–6) and Ronnie D. Lipschutz, who makes the point that '*The Matrix* can be understood as an inverted allegory of globalisation, about the consumer's alienation from physical reality promoted by commodity fetishism, the broadly advertised opportunities they are offered to purchase escapes into fantasy world, and a general inability on their part to perceive how the capitalist system operates' (2003: 92).

7  The same ambiguity is the aim for the less technologically saturated moments in the films, such as the Oracle's implication that, as Jason Haslam points out, Neo's 'identity is in fact a determined one, not the self-contained individual of Enlightenment ontology' (2005: 104).

# MEDIA INTERTEXTS AND CONTEXTS

# VECTORIAL DYNAMICS: TRANSTEXTUALITY AND COMPLEXITY IN THE MATRIX
Aylish Wood

## ENCOUNTERING THE MATRIX

Though the critical reception of the trilogy of the *Matrix* films has been one of diminishing returns, the phenomenon of the Matrix, by which I mean the extensive story-world created through multi-media products, continues to expand.[1] Much of the attention paid to the Matrix has been devoted to the trilogy, with frequent discussions of special effects, nested realities and representations of humans and technologies.[2] The Matrix, however, is complex and multifaceted, created by the intersection of numerous texts adding motivating histories, expanding and transforming through additional narratives and different multi-media conventions of story-telling. The most prominent of these texts remains the *Matrix* trilogy – *The Matrix* (1999), *The Matrix Reloaded* (2003) and *The Matrix Revolutions* (2003) – all written and directed by Andy and Larry Wachowski. But these co-exist with *The Animatrix* (2003), a collection also heavily marketed, including the use of one of the animations, *Final Flight of the Osiris*, as a teaser in the cinema prior to the global release of the DVD and video. *The Animatrix* collects together nine animations, directed at studios in Tokyo (Studio4oC and Madhouse), Seoul (DNA), and the USA (Square USA). Though all the animations draw on the story-world of the Matrix, only four were written by the Wachowski brothers – *Final Flight of Osiris*, *The Second Renaissance Part I*, *The Second Renaissance Part II* and *Kid's Story*. *The Matrix Comics* (2003) provides another resource for variations on the Matrix theme, though is itself only a selection from a larger collection of stories available at http://whatisthematrix.warnerbros.com. Excepting 'Bits and Pieces of Information' (Darrow, Wachowski and Wachowski 2003) each story was written and drawn by different combinations of writers and artists, though the contents page states: 'all stories based on concepts by Larry and Andy Wachowski.' The computer game *Enter the Matrix* (2003), the multiplayer game *The Matrix On-line* (2004) and the online fan-writing sites, while also based on concepts by the Wachowski brothers, are equally the work of game programmers and fans.[3]

The extensive list of texts outlined above points to the centrality of the Wachowski brothers as authorial progenitors of the Matrix story-world. The list equally establishes the elements from which that story-world is generated as a network of intersecting and overlapping texts. It is not simply the individual texts that produce the story, but also the connections between them. Writing in the introduction to *The Matrix Comics*, Spencer Lamm comments:

> It was Andy and Larry who suggested we do comics, back in the very first days. Not adaptations, to be clear, but new stories. We figured, 'Why create adaptations when the film already tells that particular story? Why be redundant?' Years forward, of course, the brothers would take this to new heights, crisscrossing the plots of the game *Enter the Matrix*, the anime series *The Animatrix*, and yes the comics, too, with the films themselves. (2003: 4)

As Lamm accentuates the place of the Wachowski brothers as the creative origin of the stories, he draws attention to the crisscrossing of plots between different media. However, the connections between the texts need not simply be put down to the interwoven plots, but also to the extent with which they work off and against each other as additions, reflections, prequels or sequels. The very fact that these connections in themselves begin to generate meaning, destabilises the place of the Wachowski brothers as the origin of every element of the story-world.

I will here investigate not so much the destabilised authorial status of the Wachowski brothers, but rather the distinctiveness of the Matrix as a complex text, paying particular attention to the emergence of non-linearity across the dimensions of its networked organisation. Through the idea of non-linear connections I expose the different ways these interconnections disturb the chronologies implied by transformative textual interplay, and how origins of narrative histories and aesthetic codes are put into question in the same way as the authorial status of the Wachowski brothers. In making this argument I mobilise two terms that require further definition: architecture and vectorial dynamics. Describing the textual body of the Matrix as an architecture is to some extent self-evident, as it suggests a group of elements fitting together to form a structure. But where architecture more conventionally means a stable structure, the Matrix slips between an actual and virtual presence. Actual in the sense that each element exists, both in a substantive form as a text and also as a more contingent form established through transtextual connections; virtual in the sense that not all potential connections are active, remaining possibilities rather than actualities. The architecture of the Matrix is, then, described by substantive textual elements as well as the actual and virtual connections present between them. These connections can be further conceptualised in terms of vectorial dynamics. A vector designates directionality, pointing from one location towards another, and as such is a term that can define intertextual connections. However, in this chapter I want to keep in play the idea that complex non-linear relations lead to intertextual connections able to turn back on themselves, creating dynamic circuits of connection rather than unidirectional ones.

## THE MATRIX AS COMPLEX TEXT

The world of the Matrix exists within popular culture through a network of interrelated texts. As an example of aggressively diversifying commodification the Matrix has effectively established itself in the marketplace, but the unusual configuration of its textual body marks it out as distinctive. The Matrix is a network created through a series of iterations on a story that is a staple of the science fiction genre: the relationship between humans and technologies. Through a series of involutions, convolutions and revolutions, every individual text offers a set of embellishments on that relationship. And though each of these texts can be read, seen or played on their own, encountered as discrete stories in a range of media, when taken as an interplaying set of texts they constitute an entity constructed through non-linear relations. The presence of non-linear relations in the architecture of the Matrix troubles the stability of claiming any particular element as an origin within the system.

### Hypertextuality and the Matrix Architecture

The complexity of the interplay between its individual texts distinguishes the Matrix from other co-existing multi-media versions of a story. In many cases, the multi-media versions primarily serve the function of expanding the consumer base.[4] But in addition to the different intertextual connections simply activating and mobilising audiences, they are also adaptations, transformative repetitions of elements of a story between different kinds of media. The Matrix texts are similar in that each feeds into other texts as extended stories, as backdrops, backgrounds, sequels, expansions and histories; for example, 'A Life Less Empty' by Ted McKeever in *The Matrix Comics* tells the story of a regretful hacker who opted to take the blue pill. Despite this similarity, the Matrix is a very particular instance of the process of adaptation across media boundaries, as the extensiveness of its architecture creates a potential for complex circuits of interaction lacking in other examples. The distinctiveness of this transformation is explored below by approaching the textual architecture of the Matrix as a hypertext. In his essay 'Beyond Fidelity: The Dialogics of Adaptation', Robert Stam introduces the idea of hypertextuality by drawing on Gérard Genette's ideas of transtextuality, a term which refers to 'all that which puts one text in relation, whether manifest or secret, with other texts' (quoted in Stam 2000: 65). In using hypertextuality to discuss the Matrix I extend it from a chronologically distinct, serial process of adaptation, towards one that is non-linear. This shift is achieved by drawing on some elements of theories of complexity where interconnections between the elements of a system are understood to be non-linear.

The unusual textual architecture of the Matrix presents an opportunity to explore transtextual complexities existing between different versions of the same story. Stam's article, though discussing more conventional modes of adaptation, primarily between novels and film, develops a model that is particularly appropriate to the Matrix texts as it emphasises intersections between texts as creative sites of transformation. As Stam notes:

> Adaptations can take an activist stance towards their source novels, inserting them into a much broader intertextual dialogism. An adaptation, in this sense, is less an attempted resuscitation of an originary word than a turn in an ongoing dialogical process. The concept of intertextual dialogism suggests that every text forms an intersection of textual surfaces. (2000: 64)

Amongst a range of possible intersections, Stam includes hypertextuality, where a hypertext follows another, the hypotext. While the hypotext exists prior to the hypertext, it is not necessarily the original in a series; more specifically, it precedes the hypertext which the latter 'transforms, modifies, elaborates or extends' (Stam 2000: 66). As such the hypotext can be a single text, or a cumulative one formed from a number of prior adaptations.

Though the idea of a dialogic emerging around intersecting adaptations is useful to thinking about the Matrix, Stam's version of hypertextuality also invokes a seriality that works against complexity. In establishing hypertextual interplay as a step from an anterior text to a posterior one, the repetition of elements occurring in the process of adaptation takes place via a single but chronologically distinct iteration between one text and another. Such an iteration occurs with The Remains of the Day (1993) – from the previously published novel – or The Addams Family (1991) and Charlie's Angels (2000) – from earlier television series. Even if there is a multiplicity of adaptations, for example the numerous adaptations of William Shakespeare's Romeo and Juliet, there is a seriality in the chronology of their creation.[5] Adaptations involving what might be called several orders of iteration across a range of hypotexts also retain a strong sense of seriality. The Batman films and Hulk, are hypertexts of comic versions of these superhero narratives.[6] Chronologically the films are also preceded by television series, in both live-action and cartoon formats. Taken as a body of texts they each co-exist as overlapping surfaces, and their intersections have the potential to be more complicated, with multiple points of transformation co-existing across the three texts. Nevertheless, there remains the sense of a moving through a series of texts: from comic to television to films.

## From Serial Iterations to Vectorial Dynamics

The Matrix has a different kind of textual organisation, both in the sense of intersections and chronology. The overall concept of hypertextuality remains pertinent since it has an embedded flexibility that extends to give an account of intersections based on networks, rather than a more simple seriality. The Matrix texts provide a particularly rich series of transformation through the multiple degrees of iteration across all the different media, crossing boundaries of both media and versions of stories, a point I return to more fully below. In addition, the different chronological relationship disperses the seriality of adaptation, producing a more temporally truncated circulation of meaning. John Ellis argues that 'adaptation trades on the memory of a novel … a generally circulated cultural memory' (1982: 3), but in the case of the Matrix texts the cultural memory is short-term since all its elements have appeared in the public arena between the release of *The Matrix* in 1999 and *The Matrix Revolutions* in 2003. According to the stories surrounding the elusive Wachowski brothers, while the initial film, *The Matrix*, was pitched as a stand-alone script to producer Joel Silver, following its success the two conceived of the sequel films plus the multi-media comics, computer game and animations. The absence of any clearly delineated trajectory in the creation of the Matrix makes the question of adaptation less distinct, though the idea of hypertextuality remains useful. If fidelity, as an approach to adaptation, relies on an ability to map and seek matches or mismatches between elements in related texts, hypertextualities take repetition for granted and generates meaning from the intersections between the texts. Furthermore, in the case of the Matrix, the extensiveness of intersections, which include broader cultural allusions, begins to put pressure on a serial understanding of repetition or iteration.

As a mathematical term, iteration is a form of repetition. At its simplest it repeats a particular term over a predetermined number of times, and the outcome is predictable. At their simplest, each of the Matrix texts is an iteration of the central idea of a world in which humans are enslaved by machines, and excepting the Resistance, the humans live their lives unaware of their enslavement. At its most complex, iteration leads towards unpredictable outcomes. Such is the case in chaos theory, where the original term defining the element to be repeated is itself not fully known. There is something of this complexity in the iterations of the Matrix. Each text represents an iteration of the central idea, but in addition carries over a network of hypertextualities whose points of contact exist across a number of texts as well as intertexts.[7] Although the creation myth of the Matrix may evoke *The Matrix* as the originary text, the iteration of its storyline into a multiplicity of texts that additionally cross media boundaries, generate 'multileveled negotiation of intertexts'.

The network of hypertextual intersections existing within the architecture of the Matrix disperses the seriality of adaptation by creating a non-linear organisation of interaction. The idea of non-linearity within a network of intersections resonates with complex systems. Already prevalent in thinking about biological systems, complexity theories have been extended to social systems.[8] Though I am not suggesting the Matrix constitutes a complex system in the sense of either biological or social systems, some of the language of complex modelling is fruitful in thinking about its textual system. In *Complexity and Postmodernism* Paul Cilliers lays out a set of criteria for defining complex systems. A central term is non-linearity, where the links between the different elements of a system, rather than being connected in series or parallel, are instead connected via a network: 'a complex system is not constituted merely by the sum of its components, but also by the intricate relationships between these components' (1998: 2). This distinction echoes the extended hypertextuality of the Matrix. Though it is easy to point to the different elements that make up the textual architecture of the Matrix – the trilogy of films, two kinds of computer-based games, animations, comics – the complexity of the Matrix more fully emerges in the circuits of vectorial dynamics established by their interplay.

## THE MATRIX AND DISPLACED ORIGINS

I have presented a case for seeing the architecture of the Matrix as a complex interplay of overlapping and intersecting texts. An outcome of complexity is the presence of non-linear relations between texts bringing pressure to bear on questions of chronology and origin. The displacement of origin impacts on the Matrix in a number of different ways, and will be addressed below by tracing several narrative and aesthetic examples. The blurring of narrative origins is explored by looking at the interplay between Matrix texts. *The Animatrix* includes two linked animations – *The Second Renaissance: Part I* and *Part II* – and though their combined narrative is presented as a pre-history for the *Matrix* trilogy, the nature of the connections between the animations and the trilogy problematises the apparently simple chronology of a pre-history. The question of origin is further destabilised in the narrative interplay between *Enter the Matrix*, *The Animatrix* and *Matrix* trilogy, where one text appears to fill gaps in the other. Aesthetic interplay is another aspect of the Matrix texts that reveals a slippage in origins. By looking more closely at the aesthetics of the images in *The Animatrix* the collapse of the distinct origins of textual codes can be explored. In *Beyond*, for instance, a viewer is confronted with moments when the distinction between live-action footage and animation is collapsed, a device that disturbs assumptions about origins, in this instance the origin of the images themselves.

### Destabilising Narrative Origins

One of the marketing hooks for the DVD of *The Matrix Revolutions* is the tagline: 'everything that has a beginning has an end.' Despite the apparent closure provided by the resolution of *The Matrix Revolutions*, in the wider architecture of the Matrix the question of both beginnings and ends is frequently unclear, obscured by instances of non-linearity in the textual interplay. How non-linearity disperses seriality can be exposed by a closer look at the intersections between the prequel animations, *The Second Renaissance: Part I* and *Part II*, the comic book story 'Bits and Pieces of Information' and the *Matrix* trilogy. As is by now familiar, *The Matrix* presents a story of machines controlling humans, using them as power sources, and the *Matrix* trilogy tells of attempts by the Resistance to reassert human control. The release of *The Animatrix* reconfigures the temporality of the trilogy's narration, as *The Second Renaissance: Part I* and *Part II* re-place the present of their story-world into that of future events. Taken alone, *The Second Renaissance* could simply be seen as a transformative extension of the story-world that more fully articulates the histories alluded to within the trilogy. *Part I* reworks a story prevalent in the science fiction genre, an artificial life-form achieving sentience, providing a history to motivate the events of the trilogy, while also echoing many images from the trilogy, especially around the human battery motif, as well as other films including the *Terminator* and *Alien* series. In addition to the transformative interplay established by a prequel, a number of images in both *The Second Renaissance: Part I* and *Part II* resonate with images from actual world events. The director of the animations, Mahiro Maeda, deliberately evokes images of mass violence, Holocaust bodies, Tiananmen Square and rows of skulls associated with Cambodia and Rwanda. Though it may seem crass to use such potent images to establish a history for a series of glossy action films, it is worth mentioning the director's rationale. Speaking on the DVD release commentary, Maeda states that his interest in making *The Second Renaissance* was not to simply use the history of humanity as the backdrop for a fictional war with machines, but to make a statement about the extensiveness of inhumanity throughout the twentieth century.

Despite the extensive transtextuality existing between the *Matrix* trilogy, the animations and broader cultural and historical allusions, these contract the possibilities of non-linearity, imposing an implicit ordering through intertextual referencing: the weightiness of the pre-history images mark them as precursors. This tendency is, however, counterbalanced by a more expansive move, where the stability of origin becomes a site of erosion. By introducing a pre-history for events forming the temporality of the trilogy, *The Second Renaissance* establishes a story-world that apparently pre-exists the present of the *Matrix* films. But since this pre-existence was created following the production and release of the first film, any temporal loops set up in the interplay across the two sets of texts become configured into a möbius strip. In such a vectorial dynamic the question of which came first becomes less distinct in the shift between asking which came first narratively and/or chronologically.[9] The dimensions of this circuit are further expanded by the adaptation of an image from the comic. In both *The Second Renaissance: Part I* and 'Bits and Pieces of Information' the trigger event for the battle between the machines and humans is the trial of a domestic droid, B1-66ER. Even though the trial is presented as the trigger event, its status as an origin is again not straightforward since it is embedded within a trajectory forming a looped series of networked interconnections.

The equivocation created by circular vectorial dynamics fits well with one of the overall themes of the Matrix story-world – slippages in reality. Such slippages exist in other ways within the larger architecture of the Matrix. For instance, between *Final*

*Flight of the Osiris*, *Enter the Matrix* and the *Matrix* trilogy, there are narrative gaps, narrative connections and a collapse in media specificity, a combination bringing together the conflicting effects of expansion and contraction. In the framing narrative through which a player accesses *Enter the Matrix*, two characters, Ghost and Niobe (minor characters in *The Matrix Reloaded* and *The Matrix Revolutions*), discuss the death of another – Thaddeus. The actual story of the death is unnecessary for a player to enter the game, but is told in *Final Flight of the Osiris*, the opening animation in *The Animatrix* collection. *Final Flight of the Osiris* also fills a narrative gap at the opening of *Enter the Matrix* – the first task for a player is to collect a package from the post office; in *Final Flight of the Osiris* the package is posted by Juo, who dies in her attempt to get information back to Zion. Though *Final Flight of the Osiris* fills in a gap by establishing a narrative connection with the back-story of *Enter the Matrix*, being aware of the connection is not essential to the workings of either text. The ability of one element of the Matrix to function without all the others points again to the relative degree of complexity within the system.

## Aesthetic Transtextuality

The intersections between *Enter the Matrix*, the film trilogy and *Final Flight of the Osiris*, also pose a question about transformative adaptations and the aesthetic choices made in crossing different media. Stam comments that the idea of fidelity has a usefulness in the context of discussions about how adaptations in different media retain their specificity:

> The film adaptation of a novel performs these transformations according to the protocols of a distinct medium, absorbing and altering the genres and intertexts available through the grids of ambient discourses and ideologies, and as mediated by a series of filters: studio style, ideological fashion, political constraints, auteurist predilections, charismatic stars, economic advantage or disadvantage and evolving technology. (2000: 69)

The three texts in question here are not only interesting for the ways in which they operate as iterations of the story, but also as examples where the protocols of a distinct medium are increasingly broken down forming instances of remediation. One outcome of remediation is that the potential for expansion through iteration from one medium to the next contracts as the codes of the different media collapse into each other. *Final Flight of the Osiris* was created by the animators of *Final Fantasy: The Spirit Within* (2001) and, as in the latter, the look of the computer-generated animation strives towards live-action, with figures acting, moving and, more importantly, looking as human-like as possible, given the technological limits at the time of its making. Similarly, the opening segment of *Enter the Matrix* uses live-action footage of characters. As the codes of the Matrix are transformed by their iteration across different texts, the question of origin and linearity is disturbed, but in this instance through contraction rather than expansion. As the animation of *Final Flight of the Osiris* strives for live-action three-dimensionality and an authentic human look, even echoing some of the wire-work choreography of the *Matrix* trilogy, and the game's introduction and level transitions use live-action versions of game characters, the distinctions between the media become blurred in such a way that the opportunity for transformation offered by adaptation into different media are reduced. As the aesthetic codes of all three media – animation, computer games and live-action feature film – are co-ordinated in a realist representation of live-action space, the differences between the media cease to be so apparent in the images themselves. As a result, even as the scope of the story-world expands across computer-generated animation, a computer game and special effects film, the possibilities for transformation on the level of aesthetic choices contracts since each uses codes of expression that approach rather than diverge from one another.[10]

Amongst the animations collected in *The Animatrix*, *Final Flight of the Osiris* is unusual as the only one to obviously aim for a three-dimensional computer-generated look. Indeed, several directors who provide a commentary for the DVD assert their resistance to a computer-generated look. For instance, *Program*, written and directed by Yoshiaki Kawajiri, combines two fighters stylised through anime conventions, and sets them in a world based on the imagery of traditional Japanese screen painting, a choice that flattens the depth of the image. This is achieved in part by the artwork in which much of the detail (long grass or trees) remains within a foreground of equivalent planar depth, and is set against a more indistinct background. The direction of movement is also important in exaggerating the flatness of the images. Many of the movements occur across the diagonals of the screen, and those involving transitions into or out of the screen depth still retain a flatness because the edging and shading on the figures is strong, and does not fade out as the figures move through the depth.

Such aesthetic choices reinvigorate the possibilities for transformation offered by the protocols of animation. Metamorphosis is an essential part of the medium, and is the means by which animators exert full control over the flow of images, allowing them to either invoke live-action dimensionality or to work against it. Within a body of work where the issue of spatio-temporal integrity is frequently in play, the opportunity for adaptive transformation emerges in exploiting intersections between the techniques of metamorphosis and the theme of spatio-temporal disturbance in the animations. In *A Detective Story* and *World Record* the different protocols of animation are used to full advantage to transform representative possibilities in ways that extend the narrative themes into the style of image. *A Detective Story* is a variant on the way in which agents inhabit bodies as a rapid means of moving through the physical space of the Matrix. In this version the detective Ash is shot by Trinity during an in-between moment when an agent is starting to inhabit his body.[11] Throughout the animation the sense of in-between is pervasive: Ash crosses bridges, catches trains, looks into mirrors and computer screens. The style of the animation also evokes a quality of in-between. It is reminiscent of black-and-white comics based on the realist look of noir cityscapes, and when still the figure of Ash seems to slip into the background plane because of the shading and line work.[12] As Ash shifts from stillness to motion, there is an edge of unexpectedness as he appears to step out of the background into which he had been fully integrated. This visual discrepancy creates a torsion in the image drawing attention to the rupture of spatio-temporal conventions. *World Record* features a central character, Dan, who attempts to sustain his encounter with something he realises is beyond the ordinary conventions of his world. His speed as a sprinter has allowed him to gain access to the information flow that is the digital reality of the Matrix. The strangeness of the encounter is transferred to a viewer's experience by again introducing spatio-temporal torsion into the images. In *World Record* a sprinter in motion appears to not move through space: an effect most noticeable in the head-on shots when the sprinter's actions of pumping his arms are framed, intercut with the exertion of his muscles, yet the space between the figure and background remains unchanged.

*The Detective Story* and *World Record* both use the device of deliberately mismatching movements against space in a way that keeps in play the distinctiveness offered by animation. By contrast, *Beyond* diminishes this distinctiveness, but unlike the collapse of possibilities discussed above in relation to *Enter the Matrix, Final Flight of the Osiris* and the *Matrix* trilogy, establishes an expanding rather than contracting intersection of protocols. Making the protocol boundaries indistinct serves to re-iterate the narrative theme of characters encountering the Matrix because of a glitch in the system, while also placing a question mark over the status of the images. Just as the children in the story play in a 'ghost' house where they are confounded by perturbations in spatio-temporal organisations, a viewer is confronted with images the origin of which may be live-action or animation.

Attempts to subvert the expectation of a viewer run rife through *Beyond*, with the distinction between live-action aesthetics and those of animation obscured via framing and point of view rather than through any attempt to approach the three-dimensionality of live-action spaces and figures. Instead, the animation deliberately uses techniques that mimic live-action, both in terms of its extensive and fluid 'hand-held camera' movements, 'lens flare' and subjective points of view, which are often motivated but sometimes not. As some of images used in *Beyond* were initially captured on film, which was then used as the template for the animation, the fluidity of the 'camera movements' and figure motion can be traced back to the live footage. But there is another quality to the images in which their live-action antecedents merge with the animation so that the status of the image is, very briefly, indeterminate. Taken together, the techniques create a text in which the incursions of the Matrix into the reality of the children is also made immanent for an audience. Since the sense of immanence comes into being when the status of the image wavers between live-action footage and animation, the origin of the image itself is placed under question.

## EVERYTHING THAT HAS A BEGINNING HAS AN END

The Matrix, then, is a complex text, a network of interplay between different elements creating non-linear vectorial dynamics that destabilise the status of chronologies and origins at many of its levels. I began this chapter with a discussion of the centrality of the Wachowski brothers as authorial progenitors of the extended Matrix. While they will always be a structuring presence within the network organisation of connections, solely to assert their presence as a site of meaning generation closes down other ways of looking at the Matrix. My main emphasis throughout has been to look at how the presence of non-linear relations between textual elements affects notions of chronology and origin. As might be expected from the complex architecture of the Matrix, these kinds of concerns co-exist across different layers of the textual organisation. As the architecture expands through the writing of more stories or the creation of new games, such layers become ever more multifaceted, revealing transformations operating at the levels of narrative and aesthetics, as well as characters and the extensiveness of the story-world. In keeping with the idea of complexity, however, none of the connections that trouble the status of chronologies or origin can be absolutely defined. For instance, the collapse of aesthetic codes can both expand as well as contract the possibilities of adaptive transformation, depending on the particular textual elements activated in the interconnections. One of the more vivifying aspects of the Matrix is this tendency towards both expansion and contraction. The presence of its doubled pressure animates the complexity of the Matrix, keeping in play the vectorial dynamics that are a part of its actual and virtual architecture.

## NOTES

1   Throughout this chapter I use 'the Matrix' to indicate the larger phenomenon of multiple texts based on the stories of the *Matrix* trilogy.
2   For instance, see David Lavery (2001) and Aylish Wood (2002; 2004).
3   Examples of Matrix-based stories can be seen at www.fanfiction.net. For instance, see Madolan (1999), Hunter-14180 (2003) and YukiYoshi (2004).
4   Many mainstream films, such as *Spider-Man* (2002), *Scooby-Doo* (2002) and various James Bond films, particularly *GoldenEye* (1995), have associated game versions of their story-worlds, and extend the pre-existing audience of the film; others prime an audience's anticipation – the game version of *Starsky & Hutch* (2004) was released several months prior to the film. Additional means of audience expansion includes mobilising characters from video games, comics and, of course, books. *Lara Croft* (2001) was based on the *Tomb Raider* games, *Super Mario Brothers* (1993) on the similarly named games; *Superman*

(1978), *Batman* (1989), *X-Men* (2000), *Ghost World* (2000) and *Hulk* (2003) mobilised a pre-existing audience of the comics and there are numerous examples of films based on novels and short stories.

5  English-language film adaptations include those directed by George Cukor (1936), Renato Castellani (1954) and Franco Zeffirelli (1968), as well as *West Side Story* (1961) and *Romeo + Juliet* (1996).

6  See Will Brooker (2001) for an analysis of the different textualities of *Batman*.

7  By texts I mean those forming part of the architecture of the Matrix, and I use intertexts more conventionally to mean texts referenced in someway, either by quotation or allusion.

8  For discussions of complexity in biological systems, see Humberto Maturana and Francisco Varela (1980); for physical systems, see Ilya Prigogine and Isabelle Stengers (1984); and for complexity in social systems see Niklas Luhmann (1995).

9  Though the *Star Wars* films do not have the same compressed chronology as the *Matrix* movies, a similar question might be asked about the relationship between the trilogy made between the late 1970s and early 1980s, and the second trilogy made between the late 1990s and early 2000s. I thank Catherine Grant for bringing this point to my attention.

10  Another example of non-fidelity to a media can be found in the comic collection. Neil Gaiman is the creator of the multi-volume *Sandman* series, but more recently has shifted to writing novels: *American Gods* (2002) and *Coraline* (2003). Gaiman's contribution to *The Matrix Comics*, 'Goliath', also reflects this shift as, unlike all the other stories in the collection, it is written in prose form with more marginal illustrations by Bill Sienkiewicz and Gregory Ruth.

11  *A Detective Story* is the only animation in *The Animatrix* to use the voice talent of one the stars of the live-action films as Carrie-Anne Moss provides the voice for the animated Trinity.

12  *A Detective Story* is not, however, black-and-white since colour is often used to emphasise an element in an otherwise predominant greyscale.

# 'YOU HEAR ABOUT THEM ALL THE TIME': A GENEALOGY OF THE SENTIENT PROGRAM
Andrew Shail

> The moral is, of course, that though man might create mechanical man [the Robot Maria in *Metropolis*], even the degree of humanity the machine possessed would endow it with that capacity for disobedience and revolt which has distinguished man since Adam.
>      – Iris Barry (1927: 540)

In the double-feature-length sequel to *The Matrix* (1999) released as the second and third parts of a trilogy, by changing the narrative trajectory projected by the first film to ultimately leave the Matrix intact, the directors Andy and Larry Wachowski delivered an instance of narrative pleasure related to how enjoyable being in the Matrix is – a viewer presence created both by identification with characters and by the extremely mobile real and virtual cinematography used to denote the events occurring in the world of the Matrix. The Matrix is the place where a body can move with total freedom in three dimensions, dress cool, possess all the equipment it needs, fight bloodlessly, communicate without limitations, and be both omnipotent and extremely graceful. The two sequels develop the contrast set up between the Matrix and the real world in *The Matrix*: violence in the real world is blood, pus, violent penetration, self-mutilation and being torn apart. In the Matrix, combat is graceful sparring and is largely unarmed, fluids featuring no further than the striking red mist that hangs in the air when Trinity shoots an agent in the first film, or the unseen wounds of the mansion fight sequence in the second film. The Burly Brawl and the dock battle, and the freeway chase and Neo's fight with Bane/Smith are the rough equivalents in the time indexes of the second and third films respectively, structurally iterating a key contrast between the Matrix and 'real' action and violence. In addition to contrasts between the two types of action – unarmed bloodless martial arts and reliance on weapons – and between two types of violence – losing/winning and being mutilated – this central Matrix/Zion action contrariety also contrasts agile self-control with either being flung around by sentinels or the clumsy movements of the Armoured Personnel Units. Another reason for this shift away from the fate of the Matrix forecast by the first film's penultimate image – 'System Failure' – is the sense of immortality now widely associated with digital information. While the magnetically-sensitive media layers only a few millionths of an inch thick which constitute the recording material of modern hard disk drives do not render information any more hardy than when recorded on paper, instant accessibility and duplicatability has created a widespread ambient impression amongst users of the internet that information is independent of its recording mechanism and so is therefore immortal. As a figuration of cyberspace, the Matrix destroyed or deleted would depart too far from its analogue.[1]

Of course, perhaps the most explicit rationale for the Matrix not being destroyed is that the sequels, for two reasons, involve reinventing what the Matrix is. First, the narrative of the first film predicted an unseen but diegetic destruction of the Matrix, Morpheus having explained that Neo is the reincarnation of the man able 'to change whatever he wanted, to remake the Matrix as he saw fit', the One whose 'coming would hail the destruction of the Matrix, end the war, bring freedom to our people'. The images of Neo stopping bullets, bending the building in which he destroys Smith and causing a 'System Failure' all suggest that this is coming about as the film ends. Second, a film so saturated with Baudrillardian and Foucauldian theory does not easily permit of sequels as the content is not the referent of the film. Since any sequel that showed Zion would no longer contrast the Matrix with an 'outside' of extreme contingency, showing Zion would necessitate reinventing the Matrix if it was to continue to have theoretical rather than simply diegetic significance. In the first film the alternative to the discursive reality of the Matrix was figured through the 'mini-Matrix' of the construct, the 'real world' being 'the desert of the real' that makes Neo vomit; a fantasy (Oz) as opposed to the discursive existence (Kansas), suggesting that notions of the real are a function of discourse and that disrupting the microphysics of power is only possible from inside the mechanism of control. Staging Zion involves cancelling the original theoretical significance of the Matrix. For both of these reasons reprising the diegetic world of the first film in sequels – the title of the first sequel in particular suggesting this – necessitated reinventing what the Matrix was for. But re-imagining the Matrix as a permanent place, refusing to apply the Oracle's prescient announcement that 'everything that has a beginning has an end' – a suggestion so important it featured in trailers for *The Matrix Revolutions* (2003) – to the Matrix, was also the consequence of a reading of the first film that the sequels carried out.

Initially no more than an explanation for functions of the system appearing as people, the idea of the sentient program was developed to a level in the sequels that was not predicted by the developments of the diegetic world of the Matrix in, for example, the comics that followed the first film. Whereas the agents of *The Matrix* were programs that were always hijacking a human body, through Seraph, the Oracle, the Merovingian, the Keymaker, the Architect, the Trainman, Rama-Kandra, Kamala and Sati, the Matrix in *The Matrix Reloaded* (2003) and *The Matrix Revolutions* is shown to be populated as much by those for whom it is their home as it is by its human captives. In the sequels the sentient program serves to produce a narrative for which the Matrix is not a function of a machine/human relationship, both avoiding several clichéd narrative conclusions and complicating, in advance, the less-often explored science fiction conclusion of human/machine concord by suggesting that the human resistance in the

Matrix may be secondary to a set of political relations between programs. The Matrix as a system of enslavement is replaced by the Matrix as a world with its own meanings regardless of the parameters and even purpose of the system that generates it – where Mouse the human worries that the Matrix might have got tastes wrong, the Oracle program bakes perfect cookies and loves candy. The sentient programs are the corollary of Neo's reformulation as the systemic anomaly: nothing about Neo precedes the system, yet he has, it is implied, entered a human body just as agents do. He is not a body that has been grown and then plugged into the Matrix but a program that has entered the hardware of a body. Bodies might even be irrelevant: the sequels certainly follow up the idea that it is not necessary for Neo to leave the Matrix to become the One, imparted in Morpheus' explanation in *The Matrix* that the man of whom Neo is a reincarnation was 'able to change the Matrix as he saw fit' *before* he left it.

In shifting to sentient programs as protagonists, *The Matrix Reloaded* and *The Matrix Revolutions* draw on several filmic precursors, including Steven Lisberger's *TRON* (1982), Brett Leonard's *Virtuosity* (1995), Farhad Mann's *Lawnmower Man 2* (1996) and Josef Rusnak's *The Thirteenth Floor* (1999), the latter based on Daniel Galouye's novel *Simulacron-3* (1964). The Keymaker's ability to open a way for Neo and Morpheus to the core system in *The Matrix Reloaded* closely echoes the program TRON's crusade to get the programmer Kevin Flynn to the Master Control Program. The AI consciousnesses, born in and inhabiting only cyberspace, of William Gibson's *Neuromancer* (1984) are also crucial predecessors of the sentient program, and offer a genealogy of the notion of AI which the first film, choosing to draw on other genealogies by designating AI as the machine hive-mind, did not use. However, in addition to its literary and filmic science fiction genealogies, the sentient program is as much as part of a reading of what the first film was – the notion that the answer to the question 'what is the Matrix' is 'the body as pure movement' – as it drew on generic predecessors. While Anne Cranny-Francis and Dan North suggest elsewhere in this volume that the body-puppetry with which the *Matrix* trilogy is preoccupied is of industrialised ergonomics or of virtual actors respectively, I will chart a genealogy of the body in cinema suggesting it is also that of cinema.

## THE CINEMATIC BODY

The cinematic body is a movement phenomenon. Because movement as registered by film is isolated from cause, effect, ground or force, and because the cinematic body moves in an environment of unending movements of matter, it is experienced as gravity-irrespective. Closely related to the notion that the essence of cinema is movement, this sensation of movement as perpetual also suggests both immortality and invulnerability to the cinematic body. Gilles Deleuze pointed out that a philosophical distinction made by Henri Bergson in 1907 between space and movement, between 'a single, identical, homogenous space' and movement's 'concrete duration' was intimately related to cinema (1983: 1). This body was a substantial element of what Maxim Gorky noticed at the Lumière cinematograph showing at Charles Aumont's Theatre-concert Parisian at the Nizhni-Novgorod Fair in July 1896. The world it showed was 'full of movement, the life of ghosts', a 'gray movement of gray shadows' (1985: 229), 'the movement of shadows, only of shadows … ghosts' (1960: 408) which are nevertheless also 'full of living energy and are so swift as to be almost imperceptible' (1960: 407). While the gravity-irrespective movement of *all* objects in cinema was heavily drawn on by, as Tom Gunning points out is evident in Gorky's record (2000: 318–26), a deliberate *anti*-realist screen practice that had ebbed by the turn to narrative cinema and the discursification of cinema as a representatational medium after 1908 (Gunning 1990: 93), the gravity-irrespective cinematic body and the attendant impression that this cinematic body is not the agent of its own movement persisted.

It even intensified because the movement being seen was no longer openly understood to be a result of the effect of a technology on the material filmed, instead being perceived to pre-exist what was now understood as a purely mimetic act of filming. By 1915 it was not important that 'figures seem to be one-tenth of their natural size' (1985: 227), but even in (and especially because of) a decade of film practice and film discourse, when the capacity of film to make the image seem strange was fiercely disavowed, the cinematic body maintained its supernatural, gravity-irrespective and immortal aspect. Film star Tom Mix remarked that 'when my shadow appears on the screen it seems to me there in the audience as if I were viewing the actions of a total stranger instead of the shadow of mine own self … And my shadow does things that astound me sometimes' (1915: 500). Both André Bazin and Roland Barthes have alluded to the cinematic body as ontologically undead (Bazin 1967: 15; Barthes 1980: 32). Notably, this sense of bodies as ghostly is echoed in the Oracle's description of the sentient programs in *The Matrix Reloaded*: 'Every time you heard someone say they saw a ghost or an angel; every story you've ever heard about vampires, werewolves or aliens is the system assimilating someone doing something they're not supposed to be doing.' The link between the sentient program and the cinematic body is certainly central to their aggrandisement in the sequels.

The sense of immortality attending the gravity-irrespective cinematic body can also be figured as super-heroism. One 1914 film journalist wrote that no-one looking at star Marc McDermott in evening dress for a trade ball 'would have dreamed that he had spent the previous two days attired in corduroys and a flannel shirt swinging out upon space on giant steel girders and passing rivets upon the top of a newly-constructed building frame' (Anon. 1914a: 26). In addition to describing a period of filmmaking preoccupied with action, this journalist was also, notably, describing the body produced by cinematic effect – the body 'swinging out upon space' – as existing pre-filmically. When cinema's showmanship of images designed to amaze receded underground as its representational capacity was drawn to the fore from circa 1908, the spectacular figures that derived from cinema's inability to describe the immobile were no longer discursified as a feature of an amusement. But as Tom Mix's reference to 'the actions of a total stranger' shows, the vague impression of the supernatural arising from the cinematic body did not cease.

The parameters of the growing discursive product 'picture personality/star' of the decade immediately following the reinvention of film as the 'photoplay' in 1909 indicated significant tenacity of a cinematic body understood as animated by other than its own consciousness. Popular discourse on film stars in this early period shows an attempt both to ascribe the sense of immortality to the star's body and to locate an agent behind the sense of supernatural animation. As a typical 1914 anecdote explained:

> The other day a man working on the roof of a four-storey house slipped and fell. He struck the top of a passing tramcar and bounced off into a mudcart. They dragged him out, and the crowd closed round eager to gaze on a mangled 'corpse' but they were all disappointed. The man simply shook himself, and said: 'Don't worry, people, I've been a picture-actor.' (Anon. 1914b: 311)

Film discourse of this early decade of cinematic celebrity became a catalogue of examples of immortality. In 1914 it was reported that Florence Turner had been hit by a boulder but had received only a bruised ankle (Anon. 1914c: 8). By 1915 this had reached a familiar superhero configuration – Beverly Bayne 'often performs daring feats for the camera which few would care attempt and none could successfully accomplish without Miss Bayne's nerve and physical strength' (Anon. 1915: 70) and, by 1918, cinemagoers were being informed by popular magazines that Eddie Polo could 'scientifically and effectively handle any half-a-dozen ordinary men' (Anon. 1918: 43). Edith Storey's repertoire ranged 'from riding bucking bronchos to leaping off cliffs' (Dangerfield & Howard 1921: 34). The disquieting effect of supernatural animation continued but was largely displaced into an early model of super-heroism which designated cinematic personnel as an invincible cadre.

In addition to being enshrined in popular thought about film, the cinematic body has also been a major influence on both filmmaking and film theory. For Lev Kuleshov in 1929, the corollary of his belief that the essence of cinema was movement was a theory of 'cinematographic acting' that stripped acting down from 'impersonation' to tabular ergonomics (1974: 110–12). Cinema repeats this gravity-irrespective body-in-movement regularly, from Leni Riefenstahl's *Olympiad* (1938) to Sam Raimi's *Spider-Man* (2002), with the *Matrix* trilogy demonstrating an equation between spectacle and the weightless body-in-movement (also iterated by such contemporary films as *Charlie's Angels* (2000)) from the outset. This is not to argue that these films represent 'pure cinema', but that the body they reference is a product and preoccupation of a ciné-culture. For the narrator of Virginia Woolf's *Jacob's Room* (1922), sunlight has 'equipped our brains and bodies with such an armoury of weapons that merely to

Figure 1 – *Olympiad* (Leni Riefenstahl, 1938). The animatedness of the cinematic body, and the part of framing and camera movement in this animatedness, exaggerated through total isolation from ground: a shot of a diver taken from under the diving board, with the camera inverted, played in reverse in the final cut.

see the flash and thrust of limbs engaged in the conduct of daily life is better than the old pageant of armies drawn out in battle array upon the plain' (1945: 163). It was of course cinema that, for Woolf the cinéaste, had re-tuned the observer to this pleasure. This contrast between the flash and thrust of limbs engaged in the conduct of daily life and the army drawn out in battle array is even explicitly dramatised in the sequels as the contrast between the Burly Brawl and the dock battle and between the freeway chase and the fight between Neo and Bane/Smith. From *Olympiad* to *The Matrix*, film for which the cinematic body is a referent has helped sustain the definition of the essence of cinema as movement.

## THE MATRIX

Neo's immortality – the assurance that is reached by the end of the first film that even bullets cannot harm him – is a direct statement of the cinematic body's prediction of continued movement. Its figuration as super-heroism is even explicitly present in the *Matrix* films. The One's task in *The Matrix*, which is perhaps most accurately described as destroying the Matrix, emerges in Cypher's mouth as super-heroism in the question 'so you're here to save the world?'. Neo's superpowers are the distillation of the immortal cinematic body-in-movement (the body which the narrative proves that the agents are so mistaken to think of as 'only human'), so much so that his ability to hack the Matrix as he moves through it has to disappear by the beginning of *The Matrix Reloaded*. Instead, in the two sequels Neo indulges in fights even though the end of the first film sees him reach a level of mastery over the fabric of the Matrix meaning he does not need to: the super-heroism of the immortal perpetually-moving cinematic body is always reliant on demonstration. That in *The Matrix Reloaded* Link names Neo as Superman – this popular culture reference replacing the *Alice's Adventures in Wonderland* (1865), *Through the Looking Glass, and What Alice Found There* (1871) and *The Wonderful Wizard of Oz* (1900) references of the first film with an anchor in the DC Comics superhero – indicates both how relevant the superhero is to the body discovered in the Matrix/cinema and how useful the superhero figure is in militating against other possible implications of the immortality of the cinematic body, including the disquieting impression of this body, registered by Gorky, as undead.

Inheriting the definition of the essence of cinema as movement, *The Matrix* also rendered the gravity-irrespective cinematic body as a major visual pleasure. When Morpheus explains that the sparring program and the Matrix have roughly similar rules, his one example of these is gravity. Notably, Neo's ability to control his cinematic self – his shadow – gives him the ability to totally control the figural movement irrespective of cause, effect, ground or force: to fly. All the hacker-humans have

Figure 2 – *Spider-Man* (Sam Raimi, 2002). Total isolation from force and ground achieved through 'cutting the wires'.

a degree of this ability to fly – hence the appositeness of wire work. The different degree of reality conveyed by cinematic automatism even emerges in Cypher's assertion in *The Matrix* that 'I believe that the Matrix can be more real than this world'. The Wachowskis' certainty of the need for the body in *The Matrix* to be able to fly were strong enough to compel them to import Yuen Woo-ping, master action choreographer/director of Chinese *Wuxia pian* ('hero films') and important factor in the comeback of the genre in China in the 1980s. *Wuxia pian* is one of few genres based on the conviction that flying, delivering *qi* blows, employing super-human speed, strength and responsiveness – what the cinematic body suggests, because no account exists of supernatural qualities as an effect of the apparatus, may be possible – are not impossible, and in which low budgets mean that the stars are usually already stuntmen and usually actually do everything their characters are seen to do. That one of the martial arts Neo is seen learning in *The Matrix* is 'Drunken Boxing' is a clear tribute to the Yuen Woo-ping films *She Xing Diao Shou/Snake in the Eagles' Shadow* (1978) and *Jui Kuen/Drunken Master* (1978). The five months of rigorous physical training that Keanu Reeves, Laurence Fishburne, Carrie-Anne Moss and Hugo Weaving went through before filming started on *The Matrix* – in order to replicate the *modus operandi* of *Wuxia pian* – is also a signal of the Wachowskis' commitment to physical movement occurring beyond the arena of cinematic effect.[2] The action scene in *The Matrix* before the viewer knows the diegesis is not 'real' (and the film's publicity was carefully managed to avoid the usual foreknowledge of basic plot), with its softly-crashing gong as the agent lands after the 'impossible' jump from rooftop to rooftop, is a direct extraction of *Wuxia pian*, not unremarkably because in both *Wuxia pian* and 105 years of cinema these things *are* possible. Such filmic paratexts as knowledge of Reeves, Moss, Fishburne and Weaving's martial-arts training preparation have also long been fundamental to evidencing the epistemological endeavour of cinema as distinct from simulation. Labouring this sense of film production as a logistical and physical endeavour de-emphasises the extent to which the cinematic body is an effect of the apparatus, thus again fantasising it as previous to filming. A crux of the first film is that the body in the Matrix is not just the avatar of the mind transcending its meat in cyberspace. The loosely-explained logic of injuries sustained in the Matrix having effect in the real world actually shows that the Wachowskis take significant pleasure in the mistaking of the cinematic body for the pre-filmic body: like viewers imputing cinematic effect to the pre-filmic body, they either understand or want the body in the Matrix to be the real body.

*The Matrix* also explicitly referenced the geneaology of the cinematic body in the animated figure of nineteenth-century movement-based optical toys, including the thaumatrope (John Ayrton Paris, 1824), the phenakistascope (Joseph Plateau and Simon Ritter von Stampfer, 1832), the zoetrope (George Horner, 1834), the praxinoscope (Charles Reynaud, 1877) and the mutoscope (Herman Castler, 1895). Zoetrope figures, for example, are bodies-in-movement irrespective of physical context. 'Real' films and animated films have long been differentiated by the fact that for animated films, unlike with live-action films, every frame is a single shot. By returning to the multiple cameras in a line set-up of chronophotography, bullet-time animates a figure in precisely this way and produces the narrative event around the movement of a single body. The animated figure of bullet-time is both a repetition and reinforcement of the conducting of cinema in such a way as to render real bodies as animated figures,[3] one of the documentaries on the first film explaining that bullet-time 'takes on the attributes of full-cel animation, only with people, not characters'(*What is Bullet-Time?*, 1999). Even the security of this distinction between people and characters is threatened by the fact that the four bullet-time moments in *The Matrix* are used to specify protagonists, being used twice to present Neo and once each to present Trinity, Morpheus and Smith. The most complex characters are simultaneously those presented as marionettes.

The pre-history of cinema in the optical toy was of course fractured by the discursive invention, from 1909, of cinematic celebrity. It is now an accepted aspect of film history that film actors' names were not known before 1909 not because they were being concealed or because shooting distances were too great for audiences to recognise their faces but because until this date the activity of being filmed was not understood to be acting, in part because of cinema's descent from other persistence-of-vision technologies (deCordova 1990: 33). Clearly, in a conception of cinema influenced by the discourse on acting ascendant after the explosion of narrative filmmaking from 1908, the body in cinema has not been so anonymous and so defined solely by its movement as a zoetrope figure. But the felt equivalence between the cinematic body and the animated figure has persisted. This is partially because, as Barry King explains, film incompletely digests a discourse of 'being filmed' as acting: as the cinematic character is articulated to varying degrees by editing codes, 'the project of constructing, from actor-located processes of signification, a psychologically consistent character' (1991: 170) is disrupted. King gives the example of the use of close shooting in the cinema, which 'means in effect, that the actor can signify merely because he or she has automatic or physiologically given qualities, e.g. lip shape and movement, facial mass and habitual expressions' (1991: 175).

Chronophotography also functions in *The Matrix* to explicitly state its subscription to the idea that the essence of cinema is movement. The 'virtual camera' which is actually a line of still cameras orchestrated to a single movement draws directly on the various technologies used by Etienne-Jules Marey, Albert Londe, Ottomar Anschütz and Eadweard Muybridge to precisely record animal and human motion in the 1870s and 1880s. This genealogy is invoked not just by the camera-to-subject orchestration produced by the rig of 120 still cameras used to construct the bullet-time sequences but in such normal slow-motion sequences as the lobby shoot-out, where Trinity and Neo kill all the armed police because – in such instances as Neo's one-handed handstand while shooting 3 guards – they possess the chronophotographic ability to precisely break down the increments of movement occurring at speed. But whereas Muybridge's horse with all four hooves off the ground related to centuries of producing and presenting amazing sights that had never been seen (Gunning 2000: 324), 'bullet-time' in *The Matrix* showed in the moving bullet an omnipresent cinematic movement which has, since the first developments of narrative cinema, constituted a fundamental narrative event. Bullet-time repeated the appropriation, by even the earliest potted histories of the birth of cinema, of Muybridge's invention of the zoöpraxiscope in 1879 to animate his chronophotographic stills as the originating point of a new grade of realistic rendering of movement resulting in the cinematograph: showing the moving bullet is perhaps the most intense designation of cinema as descriptor-of-movement possible. For visual effects supervisor John Gaeta the aim of bullet-time was 'slowing down time to such an extent that you really see everything around you as clearly as you possibly could'(*What is Bullet-Time?*). His description sees bullet-time not as rendering visible strange and otherwise unseen moments, but as repairing a deficiency of movement-recognition. The dramatic event remains the same – Neo, for example, is nicked twice – and nothing is shown to happen that the audience would not know to happen if they saw the shot in real time, but the cine-narrative renders visible movement in the place of the disquieting presence in audiences' minds of the reality-disrupting blank and squib. Bringing in Yuen Woo-ping also involved the *Wuxia pian* practice of surrendering control to the fight co-ordinator of not just choreography but camera set-ups and camera movement for the duration of the fight scenes, another clear signal of an intention of allowing the movement of figures rather than the film's overriding narrative to dictate the narrative event constructed in each set-piece action scene.[4]

The cinematic body becomes the basic unit and currency of *The Matrix*. The first sequence in the Construct shows viewers no horizons, just Neo and Morpheus' bodies (while not floating or flying) moving independent of any surface or ground. As Morpheus talks to Neo in the Construct, because he moves gently and because the frame obscures his lower half, the camera may either be rotating around his stationary head or rooted on the spot and changing angle to follow him as he passes, but with no background by which to judge which movement is occurring the movement of the camera and the movement of his body are indistinct – this is the ambient body of cinema and of the Matrix. Morpheus' question, 'do you believe that my being stronger or faster has anything to do with my muscles in this place?', even re-enacts the conflating, with his two use of 'my', of the body-in-cinema with the pre-filmic body, the film rendering the cinematic body as a moment of narrative pleasure by using the fact that the result of the camera's swift piecing-together of shots of action is not an unfamiliar image of a body but a super-heroic body, a body which is understood to pre-filmically possess abilities that are actually the result of editing. When the urban terrain of the jump program rushes up to Morpheus and Neo's gravity-less bodies and their camera-position from below, the camera then detaching itself from them and moving just as swiftly up, this is an extreme version of another element of the cinematic body, where it is the relation of the camera to the body that detaches body from ground.

The immortality suggested by camera-body relation also gives rise to a significant extent of the parameters of the Matrix. One of the features of the Matrix's virtual reality is that it happens in real time. That the time spent projecting one's digital image is equivalent to the time for which it exists in the digital system precisely subscribes to the reality-movement of cinema, where the 'ability' of the cinematic to move super-heroically is the result of the editing together of moments of action, but is assumed, because editing is both invisible and adheres to the 'invisible style'[5] of seamless presentation of action, to be pre-filmic, to inhere in the performing body because it has nothing to distinguish it from the body-in-performance, the body in the time-duration of the film. This is not just the reason for the building-up of a vague impression of super-heroism around the cinematic body. It is the reason Jackie Chan appears to be not just an athlete but a super-athlete; short bursts of intense action which necessitate periods of preparation and recovery and several takes to get right, when edited together with other short bursts, create a bodily achievement which the film proposes is as much a part of the diegesis as the environment being described incrementally by each shot.

Camera-movement supplements the degree to which the cinematic body's movement is experienced irrespective of cause, ground and force. When Neo dreams that Trinity jumps out of a high-rise window her free three-dimensional movement – she continues to fight in spite of falling in space – is 'orbited' by the camera position, moving from above the window, down to her face and then past her guns as she brings them round and then away from her and inside the building. Morpheus being beaten by Smith in the dirty-bathroom fight is iterated by a set of camera movements and distances that are restricted to the small room. Neo's flights from the mountains to the city and from the core building to the building where Trinity is falling both dramatise the instantaneous 'movement' from place to place of the camera resulting from editing. Neo is also married to the camera: the last few seconds of his flight from the mountains to the city is laid out a few seconds in advance by a moving camera positition. The truck-roof fight section of the freeway chase in *The Matrix Reloaded* functions to release the cinematic body from the vaguest impression of ground by combining the moving body and moving camera with a mobile surface.

## THE SENTIENT PROGRAM

*The Matrix* sequels enact a reading of the cinematic body evoked and redoubled in these multiple ways by *The Matrix*. A new and complex conception of the Matrix as a public of sentient programs is involved in such moments as the Oracle promising that Seraph will help the humans to get to the Trainman who is working for the Merovingian smuggling programs like Rama-Kandra, Kamala and Sati in and out of the Matrix. This public is even quite complex – the Merovingian represents sadism for the humans but is also rescuing programs without purpose from deletion. In addition to serving the important narrative function of expelling the machine/human conflict from the Matrix, this shift elaborates an occupant of the Matrix/cinema which does not simply create a new guise for the cinematic body of the first film. Instead, the sentient program serves to provide a 'truce' over the cinematic body.

The narrative pleasure of Neo's assertion to Smith in *The Matrix* that 'my name is Neo', by inserting a real-world name into the place where Neo is Thomas Anderson, is that of inserting a subject behind the movement of the body in the cinema/Matrix, where the movement-medium never assures the viewer that a consciousness pre-exists and orchestrates that movement. The reasserted permanency of the Matrix (in spite of both the first film's predictions of its end and the third film's ending of the war) and the act of narrative pleasure involved in demonstrating its continued existence both relate to the pleasures of the cinematic body. The capacities of the cinematic body explain why in reinventing the purpose of the Matrix the sequels do not go so far as to rescind the rule of the first film that resistance is only possible inside the Matrix: Morpheus is shown to be right to insist in *The Matrix Reloaded* that ships hacking into the Matrix remain more important than the armed forces of Zion, and Neo ends the machine/human war in *The Matrix Revolutions* by entering and bringing equilibrium to the Matrix. The narrative pleasure provided by the world's infiltrator-hackers 'swinging out upon space' and thereby discovering that they can control the abilities of their cinematic bodies is that of putting a person in place of a cinematic body whose historical discursification as super-heroic is not sufficient to install an agent behind movement experienced as occurring regardless of cause and effect, ground or force. The infiltrator-hackers' abilities above and beyond that of the unaware humans do not breach cinematic automatism – they cathartically repeat the movement-capacity of the cinematic body.

The deliberate structural juxtaposition of Matrix action and real-world violence follows directly from the first film's dialectic of the cinematic body, even to the extent that the gravity-irrespective cinematic body's ability to fly in the Matrix is precisely that which the humans lack in the dock battle, leading to them being beaten so quickly with the machines dropping the APUs and their loaders from above. The Super Burly Brawl at the end of *The Matrix Revolutions* enacts the completely independent movement of the cinematic body, continuing to reference animation as the core of this cinema and of this sense of immortality in such shots as that in which Neo's fist moves towards Smith's head through static raindrops. But even here the immortality of the cinematic body explicitly appears as troubling, when, towards the end of the Super Burly Brawl, his immortality appears as that of a zombie when he keeps getting up even when under the ground. Unlike Kevin Flynn in *Tron*, when jacked in Neo does not possess 'user power' making him superior to other programs. He does not land a blow on Seraph and is beaten by the Trainman. In learning that he is the systemic anomaly and a mirror image of Smith – the Oracle tells him that Smith 'is you, your opposite, your negative, the result of the equation trying to balance itself out' – Neo, as part of this truce, discovers that the freedoms of the Matrix which he, out of all the humans enjoys the most and which he most persistently demonstrates, only return him to the animated body.

The sentient program mediates the rewards and problems of the cinematic body as explored by the first film – this problematic of simultaneous supernatural ability and automatism. The sentient program has no assurance that there is an extra-cinematic self choosing to risk the anxieties of the cinematic body for the pleasure of perpetual movement, so encapsulating the concern that the cinema's display of a body moving irrespective of cause and effect has the superior representational claim. The sentient program is based on an open acceptance of a figure moving with no evident cause. They are the enunciators yet enunciated, those who know that they have been authored but who are nevertheless able to author anything, including deserts (the Merovingian) or a train station (the Trainman), and are able to do so according to their own political interests as opposed to the pre-determined actions of the machine/human war. In contrast to the humans who can only hack programs, only those who have been written can write: only those who are animated can use, for example, the programmer access doors. The sentient programs are those who are aware that the Matrix is a synthesised world and thus attain the degree of agency of movement in that world denied to almost all of its human inhabitants but they are also those for whom this knowledge cannot involve the ability to exit from the cinematically-animated space of movement. The cinematic body's simultaneous movement-automatism and gravity-defiance is seen, particularly in the instance of Rama-Kandra and Kamala's family, as simultaneously an effect of the system and as much a life as if pre-filmic, as if preceding the system. Only those performing this truce between movement-automatism and gravity-defiance can stably occupy the Matrix/cinema.

## NOTES

1  Even Gibson's coining of the term 'cyberspace' derived not from the existence of a virtual world but a sense of permanence to information – something like a place – implied by recent advances in information technology.

2  For more on this see Walter Jon Williams' 'Yuen Woo-ping and the Art of Flying' (2003).

3  This is also because of an ongoing intermedia relationship with the animated figure of the computer game.

4  A tendency entirely in line with the separation into units of movement made possible by the 'chapter' format of DVD.

5  The existence of the camera *does* become a factor when the screen goes blank when the Nebuchadnezzer's electro-magnetic pulse is blown, but the fact that the camera continues to exist after this reasserts its non-existence with renewed strength.

# THE RULES OF THE GAME, THE BURDEN OF NARRATIVE:
## *ENTER THE MATRIX*

Diane Carr

Much of the commercial success that *Enter the Matrix* (2003) has enjoyed is the result of its relationship with the *Matrix* trilogy, rather than the quality of play it offers.[1]
Released in May 2003, at the same time as *The Matrix Reloaded* (2003), it immediately became the fastest-selling title in its publisher's history.[2] As is typical with such
games, the action in *Enter the Matrix* centres on a characterised avatar (the game's
playable protagonist). The avatar is viewed primarily from behind as they pass through
a series of spaces that are accessed conditionally, and in a particular order, while the
player manages a variety of quantifiable resources (for example health, ammunition)
and confronts various obstacles and adversaries. The avatar has a menu of moves
– run, climb, drive, throw, shoot, punch, and so on. These potential actions are stra-
tegically triggered by the player in response to stimuli in the form of acts, events and
situations in the game. The game is made up of levels, sequential chapters or episodes
and between these are non-interactive digital animations that elaborate on the game's
narrative, relate background information and/or set up the next mission for the player
and their avatar. *Enter the Matrix* also incorporates short filmed sequences at various
points. These scenes are where the game's close links to the films are most explicit,
because they feature supporting actors and sets from *The Matrix Reloaded*. The central characters in *Enter the Matrix* are minor characters in *The Matrix Reloaded* and the
events in the game play a supporting role to events in the film. This suggests that it is
possible to trace differences in status between the game and the feature films, at a
textual level.[3] If these inequities are not acknowledged or accounted for, an analysis of
the franchise's enlistment of different media for narrative ends will remain incomplete.
The borders between the game and the films are permeable, blurred by the inclusion
of filmed sequences into the game, and by 'game-like' qualities in the feature films,
as well as by the memories and associations carried by users as they move between
these texts. Aylish Wood proposes that 'instead of thinking of *The Matrix* as a conventional film text that tells a narrative with a straightforward hero figure, perhaps
it is more useful to think of *The Matrix* as equivalent to working through levels of a
video game' (2004: 127) and Sean Cubitt points to the referential structure as less 'the
cyberspace of internet than ... that of computer games, constantly evoked in the use
of mobile phones to guide protagonists through the mazes of the city' (2004: 229). It is

one thing, however, to recognise that these texts share ground, and another to assume that this sharing is unproblematic or that the territory in question is uncontested.

## STORY AND NARRATIVE

Questions about the apparently narrative qualities of computer games have led to lively debate within computer game studies over the past couple of years. Broadly speaking, theorists examining narrative in computer games have tended to fall into one of two camps. One set accepts, more or less as a given, that computer games involve narrative to some degree, and thus they move straight on to asking 'how do games tell or generate stories?' or 'how might games evolve to tell more compelling stories?' Examples include Celia Pearce's 'Towards a Game Theory of Game' (2002), Janet H. Murray's *Hamlet on the Holodeck* (1997) and Henry Jenkins' 'Game Design as Narrative Architecture' (2002). A second set of analysts discusses narrative (or its absence) in computer games using the narrative theory of Gérard Genette (1980) or Seymour Chatman (1978). As a consequence, terms such as 'story', 'narrative' and 'plot' have distinct and precise meanings in their work. Examples would include Jesper Juul in 'Games Telling Stories?' (2001), Markku Eskelinen in 'The Gaming Situation' (2001) and Espen Aarseth in *Cybertext* (1997).[4]

In all the above examples, the analysts have produced useful, thought-provoking theory. However, because the terms at the centre of their analysis are differently defined, their various conclusions are difficult to reconcile. The aforementioned papers by Juul and Eskelinen use narrative theory to argue that computer games need to be understood as games (rather than as narratives, drama or cinema). Elsewhere, Eskelinen has responded to Henry Jenkins by indicating the ways in which the latter fails to employ similarly specific terminology: 'Jenkins doesn't define the contested concepts (narratives, stories and games) so central to his argumentation. That's certainly an effective way of building a middle ground (or a periphery), but perhaps not the most convincing one' (2002: 120). Computer games are not primarily about storytelling, yet narrative theory provides computer games theorists with an arsenal of wonderfully precise models with which to examine the organisation of perspective, event, time and action within a game-text. Yet in the article concerned, Jenkins is not relying on narrative theory. He describes computer games as spaces in which stories are spun via the actions of the player, rather than told, and he is using a concept of 'story' that is based on the work of Michel de Certeau. According to de Certeau, stories are one of the ways through which users customise spaces, and while his use of the terms 'story' and 'narrative' does not match the definitions proposed by narrative theory, this does not limit the applicability of his concepts to the analysis of computer games and play. It is easy enough to establish that these various approaches hinge on different conceptualisations of story and narrative. What is more interesting is exploring how these notions might be productively aligned. Because of its declared narrative agenda, its various failings and its rather servile relationship to a master or embedding text (a 'matrix' text, in other words), *Enter the Matrix* is an excellent game through which to explore these ideas.

## GAMES AND NARRATIVE

Perhaps the most important part of discussing the narrative aspects of any computer game is admitting that there are sizeable differences between games and narrative. Any discussion of the similarities between games and narrative needs to incorporate recognition of their distinct properties. Juul defines a game as a 'rule-based formal system with a variable and quantifiable outcome, where different outcomes are assigned different values, the player exerts effort in order to influence the outcome, the player feels attached to the outcome, and the consequences of the activity are optional and negotiable' (2003: 35). Play is a self-directed activity undertaken for pleasure or diversion, and games involve measurable outcomes (scores, wins, losses) as well as, to some degree or other, an element of chance. The game has components (chess has its chess-pieces, for instance) of symbolic value that are manipulated by the player. Games have rules, and these rules might involve time (as when the players take turns) or govern the manner in which a component can be utilised – the ways that it can move through space, for example.

A narrative, on the other hand, is 'the recounting ... of one or more real or fictitious events communicated by one, two or several (more or less overt) narrators to one, two or several (more or less overt) narratees' (Gerald Prince, quoted in Eskelinen 2001). Narrative theorists themselves argue about terms, but according to most, a narrative is made up of two parts: the story and the discourse. The story is the intangible chain of source events, while the discourse is the expression of these events (the representation of the setting and the characters that enable these events). 'In simple terms, the story is the what in a narrative that is depicted, discourse the *how*' (Chatman 1978: 19; emphasis in original). The narrative discourse is a communicative transmission within a text. It proceeds from a sending position, the implied author (the organising principal within the text), to a receiving position (the implied reader) via various conduits: narrators and narratees (Chatman 1978: 148–50). According to narrative theory, story-events are only available to us once they have been plotted in time and space and re-presented within the narrative discourse. Thus they have already happened. During play, on the other hand, events are improvised: the player instigates events in the present, as Juul (2001) has pointed out. The player may have a hand in the duration of these events, and it may be the player who decides the perspective through which these events are depicted. In other words, rather than receiving a plotted discourse, the player has a hand in plotting events (Aarseth 1997: 111–14). In the process, the player moves from the 'sender' end of Chatman's model of narrative as transmission, to the receiving end – from something like the implied

Figure 3 – *Enter the Matrix* (2003), 'The Freeway Scene': Niobe is driving, Ghost is blasting cars out of the way and Morpheus is in the distance, on top of the truck.

author, to something like an implied reader, and back again. Additionally, it is the player who decides which, if any, of these events might be 'saved', and which played over. Narrative theory helps specify the ways in which computer games are 'not narrative' and in the process, somewhat paradoxically, narrative theory proves its relevance to computer game studies.

It is one thing to assert that *Enter the Matrix* 'tells a story', and another to explain how (or how successfully) this particular computer game manages to combine narrative with game-play. In fact, it is possible that *Enter the Matrix*'s first job is to facilitate compelling play, and this aim is not helped by its commitment to storytelling. *Enter the Matrix* serves the story arc of *The Matrix* franchise, and, in the process, the game's ability to offer gamers compelling play is compromised. The game's narrative commitments overshadow its 'game-ness'. The game wraps its goals in narrative, and then pins these goals to events within *The Matrix Reloaded*. The outcome of this is that the player (in the guise of either avatar, Niobe or Ghost) is left picking up packages, running errands and making deliveries that will allow for 'big' events in the feature film to be enacted by the high status stars.

## ORDER ON THE FREEWAY

At one point in the game the player must dodge aggressive opponents while driving on a freeway, with the aim of getting the avatar Niobe and her vehicle close to a truck where Morpheus in *The Matrix Reloaded* is duelling with an agent.[5] When, after multiple attempts, the player manages to manoeuvre close enough, the mission is accomplished, play stops dead, and lustrous and spectacular images from the film take over from the blocky sterility of the game-world. The pretence is that Morpheus' acts are enabled by our (or at least Niobe's) actions. Thus the player, if they persist long enough to accomplish their mission, triggers a set of events, the culmination of which is an event in the first narrative (the feature film). But Niobe will be there on-screen, on time, in *The Matrix Reloaded*, whether the player persists or not. The knock-on effect of this is that the multiple events of play (the player's various attempts at the level, their particular, personal responses to the game's obstacles) shrink into insignificance.

There are alternative ways to reference events across texts. The 'drop' made by Jue, the heroine of *Final Flight of the Osiris*, from *The Animatrix* (2003), is directly referred to by characters in both *The Matrix Reloaded* and *Enter the Matrix*. In this case, the characters are not required to occupy the same points in time and space as Jue: the events depicted in *Final Flight of the Osiris* are referred to, rather than arrived at. Thus the animation is allowed to continue an independent existence. While there might well be discrepancies in status between this short animation and the feature films in terms of budget, medium or the evaluative perceptions of audience, at the level of the textual, *Final Flight of the Osiris* enjoys a parallel life, rather than a supporting role. The owners of *The Matrix* franchise have an online multiplayer game in development at the time of writing.[6] *The Matrix Online* will be set in the time that follows *The Matrix Revolutions*, and thus it will refer to events in the trilogy, without having to duplicate or serve them. Unlike events in *Final Flight of the Osiris*, or in the new online game, events in *Enter the Matrix* are bound to sequences in *The Matrix Reloaded*. The multiple and disposable in-game events acted out by the player (in the guise of Niobe or Ghost) cannot compete with the spectacular, expensive, singular events acted out by Neo and Morpheus.

Seymour Chatman has distinguished between 'discourse-time – the time it takes to peruse the discourse – and story-time, the duration of the purported events of the narrative' (1978: 62). The events in *The Matrix Reloaded* imported into *Enter the Matrix* are unique and singular, in comparison to the concertina-style expansion of discourse-time that is a result of the repeated play events. Thus the narrative 'now' of the filmed sequences is more coherent than the fractured, kaleidoscopic 'now' of game-play. This difference need not necessarily signal a difference in stature. If the game world was as visually compelling as the film's world, for instance, perhaps events in the game could 'hold their own' despite the proximity of filmed events. There are precedents within narrative theory for the accounting of such hierarchies. Chatman touches on the question of the relative status of events within a discourse, when he discriminates between kernels (pivotal events) and satellites (elaborative yet non-essential events). 'Narrative events have not only a logic of connection, but of logic of *hierarchy*. Some are more important than others' (1978: 53; emphasis in original). A minor plot event, or satellite, can be 'deleted without disturbing the logic of the plot' (Chatman 1978: 54). The four event strands present in *Enter the Matrix* (filmed and shared with the feature, filmed and unique to the game, digitally animated, played) take up orbits of increasing distance from the core narrative, *The Matrix Reloaded*. The events that are furthest out (the most disposable) are those that come into being through game-play. These manipulated events might be repeated many times, played over, discarded, re-routed and saved as the player struggles to achieve a particular game goal by staying on the road, dodging agents or out-shooting the opposition. The upshot of the overlapping relationship between the feature film and the game is that the player's skills, actions or strategies only have ramifications in the equivalent of a backwater.

In 'Entertainment and Utopia', Richard Dyer has written about the relationship be-tween narrative and non-narrative sequences in film musicals. Dyer argues that the two modes, in combination, evoke and then respond to the yearnings of their audi-ences. Musicals are utopian, not because they necessarily feature perfect worlds, but because they present 'what utopia would feel like' (1993: 273). For instance, a depression-era musical might involve a narrative of struggle, want and aspiration, and then counter this with non-narrative interludes, 'big numbers', where various glittering excesses (of legs, sequins, stairs and energy) churn in an outpouring of decadence and plenty. Dyer's analysis demonstrates that non-similar portions of a text can sug-gestively co-exist, and it is arguable that some computer games have managed to incorporate narrative segments in a manner that compliments game-play. In such cases the game's least variable aspects (including the pre-plotted narrative content) echo the most variable events (those that are choreographed by the player in real-time). The *Tomb Raider* series, for example, prioritises the penetration of new spaces: puzzles are solved, resources gained and monsters despatched, all so that Lara Croft can continue her journey. The player's perspective is quite confined (the 'camera' hov-ers in space behind Croft as she runs along). Space is rationed. This is balanced in the cut scenes, when real-time animations reward the player by swinging the 'camera' on great swooping arcs through the scenery. In other games, such as *Baldur's Gate* (1998), temporal factors (turn-taking, strategic pausing) are central to game-play, and these are complimented by narrative themes related to time: fate, doom, destiny. But *Enter the Matrix*, in part because it answers to an external primary text, is unable to establish any such bond between its various strands.

## SAVING BANE

Other problematic aspects of *Enter the Matrix* can be examined via the narrative theorist Genette's term 'focalisation' (1980: 186, 189–211). Focalisation involves the manner in which a narrative discourse positions or describes a narrator's perspective – perspective in the sense of 'what they see', and what they know. An analysis of focalisation involves asking 'who is the character whose point of view orients the narrative perspective' (Genette 1980: 186) and what, if any, are the limits of their vision or insight. At one point in *Enter the Matrix* the avatar character (and by extension, the player) is compelled to rescue Bane. According to *The Matrix Reloaded* – which, it is fair to expect, the player has seen, Bane is a psychotic traitor. The player cannot act on this information. On the contrary, the player is obliged to ignore what they know. As the imperative tone of this walkthrough ('walkthroughs' are game guides, written by players and distributed online) makes clear, the player who wants to progress through the game must protect Bane. 'Once these cops are down, the real battle starts. You now have to protect Malachi, Bane and Ballard on the centre walkway from the advancement of the SWAT team … Remember that if one of the rebels dies on the walkway, the mission starts over' (Sajban 2003). It is true that there are cases where a narrator within a conventional narrative form might 'know' less that the implied reader. For instance, if the narrator is a naïve child, the reader might be expected to recognise the adult intrigues as they filter through the child's innocent version of events. In a satisfying game, however, information is central to strategy, and the player acts, exercises their prerogative, and witnesses the ramifications and outcomes of their choices.[7] Yet in *Enter the Matrix*, the player has information that they are not allowed to use.

It would be wrong to assume that either the player or the avatar takes a position within the game-text that is equivalent to that of the narrator within a narrative discourse. A major reason for this is that within models of narrative the narrator is not in an orchestrating position: the narrator does not plot or generate events, as much as describe and enact events from within the narrative discourse (under the direction of the 'implied author'). The player controls the avatar (within certain parameters), and thus they have the power to instigate events, and influence their duration: to plot, at least to a degree. For this reason, it is more probable that the avatar and the user provisionally combine to occupy something like a narratee/implied reader position (when they are the recipients of 'told' events) and swing to something like a narrator/implied author position (when they instigate events). But what happens to this mobile bonding of player-with-avatar, when the player (who has seen *The Matrix Reloaded*, as well as the filmed scenes implicating Bane included in the game) is privy to information, of which the avatar must act blissfully unaware? How is the player supposed to feel about their mission to safeguard Bane? The crucial purpose of information in a game is that it will enable or arm the player. In this particular and peculiar case, the player must ignore what they know and proceed with the mission: the outcome of this is that the player is momentarily reduced from instigator to dupe.

## PLAY, STORIES, PRACTICE

As the above suggests, the game's narrative commitments compromise its playability. The game must work against itself, in order to serve the storytelling agenda of the master text. To examine the ramifications of this, of the game's 'supporting role', we return to Jenkins' article, 'Game Design as Narrative Architecture'. More precisely, we turn to the text that strongly influences Jenkins' use of the term 'spatial stories' – Michel de Certeau's *The Practice of Everyday Life* (1988). Throughout this book de Certeau describes a dynamic, generative partnership of non-equals. On the one hand are the sanctioning, legalising and delineating discourses of empowered institutions and producers. On the other, are the proliferating, ephemeral and transient practices of consumers. These practices, in fact, reposition consumption itself as a form of production. While this resistance involves a kind of empowerment, the practices are the symptom of an unequal distribution of power, and this inequity is not itself overturned by these practices. This notion is enlarged upon through various analogies.

Legal discourses describe a rented apartment, for example, but the recouping and personalising practices of the inhabitant generate a form of conversion, when they 'furnish [it] with their acts and memories'. Speakers make a language 'their own' through personality, prerogative, idiosyncrasy or accent (that is, through the act of speaking) while the grid of the modern city is remade through the uses and practices of pedestrians (de Certeau 1988: xxi). For de Certeau, stories are one of the ephemeral practices that convert plotted place into dynamic space. This distinction between place and space is important:

> [A place is] an instantaneous configuration of positions. It implies an indication of stability [whereas] a space exists when one takes into consideration vectors of direction, velocities and time variables … In short, *space is a practiced place*. Thus the street geometrically defined by urban planning is transformed into a space by walkers. In the same way, an act of reading is the space produced by the practice of a particular place: a written text. (1988: 117; emphasis in original)

Places are identified, whereas spaces are actualised. Place is associated with static and ordered clarity, and thus with a denial of temporality (because time infers motion, change, transience). Spaces involve trajectories, tactics, motion and operations. In other words, space, in contrast to place, hosts dynamic change and temporality.

Throughout de Certeau's analysis, power is associated with production, demarcation and the clarity achieved through reduction or distance, while spaces are equated with immediacy and improvisation, wit and resistance. Viewed from the top of a skyscraper, the grid of the city is an ordered plan: a place. From the perspective of the wandering pedestrians crossing paths at street level, the city is a practice: a space. Stories, suggests de Certeau, have the power to convert inert place, into the 'other': into space. Stories 'carry out a labour that constantly transforms places into spaces or spaces into places' (de Certeau 1988: 118). As this indicates, de Certeau's concept of story clearly differs from that of narrative theory; not least because he seems to use the terms story and narrative interchangeably. It should also be clear that it would be a mistake to discount his thesis because of this. It would also be a mistake to draft the two planes of narrative theory, straight onto the two kinds of phenomena detailed in de Certeau's essay – to associate plot and discourse with production and demarcation, and story-events with ephemeral practices, even if it might be possible to argue that there are analogies between the concepts.

What might be more productive is imagining how de Certeau's concept of 'practice' relates to game-play within a digital game, while his account of place, might more resemble those plotted elements within the game. As the player proceeds through a level of *Enter the Matrix*, they generate (via acts and practices) a trajectory. This trajectory through the game's space is not a singular, unwavering arc. It will vary from player to player, and from play session to session. Events are repeated, or repeated only to be altered by chance. The repertoire of the avatar's motions are played with, actions are duplicated, new potentials uncovered, and the player's level of skill increases, an alteration that will be reflected in the increased speed, accuracy or agility of the protagonist. A trajectory is dropped and resumed and repeated until that leg of the journey is completed, the mission accomplished, or the goal achieved. At which point, having attained the state demanded by the game at that moment, another piece of storytelling is unleashed with an animated or filmed slice of narrative. Play is experiential, a chain of non-static events. Narrative segments, on the other hand, are non-interactive, relatively static and pre-ordered. What this suggests is that at least within the context of this computer game, play is closer to the resistant and ephemeral tactics of the consumer, while narrative parallels the plotted strategies of the producer. And what this in turn suggests is that by harnessing the in-game narrative to an extra-gamic cinematic narrative, the authority of the determining producer-definer is amplified, while the authority of the playful consumer-producer decreases in ratio.

According to de Certeau, all consumption – whether of a narrative, a television show, a religion, or an apartment – involves creative reformulations by users. While this proviso should halt our descent into paranoid rhetoric, there is at least one other way that the producers of *Enter the Matrix* appear to have deliberately plotted for the recouping of 'practices' commonly enjoyed informally by player-consumers. The game, in a nod to aspects of *The Matrix* (1999), includes a mode called 'Hacking' on its menu. The player is invited to hack in to discover 'just how deep the rabbit hole goes' and thus unlock variation on levels, access different weapons, and so on. In other words, the hacking mode, takes the place of 'cheats'. Within gamer culture, generally speaking, cheats are discovered and gleefully swapped by players over the internet or through friends. Cheats involve informal, social, consumer practices of creative resistance; they are a tactic for reclaiming the text, for rezoning a space within the text and seemingly outside of the apparent jurisdiction of its producers. By formalising the 'cheat', the suppliers of *Enter the Matrix* effectively re-colonise it, shifting it from an alternative practice, to a sanctioned procedure.

# CONCLUSIONS

*Enter the Matrix* contributes to a cross-media narrative franchise, but it does so only by downplaying its media-specific potential: by making play events answerable to narrative events. Many action-adventure computer games do this, to one degree or another, when they incorporate backstories and narrative qualities and storytelling inserts. The difference is that not only do the play events in *Enter the Matrix* culminate in static segments of plotted discourse, but that these segments are minor events played out by minor characters in the primary narrative: an expensive and spectacular feature film. *Enter the Matrix* is not an independent sibling-text, existing in an open relationship with the narrative of *The Matrix Reloaded*. On the contrary, the events recounted in the game, are bound to the 'main event' of the first narrative: the primary, embedding narrative, the 'now' from which other events are ordered. If different media contribute to a trans-media narrative, does it matter if the various contributing texts are granted equal status? If, as argued here, these texts do not enjoy equal status, what are the ramifications for the bodies on-screen in those texts? What does that say about the status of players, relative to readers or viewers? Game-play, as an ephemeral, proliferating and creative act is suggestive of the resistant practices described by de Certeau. Perhaps, in part, this explains the necessity of containment: play acts are bracketed by the in-game narrative events. These events, in their turn, serve the master narrative. It is valid to ask these questions, but there are also various assumptions that should be avoided. In opposing game-play to narration, for instance, this argument runs the risk of reductively misrepresenting narrative as 'closed' and games as 'open'.

Consent is central to play, and playing *Enter the Matrix* involves negotiating with rules, invariables, controls and commands. The game's environment, although it appears in 3D, actually funnels the player in quite specific directions. Only some doors will open. Only some rooms offer action. Only some actions are effective, and not all acts have outcomes. Action-adventure computer games in general tend to feature fairly extensive plotting. The player, as well as manipulating events themselves, is confronted with narrative material (pre-set events that are related to the user) and characterisation. Usually the bulk of this narrative is slotted between levels as animations. *Enter the Matrix* is not unusual in this regard. But it has real trouble reconciling its various parts. Even the relationship between the various real-time segments is problematic: some are digital animations, others are on film. The overlap between the in-game events and the feature film's narrative events undermines any potential coherence between *Enter the Matrix*'s different elements. In order to 'work' as a whole, the mechanics, physics, limits and possibilities of the game-world would need to establish a degree of productive tension with the non-interactive full motion (animated or filmed) segments.

*The Matrix Reloaded* overshadows *Enter the Matrix*. The proximity of the master narrative limits the sense that the player's actions have demonstrable or alternative outcomes. This in turn limits any sense that the player is exercising their prerogative and making meaningful choices – prerequisites of compelling play experiences. The scale of the master narrative shrinks the player's sphere of influence. In other words, the manner in which *Enter the Matrix* has been drafted into the story arc of *The Matrix* cycle is detrimental to its ability to function as a game. It could be argued that by stretching *The Matrix* narrative over a range of texts and media, the producers have allowed for a variable and fertile array of spaces, which the consumer/audience can dip into, rework and explore. According to de Certeau, consumers will dive through any text, appropriating and refitting it, whatever the strategic intentions of its producers. But we have not been focusing on the many different potential acts of users, nor has any attempt been made here to document the paths taken through the series by actual players. These paths can be transcribed, collated or recorded, but de Certeau warns that any such data might only refer to 'the absence of what has passed by. Surveys of routes miss what was: the act itself of passing by' (1988: 97). What has been under consideration in this chapter are the indications that *Enter the Matrix* is host to hierarchical patterns (of temporality, events and plot). Tracing these patterns is a form of textual autopsy, not a form of fortune-telling: what these texts become in use, to their audiences, is another story.

## NOTES

1   This online review by Mugwum at Eurogamer who rated the game 4/10, is representative of the reviews for *Enter The Matrix*: 'Let's be fair: *Enter The Matrix* has almost its fair share of good bits. The hacking mode is a bit of a laugh, the combat can be quite fun (and if you haven't played *Max Payne* you'll probably enjoy it even more), it's reasonably lengthy (more than the seven hours we've seen quoted elsewhere, especially if you play it on Normal and go for both campaigns), it has slow-motion sniping and some madcap running-away-from-agents rooftop chases, and it plugs some of the gaps in and poses more brain-teasing questions about a storyline that has most of the world hooked, but it is blighted on so many levels by the blundering stupidity of its malformed stillborn design that recommending it is beyond us. The blue pill never looked so tasty' (2003: par. 15).

2   *Enter The Matrix* was developed by Shiny Entertainment, and published by Atari. Players and gaming magazines attribute some of the game's rough edges to its being rushed to meet this simultaneous release date: 'I think the production was rushed and because of this there were a couple bugs left' and 'I like the Matrix. I like everything about it except this game. You can tell this game was rushed to the shelves. There's glitches everywhere [sic]' (www.videogamereview.com: 2003). Thanks to Andrew Burn for bringing this site to my attention. The gaming press made similar statements in *Edge*: 'No doubt some of these technical shortcomings are down to the game having been rushed out in time for the film's May 15 US release (though it was in development for three years). [It shows] signs of having been put together at the last minute' (Anon. 2003: 95).

3    Looking at differences in status between the *media* (games and films) would be a separate question. Also it should be noted that I am not looking at the positive values or status attributed by fans of the *Matrix* to the game precisely because of its links to the franchise. I am not looking at the status of the directors Andy and Larry Wachowski as 'authors', what their involvement with the game means to their fans, or to the game's promoters. Nor am I analysing relationships between 'original' and subsequent texts. These are all valid questions, but they cannot be adequately addressed in a single chapter.

4    Within computer games studies circles, this debate has been differently framed, and dubbed 'narratologists vs. ludologists'; see Gonzalo Frasca (2003). For more on computer games and literary theory see Julian Kücklich (2003).

5    Players go through the game either as Niobe, or Ghost (or one, then the other). For a complete walkthrough of the game, see Sajban (2003). Interviews, trailers and screenshots are available at the game's official website, http://whatisthematrix.warnerbros.html.

6    See http://whatisthematrix.warnerbros.html. The online game is still in development at the time of writing, and so it does not feature in this analysis. As *The Matrix Online* will be an online game in which users play in a shared world it will significantly differ from *Enter The Matrix*.

7    In the game design and analysis manual *Rules of Play*, Katie Salen and Eric Zimmerman write that 'understanding choice in a game can be extremely useful in diagnosing games design problems. If your game is failing to deliver meaningful play, it is probably because there is a breakdown somewhere in the action > outcome chain' (2004: 65). They go on to point out that for the game to work, the players' choices and actions should result in 'meaningful outcomes' and that the player needs to receive clear indications that their actions have ramifications (2004: 66).

# VIRTUAL ACTORS, SPECTACLE AND SPECIAL EFFECTS: KUNG FU MEETS 'ALL THAT CGI BULLSHIT'

Dan North

## STORY AND SPECTACLE

Until relatively recently in film studies, special effects have been viewed predominantly as exercises in technological onanism – anti-cerebral spectacles bolted onto a film text to add sonic and visual punctuation for the benefit of viewers unable to concentrate on even the most linear of narratives without frequent injections of adrenalising pyrotechnics. As Scott Bukatman phrased it, 'neither participating in the satisfactory *telos* of cinematic narrative nor fully inscribed by the terms of an alternative avant-garde, special effects are doubly compromised' (1993: 13). It is difficult and unnecessary to dispute claims that visual spectacle can be used as a fig leaf to hide the shame of substandard storytelling, but since John Caughie and Sean Cubitt's special issue of *Screen* (1999), Michele Pierson's *Special Effects: Still in Search of Wonder* (2002) and Norman Klein's *The Vatican to Vegas: A History of Special Effects* (2004), there has been more evidence of a concerted critical effort to account for special effects as an integral component of the formal and thematic stratagems of commercial cinema rather than as a deleterious side-effect of its perceived deterioration. In addition, Hollywood's gleeful embrace of digital technologies for the production of photorealistic computer-generated imagery (CGI) since the early 1990s has promoted a simulationist aesthetic which has caught the attention of postmodern thinkers in a way that hubcap UFOs and rubber dinosaurs never could.

Using the *Matrix* films as exemplary texts, this chapter argues that, rather than striving to stultify and patronise the cinema audience with opiate and immersive sights, special effects technologies can stimulate the spectator intellectually by connecting text with context, image with apparatus. They should typically incite wonder at three levels: the *diegetic* (the visual effect depicts a spectacular event occurring as part of the story); the *intertextual/comparative* (the visual effect stands as an improvement upon or a re-contextualisation of effects seen within the diegeses of other films or associated media); and the *speculative* (the viewer is invited to imagine how illusory technologies will be deployed in future films or sometimes in the real world). The *Matrix* trilogy deploys almost the entire panoply of available special (physically present on the set) and visual (added in post-production) effects, including digital matte paintings, miniature models and prosthetic make-up. I will here concentrate on one particular scene from *The Matrix Reloaded* (2003) – the sequence which has come to be known as the 'Burly Brawl'. This scene allows the viewer to observe the full mobilisation of virtual actors in computer-generated backgrounds, and deliberately places the human cast in positions of conflict (diegetic and extra-filmic) with their digital doubles.

The *Matrix* trilogy has endeavoured to intertwine narrative and spectacle with minimal disruption to the consistency of either. Within the visual and thematic logic of the films, it makes sense that their diegetic focus oscillates between two separate environments, the first (the 'Matrix') seductively illusory and the other (the 'real' world) inhospitably solid, a scorched Earth whose vestiges remain beneath the sheen of an ageless and pristine simulacrum. Neo finds that he has been plugged into a reconfigured post-apocalyptic planet, and that what he thought of as his body was a digital avatar of his excorporeated mind. The view from inside the Matrix provides the spectator with all of the films' comforting filmic pleasures (the empowered spatio-temporal manipulations of bullet-time, fetish-fashion, indestructibility and choreographed violence) – what Jeffrey Sconce calls a 'hipster playground of high-action and high-fashion' (2000: 204) – while the real world is a harsh and hungry wasteland.

The films present a virtual world which, until it is recognised as illusory, conforms to the physical laws of real-world environments – for Neo and the rest of the Zion rebels, a liberating engagement with and manipulation of the Matrix begins with training the senses to look beyond the surface of the digital illusion to its true composition as an electronic construct. In this sense, the visual fabrication offered to the plugged-in humans of the Matrix is an analogue for the photorealist aesthetic which has defined the majority of the computer-generated visual effects imagery of the last decade. The proliferation of such effects has been accompanied by a popular belief that digital imaging technologies are about to usher in a new age of absolute simulation, in which the computer-generated image will be indistinguishable from filmed reality, and the mediating apparatus through which such illusions are manufactured will cease to have a perceptible presence. As Jay David Bolter and Richard Grusin put it: 'Computer graphics experts, computer users and the vast audience for popular film and television continue to assume that unmediated presentation is the ultimate goal of visual representation and to believe that technological progress toward that goal is being made' (2000: 30). However, an expensive special effect which passes unnoticed represents a large portion of the budget wasted. Visual spectacle is not experienced as pure novel spectacle, but as a comparison with extant forms of display: spectators are not asked to marvel at an independent simulacrum, but at the discrepancy between the real and its mimic. This discrepancy is the space in which visual effects can be seen to be understood by the spectator, and though it might be a gap narrowed by photorealism, extra-textual reference points help to preserve its integrity. Film texts which depend on a collaboration between visual spectacle and thematic continuity exhibit structural patterns which serve to facilitate the spectator's consumption of special effects as both diegetic occurrences and cues to contemplation of external referents.

## DIGRESSIONS AND THE PHOTOREAL

Each component of *The Matrix* franchise is linked to the whole by a series of digressive pathways. At one level these can be narrative-based connections – in *Final Flight of the Osiris* from *The Animatrix* (2003), Jue posts a message from within the Matrix which arrives in the diegetic space of *The Matrix Reloaded*, while the computer game *Enter the Matrix* (2003) features a narrative thread that intersects with that of *The Matrix Reloaded*. At another level, the digressions do not point to intertexts of the franchise but to the apparatus behind their production. More than most film cycles, the *Matrix* trilogy has fostered a network of discursive articles, behind-the-scenes footage, fan fiction, crew interviews and on-set photographs all clustered around the mainframe of an official website (http://whatisthematrix.warnerbros.com), and profusely scattered across various DVD releases. It is also worth noting that, owing to the directors Andy and Larry Wachowski's self-imposed media vacuum, the public relations work has mostly been handled by executive producer Joel Silver, and John Gaeta, the visual effects supervisor. Gaeta's eloquent commentaries on the films, and his willingness to discuss all aspects of his craft have allowed him to impose, via the media, his own technofuturist stamp on how the films are understood and which aspects of their product should be accentuated. Even if the Wachowskis serve as an enigmatic authorial core for the franchise, exerting control over how the characters progress along their storylines, Gaeta's control of the visual effects offers access to the film's technological meta-narrative of technical display via the particular emphases imposed on the text by his authorial input.

In refuting the concept of the ideal spectator acted upon by the film text as posited by psychoanalytic theory, Barbara Klinger has proposed a conception of spectatorship which incorporates digressions ranging from 'generic or narrative intertexts that school the spectator in dramatic conventions, to a host of promotional forms … that arm the spectator with background information' (1989: 4). Although Klinger does not cite them specifically, special effects offer similar digressive prompts; in fact, they derive maximum spectacular impact from their consumption as both convincing fictions and as artificial tableaux. The digressive principle is demonstrated nowhere more explicitly than in the 'Follow the White Rabbit' feature on *The Matrix* (1999) and *The Matrix Revolutions* (2003) DVDs, which prompts the viewer with an opportunity to exit the diegesis to see behind-the-scenes footage of the production techniques used in the making of a particular sequence. The white rabbit motif, borrowed from the film itself, signifies the first step in Neo's voyage of awakening to the true nature of the Matrix, and its use as an on-screen icon for revelation of the film's construction external to its crafted and involving diegesis creates a correlation between the story and the components of its enfranchisement.

Warren Buckland (1999) has discussed the development towards photorealistic digital effects which proffer an illusion so convincing that the spectator is not forced 'out' of the text by special effects which betray their origins as mechanical craftwork.[1] Aylish Wood has built upon Buckland's article to claim that digital effects can enforce the spectator's immersion in the narrative because they are not as markedly artificial as earlier types of trick effects and thus do not infringe upon the *mise-en-scène*. Comparing the miniature model shots of the Titanic in *A Night to Remember* (1958) and the computer-assisted version in James Cameron's *Titanic* (1997), she notes that 'digital effects ... [can be used to] lengthen the time that spectacular elements remain convincing before drawing attention to themselves as illusions' (2002: 372). While I concur with Wood that the increased screen time given to lingering shots of CG models serves to construct a technological meta-narrative that was not fostered by the use of miniatures, I would also argue that the proliferation of behind-the-scenes material and revelatory explication of the technologies behind the effects offsets any conviction in the illusion suggested by photorealistic CGI. At the most cynical level, this is in the service of selling DVDs with the promise of privileged secrets, or of attracting hits to members-only sections of websites, but it also keeps the spectator engaged with the diegetic technologies as reflections or extrapolations of extra-filmic developments in digital imaging. It remains to be seen whether DVD will be used to open the film text democratically, or whether its multiform pathways will be dead-ends designed to impose strict, centrally-authored interpretations upon it or to direct fans towards other purchase opportunities within the same (or co-owned) franchises. In the meantime, the digressive aspects of the film can be seen to preserve the function of special effects to draw attention to themselves without necessitating compromises in technical clarity or *perceptual realism* – a term coined by Stephen Prince to describe that distinctive facet of CGI which aligns it with photorealism by virtue of its detailed textural resemblance to its referent, but which enables it to create impossible objects, locations and characters by virtue of its extreme malleability; CGI thus creates images which are 'referentially fictional but perceptually realistic' (1996: 32).

The first step in rendering an effects sequence consumable as spectacular fodder is to segregate it from the main body of the film, or at least to accentuate its perimeters as a set-piece which forms part of the main narrative trajectory, but which can also be viewed on its own as a metatext of technological display. Michele Pierson notes that in the early 1990s, when CGI offered a novel type of visual display – prior to shedding its 'specifically electronic properties' (2002: 131) – effects sequences would be, in formal terms, 'bracketed for audiences ... as both a technoscientific tour de force for the special effects industry and a special kind of aesthetic object' (2002: 123). The implication might be that, if the stated aim of CGI is development towards absolute simulation, the special effect might come to so closely resemble the 'real' as to negate the disruptive (or distracting) properties of its inchoate incarnations, but as CGI develops an ever greater arsenal of software for the digital capture and imitation of real objects and creatures, so the spectator is equipped with an exponentially expanding set of extra-diegetic, revelatory intertexts that enhance her/his ability to decode the spectacle. The formal properties of film provide a series of opportunities to contemplate the mechanisms behind its production. These are necessities, not defects, of the cinematic viewing position.

## THE BURLY BRAWL AND VIRTUAL CINEMATOGRAPHY

The 'Burly Brawl' refers to a scene midway through The Matrix Reloaded in which Neo fights an ever-expanding army of Smiths, the rogue agent who has acquired the ability to replicate himself. Beginning with a small-scale scuffle with a small group of rogue agents, in which the principle special effects are digital wire removals and head replacements (an increasingly common procedure in which scans of an actor's head are placed over the visage of a stunt performer), the fight escalates to an almost surreal state of extremity. As Neo is called upon to parry the attacks of increasing numbers of Smiths, so the visual effects are required to replace more of the combatants with computer-generated doubles: one of the spectatorial challenges prompted by the scene is to discern the points at which the switches occur, again urging the viewer into contemplation of that discrepancy between real and rendered. Set-pieces in the Matrix films are usually built around a fight sequence and divided from the main body of the film through a variety of stylistic devices. The Burly Brawl, for instance, aside from having its own title by which fans and commentators can refer to it when discussing its particular properties as a segregant of the whole film, has a clearly defined setting, strict dress code, limited colour scheme and its own theme tune ('The Burly Brawl' by Don Davis and Juno Reactor) which is tightly linked to the pacing of the scene.[2]

The Burly Brawl can be seen not just as a highpoint of visual spectacle, but also as a thematic pivot point for the Neo/Smith equation which is resolved in the subsequent 'Super Burly Brawl' at the close of the final film. By placing such a peak of spectacle at the midpoint of the narrative, it serves to reassert the films' structure as a cohesive and symmetrical, almost palindromic three-piece set; the trilogy will primarily be viewed by fans as a single text on collected DVDs, rather than as three distinct works, with the Burly Brawl's combative stalemate at its halfway mark. While the action escalates and Smith multiplies exponentially throughout the second and third films, the monstrative elements of the films' technological meta-narrative effect a parallel development. The scene operates self-consciously as a showcase for something called 'Virtual Cinematography,' the conglomeration of digitally-rendered bodies and backgrounds offering a theoretically unlimited number of shooting angles within that virtual space.

Before 'Virtual Cinematography' became the buzzword preceding the sequels and epitomising their technical advances, The Matrix offered its viewers the signature vi-

Figure 4 – The rig of 120 still cameras used to capture the central action of bullet-time sequences in *The Matrix*.

sual trope of 'bullet-time', an effect of camera movement within ultra-slow motion which, despite occupying no more than twenty seconds of screen time in the first film, was instrumental in establishing the film as technically and stylistically innovative. In bullet-time effects, the human subject is first recorded against a green screen (so that this blank, neutral background can later be replaced by a digitally rendered set) by the rig of up to 120 cameras set to shoot in rapid sequence, providing a series of still images of the action. The bullet-time motif is the validating seal of the franchise, so it might appear that the novelty of this effect could work against the intertextual digressions that are prompted by the appearance of a technical illusion – to what other texts can it refer if its appearance is so intrinsically linked to *The Matrix* environment?

Bolter and Grusin have argued that new media forms exist only in relation to earlier configurations of techniques and technologies (2000: 50). Bullet-time sequences represent an accumulation of existing technologies narrativised and branded as a novel visual spectacle. Some of these are semi-scientific experiments such as the photogrammetric experiments of *The Campanile Movie* (1997), Paul Debevec's 150-second fly-by of the Berkeley campus featuring image-based models of many of the buildings, built by mapping the textures of the buildings captured from still photographs onto three-dimensional representations of the buildings' actual geometry and structure. This provided the impetus for the creation of virtual backdrops into which the human subjects could be composited; Dayton Taylor's 'Timetrack' camera rig, which had been patented in 1997 and tested on several television commercials, sired the (rarely credited) means of capturing the ultra-slow motion foreground action (1996). We could even trace such multi-camera chronophotographic excursions as far back as the motion studies conducted in California in the 1870s by Eadweard Muybridge, 'the man who split the second', as Rebecca Solnit would have it (2003: 7), for bullet-time can be situated within a heritage of scientific investigations into the malleability of temporal spaces. The works of Debevec and Taylor are not obvious intertexts for the vast majority of viewers, but they represent the scientific component of a ritualised convention of action sequences slowed down to allow close scrutiny (even fetishisation) of bodies in motion. So, the spatio-temporal manipulations made possible by bullet-time and later by 'virtual cinematography' are rooted in the scientific as deeply as they are part of the traditions of slow-motion: by reducing the speed of the action to a degree that borders on forensic examination, the *comparative* element of the effect is fulfilled by the production of slower motion than has been seen before.

The early version of bullet-time was not fully virtualised because it required detailed pre-planning from conceptual drawings by comic-book illustrators Steve Skroce and Geoff Darrow (Lamm 2000: 8) to computer-generated pre-visualisations of shots, followed by strict adherence to those plans at the shooting stage. The virtual camera was constrained by the practical procedures required for its use, its very virtuality a cunning illusion. In one piece of explication/publicity, Gaeta promises that the sequels' virtual cinematography was more advanced, allowing the construction of shots to be devised regardless of camera position and possible lines of movement:

We wanted to create scenes that were not in any way restricted by physical placement of cameras. We wanted to totally do away with that and create compositions where the choreography of a shot was what drove the camera. We wanted longer, flowing shots that built action to a level where the interactions of bodies would be so complex there would be no way that we could properly conceive of the cameras during shooting. Instead, we would create the master template for the choreography, and then have complete flexibility to compose shots in post-production. This act of composing, editing and rendering became what we called 'virtual cinematography'. (Quoted in Fordham 2003: 87)

Gaeta claims that the virtual camera technology was supposed to be analogous with the very technology that created the simulacrous environments of the Matrix's non-consensual hallucination. The *Matrix* films thematise technology in ways which are not unfamiliar within discourses around science fiction and cyberpunk cinema, but the visual effects serve to knit the components of the franchise together as a transmedia experience, and go beyond the usual spectacular functions of such illusions to solidify the connections between the diegetic and extra-filmic technologies. For instance, the presence of virtual actors within the films is more than a technical anomaly necessitated by the limits of human performance, but a fully integrated trope mobilising discursive elements within and without the text. 'Within the Matrix, everything is really a state of mind, a mental self-actualisation of your abilities. We wanted to visually depict that power, simulating events that Neo was part of' (Gaeta quoted in Fordham 2003: 86). The virtual actor was thus the result of discussions of superhumanism between Gaeta and the Wachowskis.

## VIRTUAL ACTORS AND CINEMATIC BODIES

It would be all too easy to fall for the suggestion that the age of the synthespian, the 'virtual actor', is imminent, and that soon human actors will interact with computer-generated co-stars without the audience realising which is which. The apotheosis of an animated character into an artificially intelligent, fully simulacrous figure indistinguishable from its carbon-based referent is technically impossible, at least in the foreseeable future, but visual effects are not definitive renderings of a character or event but indicators of the state-of-the-art, offering hints of what is likely to occur in the field of visual illusions in the future (Kerlow 2003). It is understandable that such a competitive industry needs to maintain interest in the potential of its products, but the mythos of the virtual actor has infiltrated the Hollywood blockbuster in recent years and provides an opportunity to re-iterate the three levels of wonder (diegetic, intertextual/comparative, speculative) mentioned at the start of this chapter: the computer-generated body has to fit into the diegesis unobtrusively, interacting with human actors.[3]

The Animatrix prefigures the virtual body as a site of spectatorial solicitation – the CGI striptease which opens Final Flight of the Osiris keeps one foot in the Matrix iconographic pool with its dojo fight sequence and the other in the spectacular syntax of Final Fantasy: The Spirits Within (2001) with the shared assonance of the two titles compounding the comparison. On its release in 2001, Final Fantasy was discussed almost exclusively in terms of the merits of its digital animation, but its human characters, entirely rendered digitally, were usually covered up by combat gear, largely to avoid the notoriously difficult job of animating human flesh and its distinct reflective properties and detailed textures. In the competitive arena of animating virtual actors, where every movement has to be painstakingly crafted – an uncanny flick of the hair or twitch of the nose, if mimicked precisely enough, carries as much spectacular weight as any exploding spacecraft or animatronic puppet – the digital body becomes what Norman Klein terms 'a movie-set wrapped in prosthetics' (2004: 228), but appreciation of such delicate spectacle demands that the spectator be aware of the difficulties and expense involved in their production. Final Flight of the Osiris announces itself as 'advanced' by lingering on detailed surfaces of athletic bodies in action. Viewers with a suspicious propensity towards 'close readings' of such things will notice that Jue exhibits what may well be the world's first sighting of computer-generated

Figure 5 – The virtual body of Jue in the opening scene of the entirely computer-generated *Final Flight of the Osiris* from *The Animatrix* (2003). Jue's movements were created from a combination of motion-capture from live actors and 'key-frame' animation directed by computer animators.

cellulite – the markings of a true body removed from the idealised gloss of airbrushed skin. It is technological intertexts and digressions which keep the spectator aware of the capacities of imaging systems and thus codifies such details not as 'imperfections' but as points of fascination.

Unlike other synthespianic creations such as Gollum in the *Lord of the Rings* trilogy (2001–03) or the reviled character of Jar Jar Binks in *Star Wars: Episode 1 – The Phantom Menace* (1999), where the digital body is designed to suggest organic consistency with human actors occupying the same spaces, in the *Matrix* trilogy the appearance of virtual bodies is thematically consistent, providing a visual articulation of the kinds of physical transcendence which Neo effects within the Matrix. To succeed in the Matrix (that is, to acquire the skills required to manipulate its environs spatio-temporally) is to render one's body cinematic, to abstract oneself subjectively from those around you. Neo's superiority over enemy combatants is conveyed via those most advantageous of subjectival positions: slow-motion and framing which privileges his physical prowess. He is usually at the centre of the frame, with multiple Smiths spilling out of the peripheries. Through an extra-diegetic collusion with the filmmakers, Neo/Reeves becomes powerful through a cinematisation both as a character within the story of a digital simulation, and as a star performer within a filmic space. It is when moving within the Matrix that the unplugged characters can manipulate their bodies – more specifically, their exterior appearance, what Morpheus calls 'residual self image' – to become glamourised upgrades of their organic forms, which are prostrate elsewhere, grimy and linen-clad. Expanding upon Klinger's theory of digression, this dual function of star and character is a good way to encourage the spectator's movement within and without the text, contemplating alternately the imagistic spectacle and the technology behind it. More specifically, as Andrew Shail discusses in this volume, Neo takes on the properties of a *digitally* cinematic body – he is preternaturally fast, fluid and precise in his movements. We could say that he is becoming synergised – he can assume the capacities of a computer game sprite or a synthespian, replicable and spectacular just by virtue of his very existence (as opposed to by virtue of what he actually *does*). His abilities are downloaded – he learns kung fu in a matter of seconds from a makeshift internet; this is not kung fu gathered from actual teaching, but from an imagistic torrent of information that presumably has been gleaned from electronic memories of films and videos, a genre cultist's collection of fight moves and postures. For instance, during the first dojo fight between Neo and Morpheus, Neo echoes the beckoning gesture and scratch of the nose with which Bruce Lee taunted his opponents.

The avatar which performs Keanu Reeves' more grandiose manoeuvres is built from motion capture data which records the co-ordinates of key reference points placed on a performer's body, onto which the digital form is then mapped – facial capture is also performed at very high resolution so that the image of the actor's head can be grafted onto the shoulders of the double. Skin/fabric texture capture completes the process, dressing the rudimentary figure in perceptually realistic layers of skin and clothing. It is a cinematic prosthesis, enabling the performer to enact cinemati-

Figure 6 – Virtual Neo battles virtual Smiths in virtual backgrounds during the 'Burly Brawl' from *The Matrix Reloaded*.

sation without recourse to the usual concealments made possible by tactical editing and composition which can, for instance, hide the face of a stunt double. Ordinarily, a stand-in might only be shot from behind, or in long shot, but the computer-generated doubles, possessing the faces of their subjects, withstand greater scrutiny. The camera swirls around, over and above the combatants, like a magician showing us all sides of a 'magic' cabinet, demonstrating that the customary cutaways are not required. The Burly Brawl toys with viewers' expectations about how an action sequence usually has to work around the limitations of the body. Virtual camera moves are only recognisable as such because we are viewers familiar with where and how a camera can and cannot be moved.

## AUTHENTIC KUNG FU AND 'CGI BULLSHIT'

Quentin Tarantino evidently did not enjoy *The Matrix Reloaded*. When asked about similarities between the Burly Brawl and the climactic battle between the Bride and the Crazy 88 gang in his *Kill Bill: Volume I* (2003), Tarantino was keen to distance himself from such 'CGI bullshit', even though his fight scene is as much a cinematic construction as any in *The Matrix*: 'You know, my guys are all real. There's no computer fucking around. I'm sick to death of all that shit. This is old school, with fucking cameras. If I'd wanted all that computer game bullshit, I'd have gone home and stuck my dick in my Nintendo' (quoted in Dinning 2003: 91). This inelegant but heartfelt, console-jamming analogy articulates a healthy objection to the over-use of CGI to circumvent practical problems of the production process, but Tarantino forgets that one of the reasons for the deployment of such profane digital imagery in the *Matrix* trilogy is precisely for the purposes of differentiation from the films to which it refers (or pays homage) at the conceptual level – Yuen Woo-ping served as a martial arts advisor on both the *Kill Bill* and *The Matrix* series, but the kung fu fighting between Neo and Smith represents a dramatic remediation of the choreographed combat for which he is renowned, rather than the affectionate revisiting and generic authenticity for which he was enlisted by Tarantino.

Steven Connor has suggested that cyberpunk 'blends the evocation of extravagant technological possibilities with the most hard-bitten and unillusioned of narrative styles ... which choke off the exhilaration of futurity' (1997: 135). In the *Matrix* trilogy we find a similar coupling of state-of-the-art technology with generic materials from sources distant from the influence of digitality. This matches the prevalence in cycles of effects-heavy Hollywood blockbusters for repurposing franchises which originate from crude or lo-fi media such as comic books, 2D television cartoons or any other form which is easy to upstage at a technical level: the success of films such as *The Mask* (1994), *Spider-Man* (2002) and *Scooby-Doo* (2002) can be attributed, at least in part, to their remediation of hand-drawn, paint-and-trace techniques through the three-dimensional, perceptually realistic prism of digital media. If the *Matrix* films give the impression of novelty, it is only an illusion created by the prolific remediation of a wide variety of pop cultural reference points; as Tarantino obliquely, perhaps even unintentionally, proclaims, they have appropriated certain qualities of kung fu films, comic book visuals, anime compositions and anti-corporate nu-metal posturing and technologised as if to preclude their imposition upon the new texts – there is, for instance, no homage as literal as Tarantino's borrowing of sets, costumes and even the theme song from *Shurayukihim* (1973).

Leon Hunt outlines three types of authenticating strategies employed in kung fu films in order to re-synthesise the presence of the body, which is otherwise threatened by the technological mediation between a human body and the fighter on-screen (2003: 43). These are delineated as *archival* (the authenticity of actual fighting styles and their cultural, regional and historical specificities), *cinematic* (long takes and a minimum of technical manipulation serve to document the capabilities of a trained martial artist) and *corporeal* (the performer is visibly in real danger or enduring empathetically tangible pain). In technologising the characteristics of a genre which is often embarrassed by its own reliance on technology, the fight scene is constructed around a series of generic modifications, thus fulfilling the *intertextual/comparative* duties of the visual spectacle.

The Burly Brawl is built up from a series of actions appropriated from the kung fu film's generic database, hyperbolised, digitised and virtualised. David Bordwell refers to the kung fu film's use of 'expressive amplification', whereby 'film style magnifies the emotional dynamics of the performance' (2000: 232). This helps to explain how combatants in kung fu films can appear to transcend the limits of plausibility to fight, for example, with superhuman speed (under-cranking the camera during shooting makes the projected film run slightly faster) or skill (supporting wires can help them to defy gravity). One authenticating technique the Burly Brawl employs is what Bordwell terms the 'one-by-one tracking shot', a technique of cinematic authentication through which a fighter is shown moving through a group of combatants in a continuous take. The length of the unedited shot cues the spectator to accept that the performer is demonstrating a sustained sequence of skills: often a fight would be constructed through montage using fast edits and body doubles if, for instance, the lead actor is a pop star, not a fighter (Bordwell 2000: 36). During the Burly Brawl, two such shots occur, the first performed by Reeves and a group of stunt performers, and the second performed by his digital double. One result of subjecting the real and virtual bodies to the same modes of mediation is to again foster the viewer's fascination in a discrepancy between the two, just as the kung fu fanatic will inspect the text for evidence of the star's authenticity or replacement by a diegetically anomalous but technically necessitated stunt double. When Reeves' digital copy flies through the air, the illusion is distinct from its traditional appearance because the virtual body is unfettered by the need for physical support – 'wirework' is always inflected by the body's need for the balanced weight distribution that gives it its distinctive, super-real look. In remediating kung fu motifs and visual stylings, the former represented by, for example, the peda-gogic dojo fight sequence, and the latter by wirework and choreographed combat, the trilogy constructs a dialectic between old and new that is consolidated by intertextual information.

Around the concept of virtual cinematography, the *Matrix* films have presented a series of postulations on the past and future of special effects – it is defined in relation to earlier, less starkly technologised forms of cinema (kung fu, anime) by repurposing their motifs of physical or animated display in the service of a technological spectacle; at the same time as it cites these referents, it offers a utopian idea of a type of cinema without the tethers of indexicality and practical constraints: this liberated point-of-view is equated with Neo's empowerment as a virtualised body free from the gravi-tational, physical restrictions of the real world. Just as this digital puppet (the virtual actor) is tracked onto the movements and characteristics of an organic body, so the filmic construct that is the *Matrix* trilogy has been mapped onto pre-existing formal, stylistic and technological systems. Similarly, the concept of virtual cinematography is, for the time being, a futurological illusion; though its movements are ostensibly freed from the mechanical constraints of dollies and cranes, they are guided by the residual traces of extant reference points, which dictate many of the ways in which an action can remain comprehensible and comparatively spectacular next to its generic and technical antecedents. The spectator becomes empowered with mastery of the film text by a profusion of textual exit points which offer the chance to observe the spectacle from a position that reveals its artificiality at the same time as it celebrates the seductive force of artifice.

## NOTES

1   One of Buckland's main arguments is that the dinosaurs of Steven Spielberg's *Jurassic Park* (1993) represent a visual articulation of possible world theories. Although Paul Sel-lors (2000) has refuted Buckland's thesis on the grounds that he misinterprets the precise definition of possible worlds according to modal philosophy, the article makes useful points about CGI's mimicry of photochemical properties to give the impression of real and syn-thetic elements occupying the same frame space.

2   The scene's title makes it subset of the film's secretive working title 'The Burly Man' in obscure tribute to the Coen Brothers' *Barton Fink* (1991) – *The Burly Man* is the title of the wrestling film on which Fink (John Turturro) serves as a reluctant screenwriter.

3   The virtual actor appears as a narrative element in *S1m0ne* (2002), in which Al Pacino plays a struggling film producer who replaces his temperamental star with a digital actress, who becomes a superstar. Director Andrew Niccol caused consternation from Hollywood's Screen Actors' Guild by hinting that he would cast a virtual actor in the title role, but despite scouting the available technologies during pre-production, he cast former model Rachel Roberts. Elsewhere, the increased use of digital extras and stunt doubles, sometimes as

anonymous crowds, sometimes as superheroic alter-egos – see, for instance, the reliance on virtual actors for action scenes in *Spider-Man* (2002) and *Hulk* (2003) – has led to a presumption that the synthespian will eventually take over in leading roles. In Hong Kong's *Seung Fei/Princess D* (2002), a computer game designer creates a female synthespian as the centre-piece for a game in which the player confronts everyday problems. Virtual stars such as Yuki Terai, who has starred in a series of commercials, animated shorts and pop videos, have been a common sight in Japan since the mid-1990s.

# THE TRANSPARENCY OF THE INTERFACE: REALITY HACKING AND FANTASIES OF RESISTANCE

Thomas Foster

*It's the dream of every hacker since ancient times.*
*To get root on reality. To make the natural hack.*
*— Tony Daniel (2004: 186)*

This chapter focuses on how the *Matrix* trilogy reworks a typical cyberpunk thematic: the constraints placed on agency and free choice by the programming structures that characters must negotiate. Within such constraints, agency resides in the ability to hack the rules that govern these structures, a motif that can be traced back directly to the plot of William Gibson's *Neuromancer*, which focuses on a scheme to 'cut the hardwired shackles' that keep an artificial intelligence from acting independently of its programming (1984: 132). The *Matrix* films are structured by a fantasy of feeding this kind of agency back into real-world contexts, literalising Andrew Ross' argument that hacking can provide a model for knowledges resistant to 'existing systems of rationality that might otherwise be seen as infallible' (1991: 100). Within the cyberpunk tradition of print science fiction, these constraints are most often conceived as the determination of identity by bodily particularity and as behavioral compulsions. This tradition can be traced through the thematics of 'hardwiring' in well-known cyberpunk narratives such as *Neuromancer* and Neal Stephenson's *Snow Crash* (1992), as well as in alternative texts by feminists and writers of colour.[1] The critical value of this tradition resides in its refusal either to follow Daniel Dennett in opposing hardwired or evolved instincts to neural plasticity and a capacity for learning and change (1991: 184), or to imagine that the only way to overcome our own immutable 'biological urges' is to deny the body and embrace the transcendent freedom of a 'postbiological' condition, as in Peter James' novel *Host* (1995: 159).

The *Matrix* trilogy seems to have inspired recent cyberpunk writing to apply this model to the normative power of cultural and social formations more generally, a possibility already implicit in Gibson's definition of cyberspace as 'consensual hallucination' (1984: 51). These more recent texts explore instabilities in the category of the natural, or more precisely the distinction between nature and culture in highly-mediated technological contexts. Original cyberpunk writer Rudy Rucker's most recent novel describes 'physics' as 'a matter of Style – not Law' in virtual realities (2004:

452), while Gwyneth Jones has written a series of novels involving a new technology capable of changing 'the code of reality' (2003: 30).[2] The *Matrix* trilogy's version of this fantasy centres around Neo's status as the One and his ability to modify the simulation. How do Neo's abilities differ from Morpheus' or the other members of the Zion resistance? From the Agents who police the Matrix? Is this ability an innate 'gift,' or is it a skill that can be learned, as implied by the scenes depicting Neo's training sessions with Morpheus in the first film? Is the ability to slow time or to levitate a function of technical competence and manipulation of programming code, which would seem to be the job of the Operators who remain outside the Matrix working at their computer screens, or do these abilities have to be activated from within the Matrix, and if so then how? By sheer force of will, self-confidence or mystic transcendence, as is suggested at different points in the film? The central fantasy structure of the Matrix depends on the conflation of these different possible interpretations, in order to suggest that the cultivation of scepticism and critical distance, the refusal to capitulate to the naturalness of the rules written into the simulation, can give the characters the same power over reality that root or superuser access to an operating system can give users of that system. This 'reality hacking' is a relatively conventional cyberpunk fantasy. Yet how does the trilogy engage with the problems and limits encountered by such desires for agency and resistance, within what Manuel Castells calls 'network geometries' (1998: 347)?

## DISSENTING VIEWPOINTS AND CONSENSUAL HALLUCINATIONS

*The Matrix* (1999) famously begins by introducing a series of challenges to the realism of the fictional world Neo unknowingly inhabits. Along with Neo, audiences are invited to participate in this alienation-effect, as we learn that the 'world' depicted in the film is also an illusion being pulled over our eyes, as Morpheus later tells Neo. In this way, the film associates what Michael Benedikt calls the desire for 'magic in cyberspace' with a critical self-consciousness about the constructedness of the social worlds the film's characters and its audiences inhabit. 'After all, why have cyberspace if we cannot (apparently) bend nature's rules there?' Benedikt asks, rhetorically (1991b: 128). *The Matrix* derives its most powerful effects from situating such 'violations of principles' within a seemingly mimetic artificial reality. Benedikt points out, however, that 'there is a limit to how frequent and severe [such violations] can become before credibility, orientation and narrative power begin to be lost' (ibid.). He therefore argues a virtual space can function as a site of social interaction only when 'all comers to a given domain at a given time in cyberspace are able to see/ hear largely the same thing' and, in a comment especially relevant to *The Matrix*'s representation of Trinity, Morpheus or Neo's abilities to violate the principles written into the virtual world, when 'the same direction [is] considered as *up*' for all users who wish to interact with one another (1991b: 180; emphasis in original). Benedikt emphasises, then, that in a shared virtual world data structures can only be partially customised for each individual; subsets of each object and person in the virtual world must possess consistent 'self-similarity as a norm', and he argues that it is only the possibility of combining diverse, customised 'realities' with a dependable, self-similar and unchanging space of interaction that 'allows us to achieve both the realness of the everyday world *and* the magical properties we would wish for cyberspace' (1991b: 181; my emphasis).

The Matrix tends to be associated with the tyranny of objective reality as a deceptive and externally-imposed social norm, but the ending of the final film in the trilogy, *The Matrix Revolutions* (2003), suggests that the kind of balance that Benedikt calls for is in fact the utopian goal of Neo's dissatisfaction with the virtual world of the Matrix. The only real hint of what will become of the Matrix after Neo sacrifices himself to establish a truce between the humans and the machines appears when a virtual character, a rogue program who takes the form of a young South Asian girl, commemorates Neo's death by seizing partial control of the Matrix and crafting a beautiful sunrise: as we watch this scene, the Oracle turns to the girl and asks, 'Did you do that?' This argument for a balance between individual desire or personal agency and submission to shared norms is central to Benedikt's claim that cyberspace should be understood as a third alternative to either realist, empiricist epistemologies which assume the existence of an objective, natural world, or idealist epistemologies that emphasise the 'subjective world of [individual] consciousness'; instead, cyberspace for Benedikt is part of the social 'world of objective, real and public structures which are the not-necessarily-intentional products of the minds of living creatures, interacting with each other' (1991a: 3). However, the difference between ordinary sociality and cyberspace as a shared or public space of communication and interaction is that in cyberspace 'the ballast of materiality [is] cast away … perhaps finally' (1991a: 4). In the fantasy of *The Matrix*, cyberspace does not simply dematerialise these objective social structures; instead, it renders them plastic and malleable, available for revision and editing, once we have mastered the trick of understanding them as such. In this sense, the film represents what Castells calls the reinscription of political power in informational societies as 'cultural codes' (1998: 347). For Castells, the increasing mediation of social relations through information networks results in visible political institutions being reduced to theatre and politics to 'symbol manipulation in the space of the media'. These institutions are therefore 'voided of power', which, however, does not disappear but instead becomes 'immaterial', relocated at the level of 'the ability to frame life experience under categories that predispose to a given behavior' (ibid.). The Matrix's deceptive function seems to correspond to this transformation in the operation of power.

To the extent that the film is able to plausibly rationalise its violations of narrative plausibility within the narrative itself, it is able to add an ironic, even subversive dimension to our familiar vocabularies of choice or freedom, determinism or inevitability.

For instance, in an early scene, Neo's boss lectures him on having a 'problem with authority', and tells him he has two choices, to do his job the right way or to lose his job. This scene dramatises the way in which, in real life, we are continually confronted with choices which are in fact limited and manipulated in advance to our disadvantage; Neo's boss confronts him with the fact of his (economic) powerlessness, framed as freedom of choice. This situation is implicitly posed as analogous to the illusory freedom offered by the Matrix itself.[3] At the same time, the lecture Neo receives – a counterpoint to his first conversation with Morpheus – also raises the question of what kinds of authority can be challenged: the laws of gravity or the conservation of momentum and energy, as well as capitalist efficiency? What is the point of blurring this distinction, as merely two different forms of what Agent Smith later describes to Neo as the 'sound of inevitability'? Does it displace the analysis of power and therefore the effectiveness of resistance onto a misguided object? Or does it constitute a refusal to abandon agency, perhaps even an attempt to reimagine it in ways appropriate for a network society? This resistance to inevitability, passivity and quietism has a disturbing corollary, however. Nothing is inevitable in the world of the Matrix because nothing is random, either; everything can be changed by the application of will (or perhaps skill) because everything in the Matrix is structured, designed and produced by (a combination of human and machine) will, a corollary most evident in Morpheus' unwavering belief in the predestined prophecy of the One.

The Matrix then effectively literalises the central premise of ideology critique as it has been developed within the tradition of cultural studies: that ideology works through processes of naturalisation. From this perspective, denaturalisation is then liberating, since it opens what we thought were inevitable features of the social world to intervention and change; it turns reified products back into contingent processes, or, to use Castells' terms, it makes unspoken cultural frames and codes accessible to explicit political debate. The ambiguities, ironies and inconsistencies surrounding the Matrix, the way in which the films try to keep open the question posed to Neo ('what is the Matrix?'), arise from the fact that, within this immersive simulation, denaturalisation is paradoxically re-naturalised as the foundation of (virtual) existence. To the extent that the Matrix films register this paradox, they cannot just be dismissed for mystifying the operation of power or as wish-fulfillment fantasies generated by category errors, such as the conflation of technical manipulation with the power of the individual will. During Neo's first trip back to the Matrix, as he gazes out at the landscape of the simulation that he thought he knew before, Morpheus comments 'it's unbelievable, isn't it?' This comment implies both that the realism of the simulation is so overwhelming as to be incredible, and also suggests the value of scepticism and critical thought, as in the tradition of ideology critique cited above. The positive, liberating effects of disbelieving the Matrix are emphasised when Neo asks what it means that he has all these memories that never actually happened. Trinity's reply is that 'It means the Matrix can't tell you who you are.'

This literalisation of social constructionist theories is also suggested in the training scenes that occur after Neo is removed from the Matrix. Rather than immediately return him to the Matrix, Morpheus and his crew's operator, Tank, use Neo's neural interface to load a simpler program into his brain. Neo's virtual body image appears in the middle of a featureless blank plain, and Morpheus appears to explain that they call this space the Construct. This virtual environment exemplifies what Benedikt calls a 'patently unreal and artificial' reality, a social space that does not conceal or naturalise its own status as a social product or construct. The Construct therefore reveals the fundamental nature of the Matrix itself, in a more obviously visible and spectacularised form. Morpheus draws attention to the implications of this deconstruction of reality by commenting on how Neo's appearance, his hair and his clothing, have changed. Morpheus explains the changes as reflecting Neo's 'residual self-image' and as a 'mental projection of [his] digital self'. This language tends to associate the changes in self-presentation that all the characters undergo when they enter the Matrix with constraints on their ability to take advantage of the constructedness of their virtual avatars or personae, as data structures within the simulation. Those constraints seem to include a desire for consistency in one's own identity, as well as the mediation or filtering of one's own self-image through fashion and media clichés.

At the same time, the shifts in Neo's appearance also imply a capacity for self-editing, an ability to alter the Matrix. Morpheus' reference to Neo's seemingly unconscious ability to modify his 'mental projection' is the film's first intimation of a form of agency that involves unmediated or direct manipulation of the simulation, a form of agency especially associated with Neo's supposedly unique gifts as the One – though we have in fact seen Agent Smith perform a far more radical act of editing, one that is not unconscious at all, when he removes Neo's mouth while he is being interrogated. This possibility for agency is emphasised when Morpheus takes Neo through the 'jump program', in order to clarify for Neo the ways in which he is still limiting himself by overidentifying with the realism of the virtual setting within which they have just been practicing their fighting skills. Neo is still misreading the constructedness of virtual environments and assuming that they possess the same facticity as the natural world. Morpheus confronts Neo by asking whether he thinks 'my being stronger or faster has anything to do with my muscles, in this place?' After having described the sparring program as having the 'same basic rules' as the 'programmed reality' of the Matrix, Morpheus tells Neo that what he 'must learn is that these rules are no different than the rules of a computer system. Some of them can be bent. Others can be broken.' But despite the assertion that the simulation works no differently than a computer system, the film also wants to present the bending or breaking of rules as working differently in the Matrix, to present reality hacking as working differently than hacking as such. In a normal computer system, rules can be broken only if it is possible to gain access to the programming structures, through technology. In the sparring program or the Matrix, Neo, Morpheus and the others seem able to break the rules simply by willing it

– or more accurately, by recognising that the rules are there, written into the program, rather than facts of nature. This ambiguity, the assertion that resistance resides in understanding the nature of computer systems, but that this understanding is enough in itself to constitute a successful hack of the system, is also central to the fantasy structure of the *Matrix* films.

To drive home this lesson in denaturalisation, Morpheus orders his crew's operator, Tank, to load their jump program. But the whole point of the scene that follows is that the ability to perform such death-defying feats is not written into the program, since Neo fails to make it, like everyone who tries the program for the first time. The function of the jump scene is to make it clear that the ability to violate the simulated law of gravity requires some kind of agency on the part of users inside the virtual simulation, and not just commands entered from outside. Morpheus tells Neo that he is trying to 'free your mind', and that the key to transcending the limits of the program and learning not to fall is not technical skill but simply belief, the ability to 'let it all go'. The message of the film at this point is that neither skill at coding nor the privileged access necessary to manipulate the programming languages that generate the virtual world are enough to take advantage of the flexibility, the 'magic', made possible by virtuality. This act of will is actually opposed to technical skill when Morpheus tells Neo not to think but to know he can break the rules.

The film then wants us to believe not just that the immersive environment of the Matrix elicits subjective identification and acceptance of the limits on agency imposed by the simulation, but also that the refusal to accept that illusion is in itself capable of objectively altering the programming structures of the Matrix. The films try to convince us that the way the Matrix solicits its users' belief, by mystifying the technological infrastructure that produces the illusion, can be turned against the Matrix itself, by using immersion within the Matrix as an opportunity to rewrite the rules of the simulation without any technological mediation, as if both power and resistance could take advantage of the lack of any visible interface between users and the Matrix. Part of the film's ambiguity on this point arises from the idea that a direct neural interface can be conceptualised as a 'mental projection' of a 'digital self', so that changes in the beliefs of that self might be concretised within the mental projection or virtual avatar that the system produces. But the film is equally insistent upon abstracting and universalising that capacity to affect the system.[4]

## GOING ROOT ON REALITY

As Andy Clark notes, to the extent that the Matrix functions successfully as an illusion realistic enough to solicit belief, it is difficult to understand how the rules governing the simulation can be bent at all: 'If your brain was getting its inputs from, and feeding its outputs to, this kind of immersive virtual reality set-up, there should be no room to break the laws of physics just by willing it so' (2003; par. 38). How can the film get away with this shift into wish-fulfillment, best represented by Trinity's telling Neo he cannot be dead because she loves him? I want to suggest that this shift does not simply represent a kind of generic hybridity, incorporating fairytale conventions or the magic realism of Asian martial arts films. Instead, the film's representation of immersive virtual realities gains power by analogy with the forms of privileged access to deeper levels of programming languages within a Linux or Unix open source operating system. In contrast to a proprietary OS, like Windows, where the system's source code is a closely-guarded, copyrighted form of intellectual property to which users of the system have no access whatsoever, in a Linux OS it is possible either to log in as a regular user, which permits you to run applications in ways that are already built into the operating system, or to log in as a *root* or *superuser*. Superuser access effectively allows the user to treat read-only files (that is, files that function as necessary components of the operating system) as open to rewriting and editing (as not qualitatively different from applications that the user has generated). Superuser access allows users to customise their own operating systems, assuming that they have the expertise at coding required. As any Linux user knows, however, the first piece of advice you are likely to get about superuser access is not to use it at all, no matter how tempting it may seem, since logging-in in this manner makes it very easy to eliminate or render unusable key elements of the operating system.

In applying this model to the *Matrix* trilogy, the first thing we note is that the extraordinary abilities of both the Agents and the Zionite resistance fighters can be explained as forms of superuser access, though as authorised superusers the Agents seem better able to take advantage of it. Trinity and Morpheus can jump tall buildings at a single bound, but only the Agents are faster than a speeding bullet, at least until Neo appears. However, it remains ambiguous whether these kinds of manipulations are being performed by the Agents within the simulation, in the same way that Morpheus or Neo seem able to bend the rules by believing they can, or whether the work of rewriting, of coding, is simply not visible from within the simulation, where we are told the code is processed by an image translator into a visual interface that effectively conceals the true nature of the software mechanisms that produce it. Do the Agents truly possess the agency required to transcend the terms of the simulation, or do they mask the mediated nature of this kind of agency, its dependence upon a technological interface?

Superuser access makes possible a more genuinely interactive relation to the operating system. The relevance of this analogy to Neo's abilities is made relatively explicit in *The Matrix Reloaded* (2003), when Councillor Hammonds takes Neo down to the engineering level of Zion. He points out that 'No one comes here, unless there's a problem. That's how it is with people. No one cares how it works as long as it does.' This statement accurately defines the attitude encouraged by proprietary operating systems and, indeed, by the graphic user interface itself, which attempts to reduce interactivity to the act of clicking on the icons provided by the system. The Councillor goes on to assert that he has no idea how Neo can accomplish what he does in the Matrix, but that he is sure there is a reason, suggesting that Neo merely has some unusually privileged access to the engineering level of the Matrix and that his seemingly unique gifts can be explained in terms other than the Christ symbolism that Morpheus tends to prefer.

Superuser access similarly implies a critique of the limits of what Arjun Appadurai calls 'consumer fetishism', in which 'images of agency' encourage the consumer 'to believe that he or she is an actor, where in fact he or she is at best a chooser' (1996: 42). But a more genuine form of agency can be gained only at the cost of greater demands on the user's skills and education; it is in no way a form of agency that can dispense with the mediation of the computer interface. In contrast, the *Matrix* films want to have it both ways: the virtual simulation is pure manipulation. The Matrix is control, Morpheus tells Neo, a 'computer-generated dreamworld'. But since the only reality in the Matrix is this mystification, it can be represented as a place where belief is real, and disbelief in the 'reality' users are force-fed has real, disruptive effects. The contrast Morpheus makes between Neo and the Agents stands directly opposed to Councillor Hammonds' insistence that the One's special abilities can be explained technologically. Morpheus tells Neo he will be the first to defeat an Agent, since 'their strength and their speed are still based in a world that is built on rules. Because of that, they'll never be as strong or as fast as you can be.' Recognising the limits of the rules written into the software structure of the virtual world leads to the discarding or the transcendence of those rules, rather than the ability to manipulate or rewrite them, and it is therefore at this point that the Linux superuser analogy tends to break down. This aspect of the films reasserts an essentialist, humanist ideology in order to associate specifically human forms of agency with pure freedom, in contrast to the discipline of interactivity required by human-computer interfaces (though this essentialist reassertion of a transcendent humanity is at least qualified by the compromise with the machines, the recognition of mutual dependence, that ends the final film in the trilogy).[5]

The recurrent visual motif of scrolling machine code seems designed to sustain this ambiguity between forms of agency enabled by computer interfaces and some more or less mystical human ability to transcend technological limitations. Immediately after Morpheus recounts the story of the One to Neo, there is a scene in which Cypher explains the necessity of 'looking' at the Matrix's code, rather than being immersed in the illusion, since the Matrix otherwise overwhelms users with information, in contrast (presumably) to the Construct program. This scene establishes a contrast against which the meaning of the end of the first film can be read, a contrast that defines the real difference between Neo, as the One, and the other resistance members. At the moment when Neo takes on the full powers of the One, after he has been shot in the Matrix by Agent Smith and revived by Trinity, he gains the ability to directly perceive the software code underlying the visual surface of the Matrix, without depending on a computer interface. As Neo looks around, the interior of the building dissolves into lines of code (still partially mimetically organised as a blueprint or diagram). The film then returns to a realistic depiction of the simulation, but with Neo now able to stop bullets and perform other fantastic feats, beyond even the abilities of the Agents. In this scene, Neo becomes the only character who has a direct, unmediated relationship to the mediating structures and languages that allow the Matrix to exist. None of the other characters possess this ability. Neo's paradoxically unmediated relationship to mediation expresses the central fantasy of the *Matrix* films. Neo possesses a seemingly natural ability to denaturalise the Matrix. This ability is extended to his perception of the other characters in the scene in *The Matrix Reloaded* in which Neo revives Trinity by reaching into the code that forms her virtual avatar and repairing the damage that has been done to her.

The films then define a new ideology of transparency, associated not with the unthinking acceptance of surface appearances, but with the ability to see through such realistic illusions. While immersion in the illusion naturalises appearances, Neo's ability to perceive their constructedness naturalises that ability as a function of the unaided critical faculties of the human mind, independent of any technological prosthesis or interface. The *Matrix* films tend to externalise mediation and the relationship between humans and computers in ways that oversimplify and re-naturalise those relationships. Transparency here refers not to naturalisation, but to instrumentalisation. Neo's ability to perceive the mediation of reality through software structures is conflated with his freedom to manipulate and revise those structures as he wishes, as if they did not structure his agency as well as the environment in which he exercises it, as if by changing reality he was not also changing himself in ways that he could not control or predict in advance.[6] The *Matrix* films therefore evade the self-criticism implicit in their own model of resistance and agency, an evasion that explains why Neo's critical perspective on reality does not translate into a redefinition of masculinity, for instance.

## THE PROBLEM OF RACIAL REPRESENTATION

The ways in which the trilogy tends to re-contain the more radical implications of its own model of reality hacking is most evident in the reticence the films display toward the possibility of the characters self-editing their own body images, despite the centrality of such themes in cyberpunk fiction.[7] The main example of this possibility is self-stylisation – that is, the ways in which the characters' clothing and hair change when they enter the Matrix. We might well ask whether the self-presentation of the black characters in the Matrix reflects the power of racial constructions and stereotypes: are the styles assumed by Morpheus or Niobe in cyberspace influenced by histories of racial othering, or do those styles constitute their own self-conscious resistance to those histories? How might Neo or Trinity's styles constitute a spectacularisation of whiteness, and how is that self-production affected by gender? In the scene in which he introduces Neo to the Construct, however, Morpheus suggests such changes should be understood as expressing the truth of the characters' inner selves. This interpretation works against the possibility of reading the characters' different modes of virtual self-presentation as forms of identity play, with gender and racial norms and preconceptions. In fact, the most prominent examples of the editing of virtual embodiment all involve male access to female body images, most notably the scene in which the Merovingian hacks a female character in order to transform her aloof style into a willingness to perform oral sex on him in the restroom of the virtual restaurant. This scene constitutes the dark underbelly of Neo's ability to heal Trinity by similarly hacking her body image. But the films never directly represent a character choosing to hack his or her own image, however tempting it is to read Morpheus or Niobe's virtual avatars as attempts to hack the cultural codes of racial representations and stereotypes.

The films' only direct thematising of race as a modifiable style appears in the training scenes, qualifying Lisa Nakamura's argument that the dominant convention in the *Matrix* films is to represent race as 'solid' and unalterable rather than 'fluid' (2002: 88). When Neo is first being reintroduced to the Matrix, after being rescued from his pod, the crew's operator downloads a whole set of martial arts skills directly into Neo's nervous system, his mind and body, through his interface jacks. Neo's first comment on the exhilarating effects of this sudden expertise is to exclaim 'I know kung fu!' When Neo and Morpheus square off against one another, they both reproduce iconic gestures associated with Bruce Lee, especially from the film *Enter the Dragon* (1973). Neo swipes his nose with his thumb, while Morpheus extends one hand and waves the tips of his fingers inward to invite Neo to come to him.

This appropriation of an Asian male action star's corporeal style reduces Asian-ness to a generalisable and appropriable set of signifiers, while also implying that such appropriations are attractive to both white and black men and that both white-ness and blackness might be subject to a similar transformation.[8] Since the different meanings this appropriability might have for men of different races is never elabo-rated in the film, however, the effect of such scenes is to reinforce the ways in which the denaturalisation of race, its detachment from any ontological grounding in fixed biological or anatomical features, is not liberating, but instead only imposes a narrow limit on what kinds of performances can count as 'Asian' (or 'white' or 'black'), as Nakamura argues in her analysis of identity tourism in text-based virtual communi-ties (2002: 39). Nakamura's important work on racial performance in online contexts is relevant to this reading of the *Matrix* films, since she defines how, in cyberspace, racial ideologies are defined by the disarticulation of the normative from the natural. In this sense, the Bruce Lee body language that both Neo and Morpheus use retains the normative power to define Asian stereotypes, even though that norm cannot be legitimated as natural.

The denaturalised circulation of racial stereotypes is thematised in an exchange between Morpheus and his former lover Niobe in *The Matrix Reloaded*. Niobe reminds Morpheus of his reputation as a dancer, and he replies 'there are some things in this world, Captain Niobe, that will never change'. Then he sees her new lover, and adds that there are some things that will. The dialogue here plays with racial stereotypes: Morpheus might be paraphrased as asserting that black men will always (be thought to) have natural rhythm. The scene raises the question of what the technological mediation of embodiment and race changes and what it does not change, precisely because such mediation allows us to choose what we change about ourselves and what we do not.[9] A play with the self-conscious production of race and racial stereotypes informs Morpheus' first face-to-face dialogue with Neo, most obviously in Morpheus' assertion that the truth the Matrix conceals is that Neo is a slave. The power of this line of dialogue is enhanced by the historical resonance it gains when uttered by a black actor like Lawrence Fishburne, even as the whole point of the statement is to define an experience of slavery that is generalised across racial lines, that applies to Neo as well as to Morpheus.

## CONSENSUAL HALLUCINATIONS

British science fiction writer Charles Stross argues that cyberpunk is not obsolete, but instead constitutes the framework for an ongoing dialogue within the genre. Stross characterises himself as belonging to the third generation of this dialogue, writers who re-imagine cyberpunk after the dotcom boom and bust, often on the basis of direct programming experience, and he argues such writers no longer 'romanticise cyberspace' (2003a: 86). As suggested at the beginning of this chapter, the *Matrix* films have played an important role in shaping the latest stage in this dialogue, by encouraging consideration of the critical possibilities inherent in going root on our consensual hallucinations and applying the model of hacking to social formations and knowledges. At the same time, these films show how difficult it can be not to romanticise cyberspace. The implications of such models of sociality and dissent for racial formations constitute a particularly urgent point of both danger and promise in this ongoing dialogue.

## NOTES

1  Stephenson's novel defines hardwiring as the basis of an analogy between human neural structures and ROM, or read-only memory, chips. In particular, the novel imagines that language acquisition is a process analogous to the way information placed on ROM chips 'transmutes into hardware' so that such learned skills are biologised as 'part of the brain's deep structure' (1992: 277).

2  One of the earliest examples of this shift in cyberpunk writing would be Bruce Sterling's

exploration of challenges to consensus reality in *Zeitgesit* (2000: 150). Especially among British writers, this shift is often associated with Vernor Vinge's (1993) speculations on a technological 'singularity' or ramping up of the pace of change to the point of unrepresentability, usually as a result of the achievement of strong artificial intelligence. Charles Stross, for instance, describes a 'limited local singularity' as a 'consensus reality excursion' (2003b: 275).

3   Indeed, the films raise this contradiction to a higher level when Neo learns, in *The Matrix Reloaded*, that the One is not the savior of the human race from the machines but just another control mechanism.

4   One possible source for this representation is John Varley's 'Overdrawn at the Memory Bank' (1976).

5   Laura Bartlett and Thomas Byers analyse the persistence of humanist ideologies in *The Matrix* in 'Back to the Future: The Humanist Matrix' (2003).

6   Slavoj Žižek adapts Sherry Turkle's pun on 'taking things at interface value' (which for Turkle describes a willingness to accept computer programs as persons) to define a similar postmodern 'shift in the use of the term "transparency"', though for Žižek this shift represents the mystification of computer technology under the rubric of interactivity (dependence on a GUI), rather than a mystification of the conditions of access to underlying programming structures, as I argue in this chapter (Turkle 1995: 104; Žižek 1997: 131).

7   Nakamura makes this point (2002: 80). For cyberpunk alternative, see Ted Chiang's 'Understand' in *Stories of Your Life and Others* (2002) or Cory Doctorow's 'Ownz0red' in *A Place So Foreign and 8 More* (2002).

8   This is assuming that Keanu Reeves' somewhat ambiguous racial persona is generally received as passing for white. Peter X. Feng similarly argues that 'in the Construct, everyone knows kung fu', moreover, the fight scenes are a pastiche of Jet Li's fighting style (2002: 157).

9   A similar point emerges in the climactic fight scene in *The Matrix Revolutions*, when Agent Smith characterises humanist values like peace, love and freedom as 'temporary constructs of the human intellect, as artificial as the Matrix itself', and then asks why Neo persists in the face of this insight. Neo's answer is 'because I choose to'.

# CYBER NOIR: CYBERSPACE, (POST)FEMINISM AND THE *FEMME FATALE*

Stacy Gillis

> Why aren't there any women in cyberspace?
> – Scott Bukatman (1993: 314)

Although the *Matrix* trilogy is predicated upon the quest narrative of 'the One', a male hacker-figure who is mentored by a man and whose opponent takes the form of a man – indeed, 'the Man'[1] – it is woman who is the referent of the films. The films are actually Trinity's story, as the Architect makes clear that while Neo is version 6.0, Trinity, or, more precisely and most importantly, the level of emotion she arouses in Neo, is version 1.0. Her position of power is the result of the intersection of two genres in the trilogy – cyberpunk and noir. This intersection in Trinity posits a cyborgian *femme fatale*: that is, she is an ass-kicking, leather-wearing cyberpunk, following in the footsteps of Molly Millions from William Gibson's *Neuromancer* trilogy (1984–88), as well as drawing upon a heavily stylised representation of noir femininity, exemplified by the *femmes fatales* in classic American film noir such as *The Maltese Falcon* (1941), *Double Indemnity* (1944), *The Postman Always Rings Twice* (1946) and, more recently, *Blade Runner* (1982) and *Basic Instinct* (1992). With such a weighty history behind the representation of woman in the film, it is no surprise that Trinity dies at the end of the final film; her death was anticipated from the moment she appeared on-screen, dressed all in black, with leather boots and hair slicked back hacking into a computer in the Heart o' the City hotel – where the police disastrously and erroneously claim that 'I think we can handle one little girl' – and then running away from the Law through a murky noiresque city. As a cyberpunk, Trinity the hacker might exist beyond the films' narrative but because of the films' reliance upon the tropes of the trangressive film noir heroine, she must die, despite her action-hero abilities.[2] The year before *The Matrix* (1999) was released, Yvonne Tasker was still pointing out that 'the majority of big-budget action movies continue to focus primarily on male protagonists and to position women in supportive, often romantic roles' (1998: 67). Trinity's position as the catalyst for all action in the films is one avenue by which this subordination has been recently complicated. But as her function is to support Neo both in and out of the Matrix, Trinity's meaning is ultimately contained by the inscrutable category *and* function of woman. This chapter will first locate the *Matrix* trilogy within the noir tradition before moving onto a discussion of the ways in which Trinity embodies a (post)feminist noir femininity.

## CYBER NOIR

Steven Connor argues that cyberpunk 'blends the evocation of extravagant technological possibilities with the most hard-bitten and unillusioned of narrative styles, borrowed from the historical forms of the detective story and the film noir' (1997: 135). Cyberpunk certainly articulates many of the concerns and stylistics of film noir, with its urban settings and often baroque conventions.[3] Moreover, the narrative complexity of film noir – a prerequisite of the detective genre from which it derives – is replicated in cyberpunk, with its undermining not of points of view *per se*, but of the *notion* of points of view, as identity is rendered fluid and, occasionally, irrelevant. This use of classic noir tropes as well as the hybridising reconfiguration of these tropes marks cyberpunk as not so much film noir as postmodern noir or cyber noir.[4] The slippage here emblematises the ways in which noir is, as Steve Neale would have it, 'in essence a critical category' (2000: 153). That is, noir should be understood as a fairly vague category, but one that is necessary in order to comprehend not a genre, but an aesthetic. If noir is an aesthetic then we should be seeking to understand how it works as a discursive critical construction. Slavoj Žižek speaks to this concern:

> is 'noir' a predicate that entertains towards the crime universe the same relationship as towards comedy or western, a kind of logical operator introducing the same anamorphic distortion in every genre it is applied to, so that the fact that it found its strongest application in the crime film is ultimately a historical contingency? To raise these questions is in no way to indulge in hair-splitting sophistry: my thesis is that the 'proper', detective film noir as it were *arrives at its truth* – in Hegelese: realises its notion only by way of its fusion with another genre, specifically science fiction or the occult. (1993: 200; emphasis in original)

Although it is particularly apposite for an analysis of the cyberpunk Trinity as a *femme fatale* that Žižek should point towards science fiction as one of the ways noir 'arrives at its truth', his argument designates the ways in which we should understand noir as an aesthetic rather than a genre.

Using noir, then, as a critical term, I want to label the way in which the *Matrix* trilogy uses noir aesthetics. While there is a necessary stylistic shift in *The Matrix Reloaded* (2003) and *The Matrix Revolutions*, (2003), as more attention is given to life on the ships and in Zion, the *Matrix* trilogy draws upon film noir to articulate its notion of life within the Matrix. This is notably an urban experience, to the extent that when Neo asks Link for directions when tricked by the Merovingian in *The Matrix Reloaded*, he is told that Trinity and Morpheus are in 'the city' and knows immediately what city this is. The city is a powerful force in both cyberpunk and film noir, acting to contain the action but also to identify it. Scott Bukatman identifies *Blade Runner* as future noir, the 'quintessential city film: it presents urbanism as lived heterogeneity, an ambiguous environment of fluid spaces and identities' (1997: 12). The *Matrix* trilogy complicates this intersection of noir and cyberpunk in that the city spaces are ambiguous because they are impenetrable. While the city in *Blade Runner* is a pastiche of recycled styles, the daylight city in the Matrix is comprised of clean, cool lines that do not make any cultural or historical references. This city is not the layered city of *Blade Runner* nor the Sprawl of Gibson's *Neuromancer*, but a city with straight lines, the multiple mirroring surfaces which reflect the viewer's gaze and disallow penetration. Bukatman argues that urban space and cyberspace enable a mutual understanding:

> In cyberspace the density of the central, inner, city became an analogy for the dispersed matrices of information circulation and overload, while cyberspace itself presented an urbanism stripped to its kinetic and monumental essentials. Cyberspace exaggerated the disorienting vertigo of the city, but it also summoned a powerful controlling gaze. (1997: 47–8)

But when the urban space is cyberspace, this relationship becomes fraught. While the code trickling down the screen at the beginning of the *Matrix* films is a 'real' articulation of cyberspace, we understand the cyberspace of the Matrix to be an urban space which is impenetrable; not because it is a riot of styles and pastiches, but because it is full of mirrored surfaces. Where this city differs from earlier cyberpunk urban spaces is in its ability to not confuse users of those spaces. This is crucial because although the *Matrix* films posit urban space as cyberspace, they also draw upon the city of film noir. This is accomplished quite carefully in the first film as the mirrored surfaces will only function in the day. During the night, the city becomes the city of film noir, with seedy hotels, alleyways and underpasses. The rain-slicked roads and dark underpassages speak to a history of noir aesthetics which find their apex in the final fight sequence between Neo and Smith.

These references act to locate the narrative within the noir tradition. Elizabeth Cowie notes that in film noir, 'a narrative of an external enigma ... is interwoven with or supplanted by another which focuses on the personal and subjective relations between the characters ... Additionally, the element of fate, of chance and coincidence ... is also central to the film noir' (1993: 130). While the elements of chance and coincidence here speak to the Merovingian's understanding of computer programming and hacking, the *Matrix* trilogy's positing of the enigma of the Matrix is, indeed, interwoven with and occasionally supplanted by personal relations. Noir – as an aesthetic – posits individuals as caught in an existential maze, decoding clues and seeking signs of an exit. This speaks to the experience of being both plugged into the Matrix from a pod and from the ships at broadcast level. Individuals are caught up in a puzzle, both those in the Matrix following the clues – as Thomas Anderson does at the beginning of *The Matrix* – sent to them from those working from Zion and the hackers seeking to circumvent the Matrix. Neo is always trapped – even more so when he is expelled from the Matrix for the first time and finds that he is 'the One', a fate which he cannot avoid. Similarly, the tough guy in film noir – often the gangster with existential neuroses – can be found in Agent Smith, who, although he denies it until his final fight with Neo, seeks to – but cannot – understand 'why'. Smith tells Morpheus in *The Matrix* that 'human beings define their reality through misery and suffering', speaking to 'a disturbing vision [of noir] … that qualifies all hope and suggests a potentially fatal vulnerability' (Telotte 1989: 86), a vulnerability which both Neo and Smith act out. If this vulnerability is revealed through the pursuit of understanding of an external enigma, and if the *Matrix* films articulate the Matrix as an enigma, then this unrepresentable enigma – or the 'Real' – is figured in the films, as in much of film noir, as woman.

## CODING FEM(ME)ININITY

The seminal essays in E. Ann Kaplan's *Women in Film Noir* (1978) shifted critical interest from the noir hero to the aesthetic's articulation of woman as desirable but dangerous. In film noir, women are, for the most part, defined through their sexuality and through their relationships with men. The genre seeks to obscure the ways in which women are thus sexually defined through representing them as intelligent and, occasionally, physically powerful. Tasker identifies four significant aspects of the *femme fatale*:

> First, her seductive sexuality. Second, the power and strength (over men) that this sexuality generates for the *femme fatale*. Third, the deceptions, disguises and confusion that surrounds her, producing her as an ambiguous figure for both the audience and the hero. Fourth, as a consequence the sense of a woman as 'enigma', typically located within an investigative narrative structure which seeks to find 'truth' amidst the deception. (1998: 120)

The *femme fatale* – whether it be Phyllis Dietrichson in *Double Indemnity* or Bridget Gregory/Wendy Kroy in *The Last Seduction* (1994) – functions as the axis of the narrative. Cyberpunk draws upon the tropes of the *femme fatale* to articulate femininity so that the predominant image we have of cyberpunk is of the sexy chick who can kick ass but whose sexuality is dangerous, from Molly Millions and her razor-nails in *Neuromancer*, to to Y. T. and her booby-trapped vagina in Neal Stephenson's *Snow Crash*.[5] Moreover, in cyberpunk, as in film noir, family bonds are often absent or negative, demonstrating the destructive power of the *femme fatale* with regards to family life and to patriarchal discourse.

In the *Matrix* trilogy, the notion of family is disrupted by the existence of the Matrix, which, in removing sexual intercourse from the procreation cycle, circumvents the patriarchy. These are films which speak to the noir fear of all-devouring woman, particularly in the representation of the foetus fields which are nurtured by spider-like machines and in the Medusa-like sentinels: 'The name of the enemy, after all, is the Latin root of the English word mother (as well as of matter). The Matrix is represented as a kind of parthenogenic – which is to say autochthonous – mother, a mother that is not a mother, by virtue of being able to produce new life without the role of the male' (Kimball 2001: 191–2).[6] Neo is literally birthed by the machines – after all, *inter faeces et urinam nascimur* – and also virtually each time the Matrix is rebooted, creating another version of himself. With a system that thus replicates motherhood – but never fatherhood – the patriarchy is revealed to be redundant. In these films, then, it is little surprise that patriarchal power is asserted through the control of woman within the narrative, a control that draws its strengths from the noir tradition. The relationship between technology and the *femme fatale* has been remarked upon by Mary Ann Doane as a feature of modernity, an anxiety which is the result of new ways of understanding sexual difference:

> this is the moment when the male seems to lose access to the body, which the
> woman then comes to *overrepresent*. The 'working body' is 'confiscated by the
> alienation of machines' … Consequently, it is appropriate that the *femme fatale*
> is represented as the antithesis of the maternal – sterile or barren, she produces
> nothing in a society which fetishises production. (1991: 2; emphasis in original)[7]

Woman's sexuality, then, becomes the overriding characteristic of the *femme fatale* as this is a sexuality which does not lead to procreation; a sexuality which is devoid, therefore, of meaning in patriarchy. Moreover, the way in which the *femme fatale* is often referred to as a dangerous spider, weaving its web, has resonances with late twentieth-century and early twenty-first-century understandings of cyberspace as 'the Web'. The designation of dangerous women as spiders draws upon the Greek myth of Arachne, much as the action heroine has been designated as a modern-day Athena.[8]

The specific dangers of the *femme fatale* are also clearly indicated to Neo when he enters what he believes to be the Matrix for the first time since his expulsion. A classic *femme fatale* in a red dress, created by a geeky male hacker on the Nebuchadnezzar, is used to teach him the potential pitfalls of the Matrix. He is thus tricked by this cypher of a woman literally wearing the Western colour of warning and morbidity, dressed and coiffured in a classic 1950s aesthetic. Sarah Street notes that the woman in the red dress is a 'classic representation of the feminine as a trap, as dangerous yet seductive. The colour red of course stands for sexuality and blonde hair is associated with the *femme fatale* of the film noir genre, a signifier of the perilous "spider woman" who threatens and disturbs the male characters' (2001: 86). The films thus relies upon the *femme fatale* – the dangerous unknown – in their depiction of woman. This is perpetuated by Persephone, whose sexualised outfits and behaviour mark her as a *femme fatale* – albeit a computer program – with smouldering sexuality in her glance and potential betrayal in a kiss. She uses her sexuality to get what she wants – a passionate kiss from Neo. Trinity – the only leading female character in all three films – is cast in this mould, as both desirable and dangerous. It is Neo's desire for her that leads him to 'choose' the pre-programmed pathway as designated by the Architect and, ultimately, to death. Even Smith/Bane has been entranced by her, saying in *The Matrix Revolutions* that 'no one ever got away from me as many times as you did. Every time I thought it was the last.' But as Doane has noted, the *femme fatale*'s power is of a 'peculiar sort insofar as it is usually not subject to her conscious will, hence appearing to blur the opposition between passivity and activity. She is an ambivalent figure because she is not the subject of power but its *carrier* … she has power *despite herself* (1991: 2; emphasis in original). Trinity falls in love with Neo, thereby setting in motion the events of the two sequels – and Neo's death. But she has had no choice in the matter as the Oracle has told her she *will fall* in love with the One and she defers to Morpheus' belief that Neo is, indeed, that individual or function. Thus Trinity is paradoxically both full of power – in that she is the catalyst for the film's dénouement – but also powerless within this position of power, the classic *femme fatale*.

Trinity's clothing also powerfully articulates tropes of the *femme fatale*. Elsewhere in this volume Pamela Church Gibson discusses the spectacle of costume in the films but I am here concerned with the way in which costume is used to locate Trinity within the *femme fatale* tradition. Martina Lipp describes her as hypersexualised (2004: 21), whereas Street positions her as fetishised:

> Trinity's black shiny suits suggest a sexual, androgynous look which unsettles her more conveniently feminine persona on the ship; in a Freudian reading, however, her clothes are fetishistic, serving to allay male fears of castration in their sexual, phallic appearance … the tightness of her costume when she is in the Matrix is nevertheless suggestive of fetishistic pleasure through constriction. (2001: 96)

However, the sequels do not fulfil any of these promises. Trinity's clothing does not accentuate and sexualise revealed skin, in the way that Persephone's does. Furthermore, any fetishistic pleasure is obviated by the S&M club in *The Matrix Revolutions* in which Trinity's clothing is revealed to be, if anything, rather mundane.[9] What Trinity's clothing does is not reveal but contain her body. In the Matrix, Trinity is always dressed in black, another surface which does not allow the gaze to penetrate. Her outfits of PVC and leather may be body-hugging but are not overtly sexualising. The corsets which Trinity wears may be tight but they never allow her breasts to escape – or even to threaten an escape – and although she wears black leather boots, they are flat-heeled and merge seamlessly with her outfits, again deflecting the gaze. Her clothes are stylish, like the clothes of the *femme fatale*, but are not overtly sexualising. This contradiction in Trinity indicates the ways in which, although she engages with the tropes of the *femme fatale*, she is also bound by the conventions of another archetype, the action hero.

One reason for Trinity's clothing being so functional is because of her sheer ability to kick ass; she thus requires clothes that are, indeed, functional. If the film's ideology of femininity is informed by the *femme fatale*, it is impossible to deny that its visual representation of the same emerges from a conglomeration of comic books and contemporary action-hero films. The sexy female ass-kicker has a history in such television figures as *The Avengers*' Emma Peel (1961–69) and *Wonder Woman* (1976–79) – images of powerful women, however, which stress their femininity and their sexuality as well as their power.[10] Several recent collections, such as Frances Early and Kathleen Kennedy's *Athena's Daughters* (2003) and Sherrie Inness' *Action Chicks* (2004), have drawn attention to the portrayal and appeal of indomitable and uncompromising female heroes. The contemporary female action hero, as Inness points out in reference to *Buffy the Vampire Slayer* and *Xena, Warrior Princess*, is predicated upon the notion that 'being aggressive is desirable, and women should not wait for men to save them' (2004: 15).[11] Trinity draws upon these representations, as well as on the powerful representations of Ripley in *Alien* (1979) and Sarah Connor in *Terminator 2* (1991), as the attention in the action sequences is not on Trinity's body but on Trinity as movement, a crucial distinction.

Jenny Wolmark comments upon the play of gender identity in *The Matrix*, arguing that Neo 'lacks the spectacular body that audiences have come to expect of a male action hero, a role that is more overtly overtaken by the female character Trinity … as the opening sequence of the film establishes Trinity in action-hero mode' (2002: 84). Indeed, when they first meet in *The Matrix*, Neo says he has heard of Trinity's cracking of the IRS database and says 'It's just – I thought you were a guy,' to which she responds 'Most guys do.' This statement ironically underscores the tensions surrounding the (masculine) strength of the female hero. The gender ambiguity here is further played up by ephebic facial features of both Trinity and Neo who – at least when in the Matrix – look remarkably alike.[12] Thus, if, as Tasker has argued, 'cinematic images of women who wield guns, and who take control of cars, computers and the other technologies that have symbolised both power and freedom within Hollywood's world, mobilise a symbolically transgressive iconography' (1993: 132), then Trinity, as an über-hacker, is potentially highly transgressive. But her transgressive and myth-making job as a hacker, working on the Nebuchadnezzar, is increasingly displaced throughout the trilogy by her 'real' job, that of taking care of Neo so that he can do his work of being 'the One'. In this way, like film noir, although the *Matrix* trilogy articulates a notion of potentially powerful female agency, the narrative must ultimately contain it.

## (SIMULATING) THE *FEMME FATALE*

Trinity is a paradox, with the physical abilities of the ass-kicking action hero contained within the *femme fatale*. This points up the precariousness of the endeavour of defining the *femme fatale* as anything other than a critical category or an aesthetic, much like noir. But how does this new articulation of the *femme fatale* speak to contemporary debates about gender and sexuality? Elyce Rae Helford argues that female action heroes are 'part of the myth of the American Dream, of transcendence, of individual greatness done for the good of others. Thus, female heroes function well within the individualist discourse of postfeminism' (2000: 294). This (post)feminist discourse prioritises individual efforts rather than group activism, thereby distinguishing it from the (second wave) feminism of the 1960s and 1970s.[13] This goes some way towards explaining the paradoxical complexities of Trinity. Unlike Neo, Morpheus or Niobe, Trinity is not fighting to save Zion, she is fighting for Neo.[14] Her function within the films is first to confirm Neo as 'the One' – through falling in love with him – and then to ensure that he is able to fulfil the functions of this particular anomaly. The traditional noir trope is of the woman who induces a man to kill another man and this is what Trinity does, helping Neo to realise his potential to kill (or, at least, reboot) the symbolic order of the Matrix. She must die at the end, both to contain her transgressive potential and because it would not be possible for her to outlive Neo given that her function is bound up in him.

One way of understanding Trinity is as a simulation, 'a reflection of a profound reality' (Baudrillard 1981: 6) of the *femme fatale*. That is, if the *femme fatale* is the articulation of deep-rooted fears and concerns about the conjunction of femininity, sexuality and power in the patriarchy, then the use of the *femme fatale* as an articulation of femininity in the *Matrix* trilogy is an indication of how dangerous woman is perceived to be, both in and out of cyberspace. Drawing upon that tradition but not working for her own ends, as the traditional *femme fatale* does, Trinity lives for Neo, not for herself. Initially, she is a powerful figure: confronted by a gun-toting Agent on the roof at the end *The Matrix*, it is Neo who calls to Trinity for help; later she responds to his apparent death by ordering him, like Christ ordering Lazarus to arise (John 11: 43), to 'now get up!', which Neo promptly does. But her agency within the Matrix is slowly eroded so that, by *The Matrix Revolutions*, she potentially endangers herself, Morpheus and Seraph by losing her cool with the Merovingian when he tells them he wants the eyes of the Oracle. 'I haven't got time for this shit', she says, and draws her gun on the Merovingian. It is only the intervention of *femme fatale* Persephone which gets Trinity the information she wants: how to save Neo. Trinity's declining agency and loss of cool in the Matrix is matched by her actions outside of the Matrix, where she is, in effect, a handmaiden to Neo, bringing him food and sexual relief. The tension between this role and her function as an ass-kicking cyberpunk indicates that she is merely acting out the style of the *femme fatale* in the Matrix, thus speaking to the postfeminist backlash fears of powerful women.

Doane argues that the *femme fatale* is the result of the fear of the loss of self, best represented as castration anxiety: 'The power accorded to the *femme fatale* is a function of fears linked to the notions of uncontrollable drives, the fading of subjectivity and the loss of conscious agency ... Her textual eradication involves a desperate reassertion of control on the part of the threatened male subject. She is not the subject of feminism but a symptom of male fears about feminism'(1991: 2–3). Trinity plays the part of the *femme fatale* in the films so as to allow the Matrix a model of femininity which can be controlled. In the masculine psyche, 'Woman' is a fantasy, one which is the cause of desire but also that around which his desires circulate. Thus, a masculine subjectivity is always separate from this object and the masculine subject is always whole, always in the position of the phallus. The *femme fatale* is both this object of desire but also, for a time, escapes castration and is an exception to the Law. However, Trinity cannot achieve this and it marks her as *acting as* rather than *being* a *femme fatale*. She is, in fact, verbally castrated in *The Matrix Revolutions* when Neo – whose name cannot be sensibly abbreviated – repeatedly refers to her as Trin, thereby obviating the powerful Judeo-Christian significance implicit in her chosen hacker name. She must also be textually eradicated – her heart obscenely penetrated by the technology which she had previously chosen as a hacker to penetrate her head – thereby marking her as the Other.

This Other to be brought under control is a common feature of Enlightenment rationality, which finds its definition through the designation of the non-rational as non-masculine. As Linda Alcoff summarises, man positions woman to be 'defined, delineated, captured – understood, explained and diagnosed – to a level of determination never accorded to man himself ... Despite the variety of ways in which man has construed her essential characteristics, she is always the Object, a conglomeration of attributes to be predicted and controlled along with other natural phenomena' (1995: 434–5). This opposition is played out in the representation of female power and sexuality in the *Matrix* films. The Oracle, an intuitive program who takes the form of a cookie- and candy-loving earth-mother, is in fact designated as the mother of the Matrix by the self-designated father of the Matrix, the Architect, but she sarcastically says 'please!', as if angry with such a definition. Despite her anger, 'the Oracle is aligned with femininity, domesticity, Africa, spiritualism and the past' (Spigel 2001: 399). This controlling of female sexuality and power is made even more apparent with the Merovingian's ability to hack the Matrix in order to create female sexual desire. In *The Matrix Reloaded*, he codes a slice of chocolate cake and sends it to a Veronica Lake look-alike, explicitly referring both to the tradition of the *femme fatale* but also to the similar-looking *femme fatale* in the red dress Neo encountered in *The Matrix*.[15] One of the few glimpses the viewer has of the body-as-code is of the Veronica Lake look-alike's vagina literally exploding. Yet the sexual desires of this woman are contained within controlled subservience to a male notion of desire, in that she performs fellatio on the Merovingian. Neo is similarly scared of female sexual desire; when Trinity reaches orgasm during the sex scene in *The Matrix Reloaded*, he is rendered impotent by the way in which he associates it with a vision of death. Female sexuality and power is thus coded, in these films, as something to be feared. Woman remains an inscrutable enigma, who must be reduced to a function to be controlled.

Moreover, if, as stated above, the technology of the Matrix is read as feminine, it can also be read as feminising all that is within it. That is, it defines, delineates, captures and ultimately determines all that is within it so that the 'subjects' of the Matrix are 'controlled along with other natural phenomena' (Alcoff 1995: 435). The Matrix is, after all, the Real, a state in which there is nothing but need, something to which the films allude in the name of the restaurant – *Le Vrai* – in which Neo, Morpheus and Trinity first meet the Merovingian, who expounds upon the necessities of food and sex, even in a virtual world. This need is visually articulated in the image of the baby fed by tubes in *The Matrix*, literally fed by other humans without their knowledge. The penetrability – for which read feminine – quality of the subjects of the Matrix is made clear by the ease with which Agents can take over bodies. In *The Matrix Reloaded*, Smith says that 'the best thing about being me is that there are so many of me', referring not only to his ability to penetrate and assimilate, in a Borg-like fashion, bodies and to make them over in his likeness, but also to the power of the patriarchy. If those who are in the Matrix have been feminised then it stands to reason that the machines are masculine. Despite the machines having a largely feminised representation throughout the films, when Neo actually speaks with the machines, it takes the face and the voice of a man, clearly indicating who *is* and *has* the real power.

## 'HISTORY IS A NIGHTMARE FROM WHICH I AM TRYING TO AWAKE'

It is little surprise that the films largely rely upon representing women through explicitly drawing upon a noir aesthetic which has traditionally contained the transgressive potential of women. Trinity – as both the ass-kicking cyberpunk and the *femme fatale* – articulates the contradictions contained within current notions of gender, sexuality and (post)feminism. Ultimately, this means that she is nothing more than a muse, nothing more than the emotion she inspires in Neo: 'The One as the central figure of a given structure only becomes the One, only attains that value, retroactively, with the appearance of the Other ... She determines the One through her desire, the mystery that Western epistemology with its Judeo-Christian foundations has located in the figure of Woman' (Wegenstein 2002: 342). Even when dying, Trinity is forced to take care of Neo, to help him achieve his goal, despite not knowing what this is herself: 'I can't go with you, Neo. I've gone as far as I can. I've done all that I can do. Now you have to do the rest. You have to finish it.' She then wrests one last bit of agency from Neo when he tells her that she cannot die; her response is 'Yes, I can.' Trinity must die because she has been the *femme fatale*, she has been the emotional centre of the narrative for Neo. Arguably she never fulfils her function – although she does the stylistic tropes – of the *femme fatale* because all that she does is for Neo and never for herself. But the complexities of this contemporary representation of femininity as the *femme fatale* speak to the way in which this critical category, like that of noir, is much more complex than has been previously understood. That the over-determined aesthetic of cyberpunk draws upon an over-determined aesthetic of femininity is an indication of the way in which we should understand the *femme fatale* not as archetype, but as a constellation of tropes and characteristics emerging from concerns about women and power.

## NOTES

1  The 'Man' here refers both to the Agents, programs who take the form of 1950s American government agents, and to the Architect, whose similarity to Sigmund Freud, the 'father' of psychoanalysis cannot be disputed.

2  For an alternative reading, see Martina Lipp who argues that 'Trinity's death could also be interpreted as the glorious end on the battlefield traditionally associated with male heroic warriors' (2004: 29).

3  *Blade Runner* and *Neuromancer* are the more obvious examples of this articulation and a more recent example can be found in Neal Stephenson's *Snow Crash* (1992), with its franchulates and Burbclaves.

4  I am aware that postmodern noir has been used in reference to a specific sort of film, such as *Basic Instinct* (1992) and *Disclosure* (1994), in which 'evolving discourses around both masculinities and femininities [are addressed] through the conflation of sex and work in the figures of a feminised/persecuted hero, an aggressive *femme fatale* and the independent career woman' (Tasker 1998: 134). I am using the term 'postmodern noir' as an indication of why noir should be understood as an aesthetic, not a genre. The conflation of postmodern and cyberspace is commonplace, with cyberspace commonly regarded as articulating the conditions of postmodernity.

5  I am here referring to the predominant masculine strand of cyberpunk fiction. See Mary Flanagan and Austin Booth's *Reload: Rethinking Women and Cyberculture* (2002) for an analysis of the female-oriented strand of cyberpunk.

6  A. Samuel Kimball notes that it is 'Morpheus who induces the body of the Matrix to discharge its fetus' (2001: 191). This emphasises the masculine qualities traditionally associated with hacking.

7  Doane also highlights the way in which science fiction is concerned with reproduction, representation and history (1990: 163–76).

8  I am grateful to Rebecca Munford for bringing this point to my attention.

9  For an example of a fetishised female action hero, who combines the comic book exaggeration of physical attributes with soft pornography, see *Barb Wire* (1996).

10  Helford argues that the 'female action-adventure hero is composed equally of herstory, affirmative action, equal opportunity and repudiation of gender essentialism and traditional feminine roles' (2000: 293).

11  In addition to these two collections, also see Mimi Marinucci's 'Feminism and the Ethics of Violence: Why Buffy Kicks Ass' (2003).

12  The similarity in the features of Carrie-Anne Moss and Keanu Reeves was presumably a casting decision.

13  See Stacy Gillis, Gillian Howie and Rebecca Munford's *Third Wave Feminism* (2004) for more on the debates surrounding postfeminism and third wave feminism; see Stacy Gillis and Rebecca Munford's *New Popular Feminisms* (2006) for more on (post)feminism.

14  Lipp argues that Niobe's 'strength and independence could also be attributed to the fact that she is not caught in any intense relationship with one of the male characters' (2004: 18). Niobe offers an assertive but abbreviated counter to Trinity, with her ability to hack the Matrix, pilot a ship and actually choose her sexual partners. It is Niobe who brings in the vital information from the *Osiris*, who catches Morpheus when he falls from the van in *The Matrix Reloaded* and who gives her ship to Neo in *The Matrix Revolutions*. That it is a black woman who is able to step outside of the confines of the *femme fatale* is beyond the scope of this chapter but is a matter for consideration.

15  These two similar-looking women who both look like *femmes fatales* are played by different actresses, indicating the interchangeability of woman both in the Matrix and in the patriarchy.

# THE POLITICS OF MODERNITY AND POSTMODERNTY

# PLAYING IT COOL IN *THE MATRIX*
Claudia Springer

Released in 1999, *The Matrix* was lauded for its dazzling visual style powered by innovative special effects. Its enormous success bathed it in an aura of novelty and tended to obscure its nostalgic ethos and its similarities to earlier films. For, despite its breathtaking effects, the film hearkened back a half-century to the 1950s, a decade obsessively recycled by American popular culture. Fredric Jameson refers to the 1950s as the 'privileged lost object of desire' for Americans (1991: 19), pointing up the postmodern inability to imagine the future and the consequent obsessive cinematic recycling of stereotypes meant to evoke a mythical historical time called 'the fifties'. Rebellious youth, technological thrills, loss of identity and conflicted relationships with mother figures were themes transported from the century's middle to its end. *The Matrix* and its two sequels are immersed in the cultural beliefs and film conventions of the 1950s. Nowhere is the *Matrix* trilogy's evocation of this decade more apparent than in its reenactment of young white Americans appropriating black cool. It is a distinctly Hollywood conceit to suppose that a style produced during centuries of black suffering should be bequeathed to a young white man who alone has the ability to use its powers to save humankind from extinction.

*The Matrix* not only looks cool, it is also about the attainment of cool, about the transformation of a geek into an icon of incomparable cool. Thomas Anderson is a nondescript company drone, the 1990s' version of the man in a gray flannel suit, indistinguishable aside from his dissatisfaction with his monotonous life, from the other clean-cut corporate employees who labour at identical desks in their office cubicles. Anderson is also a loner and misfit computer hacker who spends his free time alone at home. But he is destined to escape geekdom and become Neo, an incomparably stylish and composed master of his surroundings. *The Matrix* follows the process of his transformation into a man who is impervious to pain, who can dodge bullets effortlessly, who struts through the city with supreme nonchalance clad in a black trenchcoat, and whose insouciance becomes transcendent as he soars upward through the sky, leaving the phony city below. Anderson's transformation from computer geek to superhero reenacts the familiar scenario popularised by comic books but dating back to earlier Übermensch aesthetics of an unexceptional person's metamorphosis into an undefeatable powerhouse, a well-worn but still attractive fantasy.

## COOL IN CONTEXT

It is the manner in which Anderson attains his stylish new identity that reveals the trilogy's reenactment of a cultural phenomenon from the 1950s. It was during that decade that black cool found favour with disillusioned white people who appropriated it for their own use, as they were also appropriating blues and jazz music. 'One thing is clear,' write Dick Pountain and David Robins, 'by the 1950s whites wanted to be Cool too' (2000: 42). Cool was an attitude well-suited to express rejection of the decade's regimented conformity, and it was taken up by the Beats, bohemians and other disaffected rebels. But cool did not emerge from a vacuum; it has a history steeped in the black American experience. As Pountain and Robins point out, cool's history is multifaceted and has taken different forms in different parts of the world, but the American version is rooted in a charismatic stance brought by West Africans forced into slavery. Robert Farris Thompson defines the ancient West African Yoruba and Ibo concept of *itutu* as cool, 'a strong intellectual attitude, affecting incredibly diverse provinces of artistic happening, yet leavened with humour and a sense of play' (quoted in Pountain and Robins 2000: 36). Cool was transformed in the New World where it was used as a subtle attitude by slaves to assert their autonomy and express contempt for slave owners. Pountain and Robins contemplate cool's meaning for slaves:

> Clinging to Cool ... afforded them a symbolic territory beyond the jurisdiction of their white owners – a secret, shared, black (and at that time almost exclusively male) discourse. All that their white owners were allowed to see were caricatures of subservience, heavy with irony, behind a Cool mask that concealed the contempt and rage that the slaves felt, the frank expression of which would have brought down harsh physical punishment. (2000: 38)

Unlike African *itutu*, which 'belonged to the realm of the sacred', American cool was a secular attitude honed during the early part of the twentieth century by 'those descendents of Africans ... who played jazz and blues, and who deployed Cool as a body armour against the discrimination, patronisation and neglect they experienced from the mostly white-owned entertainment business' (Pountain & Robins 2000: 41).

White patrons encountered cool in black jazz clubs during the 1920s, and black jazz musicians were at the forefront of cool during the next several decades, a cool which, as Nelson George has it, included 'a certain sartorial elegance, smooth charm and self-possession that ... suggested a dude that controlled not only himself but his environment' (quoted in Dinerstein 1999: 241). Cool entered the mainstream of white society during the 1940s 'via the urban crime folk tales of Dashiell Hammett, Raymond Chandler and the film noir genre' (Pountain and Robins 2000: 42). White cool in the 1950s was defined by the Beats (Jack Kerouac, Allen Ginsberg and William Burroughs), by Elvis Presley, and, for viewers of American films around the world, by

Montgomery Clift, Marlon Brando and James Dean. It was during the 1950s that white hipsters used cool to announce their refusal to join a compliant work force striving to obtain the American Dream. New styles of masculinity emerged on screen and on the streets in the 1950s as a backlash against the dominant ideal of the corporate cog. The urban loner who had his origins in film noir, the sensitive self-doubter in melodramas, and the weary, introspective hero of psychological westerns introduced unconventional men for whom the status quo was a burden.

## SIGNS OF COOL

Thomas Anderson's transformation into Neo in *The Matrix* references the appropriation of black cool by whites, for the film relies on black characters to guide its white protagonist toward truth and fashion flair. Although Keanu Reeves is biracial – Asian and white – the film does not present him in those terms, and his role in relation to the film's black characters evokes the 1950s paradigm of white malcontents learning from black trendsetters. It is black characters who reveal the artificiality of what passes as the world, and they lead their white protégé to the last vestiges of reality, in the process imbuing him with the telltale signs of cool. Neo learns sartorial style and nonchalance from Morpheus, his hip black guide who shares his name with the Greek god of dreams and proves he is a hipster by teaching Neo the difference between phoniness and the real thing.

> Stuck in an unsatisfying work situation, without a partner or friends, Mr. Anderson embodies the stereotype of a dazed and confused Generation X-er. Through Morpheus' tutelage (and a little red pill) and guidance, as well as that of The Oracle and Sati, Mr. Anderson is transformed, from a depressed and scared man to a Jesus-like savior. His relationship with a black man and two women of colour provide meaning to his life, while providing his own redemption. (King & Leonard 2004: 43)

Morpheus leads Neo away from fakery and instructs him in living an enlightened life, in seeing clearly and defending himself with lightning speed and dexterity against the forces of deception. Indeed, what Morpheus makes clear is that it is not so much the artificiality of the Matrix that is its problem, but its utter lacklustre conventionality. Tellingly, its defence force, the Agents, are dressed in identical black suits, the ultimate Western conformist attire, and their uniformity is proven in *The Matrix Reloaded* (2003) when Agent Smith self-replicates into hundreds of duplicate copies. Morpheus is cast in the role of leading Neo out of his unfashionable doldrums to the latest style, the newest, hippest, most happening scene.

Ironically, it is the plain old real world that Morpheus strives to attain. The goal is mundane, but the style – the cool mystique – is compelling. Even in the face of staggering odds, Neo embodies the 'relaxed intensity' at the heart of cool (Dinerstein

1999: 241). His demeanor epitomises self-control and his speech is terse and unemotional. He and his partner in cool, Trinity, communicate in a clipped, telegraphic style and their sexiest moments occur when they walk knowingly into danger with long, relaxed strides, their faces utterly composed and opaque, and their lean bodies, clad in black leather, held erect and defiant. When Neo loses his sight in *The Matrix Revolutions* (2003), he accepts his blindness stoically and even develops a sightless way of sensing his surroundings, the kind of sixth sense implied by cool's aloof detachment. His unruffled poise functions narratively as defiance toward the agents, but its more important role is to impress the spectator.

## COOL'S CROSSOVER

Wrapped in science fiction futurism, the film is actually a throwback to a time when bored young white men and women seized a black style to escape conformity and imagined themselves electrifyingly charismatic. Norman Mailer analysed the phenomenon in *The White Negro*, and the *Matrix* trilogy is uncannily reminiscent of his swaggering version of cool's crossover into white America. The trilogy's drab unsatisfying world is suggestive of Mailer's description of post-Second World War life as 'the years of conformity and depression. A stench of fear has come out of every pore of American life, and we suffer from a collective failure of nerve' (1957: 2). In the films, as in post-war America, people are cowed into submission by an overwhelming technological threat. Here the *Matrix* trilogy aligns itself with those science fiction fears of the 1950s – fears of the bomb and the related threats of mutant life forms, alien invasion and malevolent anti-human technology. The *Matrix* films' premise that humans were defeated by machines in a devastating war evokes the Second World War as the defining moment that drained vitality from American society and spread the spectre of death throughout a world stunned by the monumentally destructive power of atomic weaponry. The films' only hope is that a few individuals will resist conformity in the manner of the hipster who adopted the role of the dissenting loner. 'You can't interview a hipster', states a *Harper's Bazaar* article in 1957, 'because his main goal is to keep out of a society which, he thinks, is trying to make everyone over in its own image' (quoted in Mailer 1957: 1).

In the *Matrix* films, the AI regime has literally remade everyone in its own image of what a smoothly functioning human society would look like. The American hipster's distrust of the status quo might have seemed paranoid during the 1950s, but paranoia is the only appropriate response in the trilogy. What we get in the films is a literal incarnation of the kind of bloodless society of drones that hipsters loathed. Mailer writes that for the hipster, 'new kinds of victories increase one's power for new kinds of perception; and defeats, the wrong kind of defeats, attack the body and imprison one's energy until one is jailed in the prison air of other people's habits, other people's defeats, boredom, quiet desperation and muted icy self-destroying rage' (1957: 3). In the films, human energy is literally imprisoned in vats and Thomas Anderson leads an illusory life of boredom and quiet desperation until he is rescued by Morpheus, just as in the 1950s hipsters imagined themselves rescued by the example set by black Americans whose profound alienation from mainstream culture was longstanding.

> And in this wedding of the white and the black it was the Negro who brought the cultural dowry. Any Negro who wishes to live must live with danger from his first day, and no experience can ever be casual to him, no Negro can saunter down a street with any real certainty that violence will not visit him on his walk ... The Negro has the simplest of alternatives: live a life of constant humility or ever-threatening danger. (Mailer 1957: 4)

During a time when Jim Crow laws and lynchings still existed, black Americans did indeed face constant dangers. Their marginalisation from the American Dream success story made it possible for them to adopt a detached perspective on its ideology. Paul Oliver writes that 'in spite of the advances made during the post-war years, Blacks in the 1950s were still predominantly employed on unskilled or semi-skilled labour, and the educated intelligentsia represented a very small minority' (1990: 283). African-Americans were, for the most part, excluded from the American Dream and faced continual racist harassment.

## THE MYTH OF AUTHENTICITY

Morpheus and his band of outsiders in the *Matrix* trilogy also see the truth behind the artifice, but the trilogy does not provide a historical context for Morpheus' acute perceptions. Instead, the premise of the films is that black people are closer to reality than white people, are in fact 'more real' than white people. This notion, widely disseminated in Eurocentric colonialist ideology, is dependent on a rigid classification of races based on supposed distinguishing traits. Among the binary oppositions established by this system is the contrast between white intellect and black physicality: between brain and body. Following from this is the myth that black people are less cerebral, closer to the earth, more natural, 'more real'. James Snead argues that

> the history of black film stereotypes is the history of the denial of history in favor of an artificially constructed general truth about the unchanging black 'character'. We are being taken out of history into the realm of myth: things which never change, which were so at the beginning, are so now, and ever shall be. (1994: 139)

Indeed, in the first film, Morpheus' small group includes both black and white rebels, but the black characters are coded as more 'real'. Two young black brothers, Tank and Dozer, for example, were born from a human mother, unlike the vast majority of humans who are seeded in vats. They also come from Zion, the last outpost of human civilisation located near the earth's still-warm core, intensifying the impression of their 'realness'. Moreover, Zion, we learn in *The Matrix Reloaded*, is populated predominantly by black people.

A racist paradigm associating black people with authenticity and life and white people with artifice and death runs throughout film history. Richard Dyer points out that in mainstream film, 'white power secures its dominance by seeming not to be anything in particular, but also because, when whiteness qua whiteness does come into focus, it is often revealed as emptiness, absence, denial or even a kind of death' (1988: 44). 'Life' is often associated with black film characters and typically, he writes,

> tends to mean the body, the emotions, sensuality and spirituality; it is usually explicitly counterposed to the mind and the intellect, with the implication that white people's over-investment in the cerebral is cutting them off from life and leading them to crush the life out of others and out of nature itself. The implicit counterposition is, of course, 'death'. (1988: 56)

This conventional cinematic opposition between black 'life' and white 'death', which has antecedents in literature and art, has created a situation in which

> through the figure of the non-white person, whites can feel what being, physicality, presence, might be like, while also dissociating themselves from the non-whiteness of such things. This would work well were it not for the fact that it also constantly risks reminding whites of what they are relinquishing in their assumption of whiteness: fun, 'life'. (Dyer 1997: 80)

In *The Matrix*, white predilection for artifice is on display in Cypher, a white member of the rebel crew who betrays his rebel colleagues in order to return to the comforts of the artificial Matrix, and in the trio of white agents with icy demeanors and an abhorrence for human smells who want to kill all humans. *The Matrix Reloaded* extends the white predilection for death with bleached-white twin killers who periodically transform into swooping ghost-like figures. *The Matrix Reloaded* displays black 'life' in a scene reminiscent of countless Hollywood jungle melodramas when the predominantly black population of Zion engages in frenzied dancing to the pounding rhythm of drums. In Hollywood, the war between artifice and reality is drawn along racial lines.

## MASTERING COOL

While the specifics of black history are elided, race and history are evoked when Morpheus uses language reminiscent of slavery to describe the human predicament under computer control. He reveals the hidden truth 'that you are a slave, Neo. Like everyone else you were born into bondage, born into a prison that you cannot smell or taste or touch, a prison for your mind.' He also asserts that 'as long as the Matrix exists, the human race will never be free'. His references to slavery and bondage and the struggle for freedom evoke African-American history, as does the haven provided by his underground barge reminiscent of the Underground Railroad's network of assistance for escaping slaves. Yet the film's hero is not black but a white apprentice. Neo's role is highly over-determined, not only evoking the second coming of Christ but also the bringer of salvation to American slaves. The coming of 'the One', says Morpheus, will 'bring freedom to our people'. In a common Hollywood pattern, black suffering and struggles are appropriated by a white protagonist. Neo the white neophyte is initially helpless – partially-blinded, afraid of heights, weakened by atrophied muscles – but eventually surpasses his black mentor's bravery and combat skills, rescuing him in both *The Matrix* and *The Matrix Reloaded*. Neo's co-optation of black history and identity evokes Norman Mailer's similar turn when he claims that 'the hipster had absorbed the existential synapses of the Negro, and for practical purposes could be considered a White Negro' (1957: 4). To hide the irony that a geeky young white guy is 'the One', the savior who will lead 'our people' out of bondage, *The Matrix* has Morpheus willingly choose to sacrifice himself to save Neo. As Linda Williams wryly observes about the continuing presence of the Uncle Tom figure in such films as *The Green Mile* (1999) and *Hurricane* (1999), 'a reconfigured version of the Tom scenario still seems to be necessary to perform melodrama's moral legibility' (2001: 303). The fact that Neo saves Morpheus does not change the fact that the film appropriates African-American history for a story about a young white man's heroism.

Neo's acquisition of cool accounts for some of the film's most breathtaking moments. With his brain plugged into a computer while his body reclines in a chair, he absorbs martial arts skills directly from computer programs and, under Morpheus' tutelage, learns to become a first-rate fighter who understands the necessity of restraint and the power of efficiently directed movement. After some initial fumbling, he achieves an extraordinary level of control. This is cool.

> Being cool obviously means being in control and invulnerable in the face of crushing odds. It means weaving a web of insensitivity to pain and trouble that cannot be cut through by knives, clubs, guns or words. The tough side of cool is that it involves risk-taking. To remain cool against well-armed police is to risk injury, imprisonment, or death … The cool male can act and talk in a smoothly controlled fashion even in the tightest of corners. He can remain detached even in the face of emotionally charged situations. Playing it cool is a survival technique and a risky business. (Majors & Billson 1992: 30)

Despite the irony that Neo's body is inert, it is his remarkably energetic martial arts combat with Morpheus that defines his metamorphosis. These sequences are a cinematic tour-de-force, but behind the cutting-edge style lies Mailer's description of the hipster's cool mode. Mailer writes that for the hipster, 'the emphasis is on energy' because hipsters 'are nothing without it since they do not have the protection of a position or a class to rely on … So the language of Hip is a language of energy, how it is found, how it is lost' (1957: 11). Hip vocabulary thus relies on words like 'go', 'make it', 'with it' and 'swing'. The *Matrix* trilogy makes good on Mailer's claim that movement is fundamental to the hipster creed. From the opening sequence of the first film when Trinity defeats the agents pursuing her by leaping and twirling and bouncing off walls and ceilings, the films are a swirl of energetic momentum. Neo's energy eventually surpasses everyone else's to the degree that he can move faster than a speeding bullet in *The Matrix*, can fight off hundreds of Agent Smiths with lighting efficiency in *The Matrix Reloaded*, and, even without the use of his eyes, can once and for all defeat Agent Smith in *The Matrix Revolutions*.

## RACIAL STEREOTYPES

The rebels of Zion are united in their desire to save humanity from imprisonment in the Matrix, but they are divided by their attitudes toward Neo, and the debate hinges on faith. It requires faith to believe that Neo is 'the One', and not everyone believes, as there is no objective proof. Instead, there is the Oracle, a soothsayer who prophesies the rebels' future. Morpheus, the staunchest believer in Neo, takes Neo into the Matrix to meet her after building up his, and our, anticipation that she will be a mysterious figure. Instead, she is a matronly older black woman living in a graffiti-splattered low-rent urban apartment building. Neo is ushered into her kitchen and finds her wearing an apron and baking cookies. She puts him at ease by speaking to him in a soothing voice and checking his throat and ears like a mother concerned about her little boy's health. The Oracle is a good mother who counteracts *The Matrix*'s acutely matriphobic depiction of human entrapment in womb-like containers from birth to death. Not a possessive mother figure, the Oracle happily predicts the love between Neo and Trinity and sends Neo away with a freshly baked cookie. She thus becomes Neo's second black mentor. She rounds out his education by imparting wisdom, and, in *The Matrix Revolutions*, she indicates approval of the cool cat he has become by telling him that 'you were like a jittery June bug, and just look at you now!' However, her apron, ample figure and her kindhearted fussing are traits of the Hollywood mammy and perpetuate a longstanding stereotype associated with black women. The Oracle's patiently supportive role and mystical powers place her among other similar black film characters who function to ensure a white protagonist's survival and success, what Spike Lee calls 'the magical mystical Negro' (quoted in Kuffner 2001: 1). Lee explains that often films feature 'magical Negroes who appear out of nowhere and have these great powers but who can't use them to help themselves or their own people but only for the benefit of the white stars of the movies' (2001: 5). Even when they are not invested with magical powers, black characters in contemporary Hollywood films often have the same stereotypical Uncle Tom, Stepin Fetchit and Mammy roles that date back a century to early shorts. Lee acutely observes that contemporary films might 'dress it up, they're slicker about it, it's much more sophisticated, but when you analyse it, it's the same old shit' (ibid.).

The historical pattern he refers to is analysed by Snead, who identifies three cinematic tactics for perpetuating racial stereotypes: 'mythification, marking and omission' (1994: 143). Ahistorical stereotypes are disseminated through mythification, racial difference is unambiguously asserted when blackness is heightened through marking, and the infinite variety of black experiences is hidden through omission. The Oracle exemplifies the mythic figure. Krin Gabbard refers to her as 'supernaturally nurturing' and deplores the tendency for white filmmakers to give us 'a silly dream of black angels outside the everyday world but readily available when white characters need help' (2003: B16). He points out that these films tap into white guilt over slavery by promoting the classic fantasy that 'the guilt for all those centuries of hatred and oppression can be wiped clean if the white man can find...the love and devotion of a powerful, dark-skinned man' (2003: B16). Morpheus and the Oracle send that message, mobilising all of their special powers to ensure Neo's survival but their success can only be gauged by Neo's independence from them. In *The Matrix Reloaded* they are still present to guide him, but their authority is now questioned, his level of cool having superseded theirs.

The *Matrix* trilogy's religious fervour might seem to contradict their commitment to the ethos of the hipster, but, on the contrary, Norman Mailer links the hipster's sensibility with religious conviction via existentialism:

> One must have one's sense of the 'purpose' – whatever the purpose may be – but a life which is directed by one's faith in the necessity of action is a life committed to the notion that the substratum of existence is the search, the end meaningful but mysterious; it is impossible to live such a life unless one's emotions provide their profound conviction. (1957: 4)

The *Matrix* trilogy includes existentialism in its religious and philosophical hodge-podge with its emphasis on individual choice, which in the second and third films is layered onto the first film's spotlight on destiny. Existentialism culminates in the final rain-splattered showdown between Neo and Agent Smith in *The Matrix Revolutions* when Smith asks Neo why he perseveres, and Neo responds, 'because I have a choice'. Neo has become super-cool and proves he can integrate the lessons of Christianity, Buddhism, postmodernism and existentialism passed on to him by the Oracle. But by making the Oracle the axis of their religious and philosophical content, the films play on the notion that black people are more spiritual. Black spirituality, like black life, is an assumption based on the myth of an intuitive black connection with nature and the mysteries of the cosmos. Whites, in this opposition, are characterised as too rational to apprehend hidden truths. Black spiritual guides in contemporary films are just another aspect of lingering colonialist ideology.

Complimentary depictions of the myth of innate black spirituality are just the other side of the coin of derogatory depictions. Stereotypes can be transmitted by 'positive' representations of the Other as much as by 'negative' representations. Edward Said supports this point when he writes about Orientalism that

> Many of the earliest oriental amateurs began by welcoming the Orient as a salutary *derangement* of their European habits of mind and spirit. The Orient was over-valued for its pantheism, its spirituality, its stability, its longevity, its primitivism and so forth ... Yet almost without exception such overesteem was followed by a counter-response: the Orient suddenly appeared lamentably under-humanised, antidemocratic, backward, barbaric and so forth. (1978: 150)

Black spirituality is evoked in the *Matrix* films not only by the Oracle but also by the use of Zion for the underground city of free humans populated primarily by black people, suggesting the dream of Christianised slaves to find a safe haven in 'the promised land' and the Rastafarian belief in a utopian society. Zion contains another black mentor, real-life African-American philosophy professor Cornel West in the role of a council member. And the mostly black residents of Zion let loose with a Dionysian revel. Their wild dance is crosscut with Neo and Trinity making love, with the parallel editing suggesting that the white couple are caught up in the orgiastic excitement. Unbridled black physicality is yet another cliché in the trilogy's version of a young white man's assumption of the mantle of cool.

## OBFUSCATION

It is one of the trilogy's ironies that it obfuscates its appropriation of black history whilst it claims to eliminate obfuscation from humanity. The Matrix functions as a concrete version of ideology, a false set of beliefs literally plugged into imprisoned brains, and it is remarkably successful in keeping the vast majority of humans, who do not know any better, satisfied. The AI regime unleashes its Agent Smith program only because Morpheus and his band of rebels are determined to free humanity from the Matrix's illusions. The Agents are the coercive branch of the AI regime, its police force, called upon to crush resistors when the Matrix fails to placate them. Louis Althusser, writing about the workings of modern capitalist societies, concluded that brute police and military force were usually not necessary to control subjects who were kept adequately submissive by such 'ideological state apparatuses' (ISAs) as schools, churches, the legal system and the arts. As long as people accept the status quo version of reality disseminated by the ISAs, those in power need not fear: 'The vast majority of (good) subjects work all right "all by themselves," i.e. by ideology (whose concrete forms are realised in the ideological state apparatuses). They are inserted into practices governed by the rituals of the ISAs' (Althusser 1971: 181). While the trilogy exposes the ideological stranglehold imposed by its AI rulers over humans, it simultaneously inserts its spectators into ideology, for cinema is one of the most powerful of ISAs.

With its mythification and its reliance on colonialist racial oppositions, the trilogy thus inserts spectators into an ideology of race that has perpetuated racist injustice for centuries. Although major roles are taken by black actors, the films do not evince knowledge about the historical and cultural contexts for its representations. They locate themselves within a racial discourse that erases the specifics of black history and assumes the presence of innate black traits. As such, it is part of the powerful system governing contemporary race relations, for, as Michel Foucault, who rejects Althusser's notion of ideology, explains, power does not emanate from a nefarious ruling elite; rather it is produced at all levels and circulates throughout the social order:

> The omnipresence of power: not because it has the privilege of consolidating everything under its invincible unity, but because it is produced from one moment to the next, at every point, or rather in every relation from one point to another. Power is everywhere; not because it embraces everything, but because it comes from everywhere. And 'Power', insofar as it is permanent, repetitious, inert and self-reproducing, is simply the over-all effect that emerges from all these mobilities, the concatenation that rests on each of them and seeks in turn to arrest their movement. (1978: 93)

According to Foucault's model, the trilogy's resolution, when Neo travels to Machine City, the centre of AI power, and strikes a deal that authorises him to annihilate the rogue program Agent Smith, is an unlikely scenario for emancipation. Agent Smith's demise leads to the implication of human freedom in a bucolic green and grassy ending, a visual release from the films' previous gray dystopian palette. It is a utopian dream in which power instantly dissolves and is replaced by a new liberated era. History, however, suggests that power and its attendant discourses are threaded far too intricately throughout society for this sort of instantaneous freedom.

## SELLING COOL

In the 1950s, hipsters fancied that their cool mystique provided an escape from the tainted commercial world. Their dream was short-lived, for by the beginning of the 1960s the advertising industry was already embracing the language of cool. Thomas Frank argues that by the late 1950s, advertisers were chafing against their decade's stale and unimaginative commercial strategies. The advertising industry did not so much cynically co-opt the 1960s counterculture as anticipate it in an attempt to find more creative ways to appeal to consumers. Hip consumerism was the answer, a consumerism 'driven by disgust with mass society itself' (1997: 28). Advertisers were 'drawn to the counterculture because it made sense to them, because they saw a reflection of the new values of consuming and managing to which they had been ministering for several years' (1997: 26). Counterculture youth in the 1960s defined themselves in part by their shared styles in clothing, music, art and other 'lifestyle' symbols. Their goal was to distinguish themselves from their parents, and consequently they comprised a market ready and willing to buy fashionably defiant accoutrements. Corporate capitalism received a boost from this eager new market and from the discourse of hip that opened up new advertising approaches. Americans were exhorted to 'be different', to 'buck the trend', to 'be themselves', to 'be a rebel' by purchasing a particular product. It helped that cool exalts the new and disdains the old, an attitude conveniently consistent with corporate capitalism's strategy of planned obsolescence. Cool had been conquered, and it continues to provide much of the imagery and language of advertising to this day. Determined to be at cool's cutting edge, corporations today employ market researchers to 'cool hunt' by scouring the world's youth cultures to find the next exploitable trend.

It should therefore come as no surprise that the trilogy's commitment to cool is itself a marketing strategy. The first film was a phenomenal success for AOL Time Warner, and although the two sequels were less of a sensation, the trilogy as a whole has been hugely profitable. The irony, as Frank Rich points out, is that AOL Time Warner, 'the powerful machine behind the films', accomplished the equivalent to the AI regime's deceptive manipulation of human brains while it drained human energy as a power source; it 'pulled off a comparable feat by plugging the country into its merchandising program for *The Matrix Reloaded* to loot our wallets' (Rich 2003: 1). Media giants like AOL Time Warner continue to consolidate their ownership of the entertainment industry with FCC approval, eliminating competition while seizing monopoly control.

> The most flaring paradox of the *Matrix* project, of course, is that while it proposes a fictional programme for liberating ourselves from a dominating system – implicitly global capitalism and the entertainment complex – there isn't a single commercially available piece that doesn't somewhere bear the inscription '© Warner Bros.'.
> (Romney 2003: 27)

Media conglomerates are today's ruling powers, with immense influence over what we see, hear, know and think. We live in their matrix. What better device to obscure their power than the figure of Neo, the underdog hero who fights the forces of omnipotent control, all the while embodying unsurpassable cool. With the *Matrix* trilogy, a media giant wrapped itself in cool like a 1950s hipster, only corporate hipsters do not fight the power. They are the power.

# MOVING *THE MATRIX*: KINESIC EXCESS AND POST-INDUSTRIAL BEING

Anne Cranny-Francis

'Follow the white rabbit.'

*The Matrix* (1999) is movement, establishing the kinesics that characterise the trilogy generally and make their viewing a breathtaking experience. From the opening scenes of the first film to the final battle between Neo and Smith, and then Neo's Superman flight over the Matrix simulation, the movement in the movie – of text and of people – creates the narrative that is the movie's structuring device.

## MOVEMENT AND MEANING

In 1844 the English artist J. M. W. Turner first showed his painting, *Rain, Steam, Speed – The Great Western Railway*, in which a shadowy train shape is seen through a veil of rain, rushing through the countryside like a great demon. The deflection of rain by the train is used to convey the impression of speed – a speed of movement not previously available to most people. This powerful image signified the changes – technological and social – that had changed the face of the English countryside. The steam engine of the train placed within the rural idyll of Britain is a figure for the transformation of both technology and the society it generates. Its movement is a restless and violent trajectory forward; it is both impervious to and in conflict with the natural world through which it plunges. This is a painting of power that has moved beyond the control of the humans who created it. As Jack Lindsay notes, the engine is painted in such a way that it is ahead of the point at which linear perspective would locate it (1985: 150). It – and the technology it represents – violates older timespace constraints.

By the end of the nineteenth century steam technology had compressed older timespace so that new kinds of movement were possible – travel beyond the locale of a village; relocation of people and communities for the purposes of work. And this movement was not simply enabled but enforced. The technology that moved the steam railway engine also moved the steam harvester and other farm machinery that made many traditional farming practices redundant. Technology, movement and power created social change – the development of huge slum communities in the rapidly expanding nineteenth-century cities, the demotion of skilled rural labourers into unskilled factory fodder. Moreover, by the end of the nineteenth century, new visual technologies were creating movement in new ways. Early forms of time-lapse photography by E. J. Marey, Eadweard Muybridge and others represent movement incrementally, as a series of integral movements that blur together in human perception to create a fluid bodily movement. And so the graceful fluidity of human bodily movements is shattered, converted to a mathematical progression that we see (ironically or not) in contemporary representations of the primitive robot. These are the movements of a puppet, tied to the will of a puppeteer.

Paintings by early twentieth-century Futurist artists such as Carlo Carrà, Umberto Boccioni, Anton Giulio Braggaglia and Giacomo Balla create movement in the same way. Their paintings show movement as a series of superimposed images that the eye interprets as motion: Braggaglia's *Young Man Rocking* (1911) and Balla's paintings, *Dynamism of a Dog on a Leash* (1912), *Little Girl Running on a Balcony* (1912) and *The Violinist's Hands* (1912) all use this technique. Gino Severini in his 'The Plastic Analogies of Dynamism – Futurist Manifesto 1913' wrote that '*the stylisation of movement ... is one of the most immediate manifestations of life* (1973: 124–5; emphasis in original). This 'stylised' movement generates a perception of human being that aligns it with the demands of contemporary technology – as Fritz Lang's *Metropolis* (1926) exposed so painfully a decade later.

This was the humanity – the human movement and being – that enabled the factory to operate: the assembly line operator who was required to make the same pre-

Figure 7 – Giacomo Dalla, *Dynamism of a Dog on a Leash* (1912).

Figure 8 – Fritz Lang, *Metropolis* (1926): The worker subjected to the time-clock.

cise movement thousands of times, over and over, in a soul-destroying repetition. Yet, despite its inhumane applications, the Futurists were fascinated by the power of this new technology, and Filippo Tommaso Marinetti's 'Founding and Manifesto of Futurism 1909' demonstrates this with a series of violent predictions:

3.   ...We intend to exalt aggressive action, a feverish insomnia, the racer's stride, the mortal leap, the punch and the slap...

9.   We will glorify war – the world's only hygiene – militarism, patriotism, the destructive gesture of freedom-bringers, beautiful ideas worth dying for, and scorn for woman.

10.  We will destroy the museums, libraries, academies of every kind, will fight moralism, feminism, every opportunistic or utilitarian cowardice.
     (1973: 21–2)

The movement Marinetti glorifies is not simply faster or smoother, but 'aggressive'; that is, constituted in terms of human affect – and specifically of violent affect. This movement is generated by insomnia – a pathological inability to be at rest, rather than a love for motion. Movement, for the Futurists, is linked to human modes of being, not just to the technology that produces it. Further, Marinetti specifically relates the technological transformation of movement (into speed, or into mathematical increments) to social and cultural attitudes – an embrace of militarism, rejection of women and scorn for all liberal political ideas and ideals. In other words, the Futurist Manifesto articulates the relationship between (attitudes to) movement and social and cultural life. How we move, and how we perceive movement, are generated by the technologies we use.

## EMBODIED MOVEMENT

When late nineteenth-century photographers began to use cameras to capture movement in a series of static images, they effectively created the way we see, and experience, movement. Human labour was no longer deployed as a fluid, self-directed process but was reconstructed as a series of machine-directed movements. The human body was accordingly transformed from a self-directed organic being, into a technological being whose *hexis* (or embodied practice) was generated by the demands of the machinery of labour. We see (literally) this understanding and perception of human movement throughout the twentieth century – in the movement attributed to mechanical beings. Visually the jerky movements of the robot recall the motion of a puppet, whose control is in the hands of the puppeteer. The robot was under the control of its human creator, and chaos resulted if it somehow achieved autonomy. In science fiction literature this possibility had to be contained by the development of the Laws of Robotics – in Isaac Asimov's *I, Robot* (1950) which spelled out the inability of the robot to act against the best interests of humans. This reflects disturbingly back on nineteenth- and early twentieth-century constructions of incremental (robotic) movement and the authoritarian logic it embodies – and which we see most explicitly in the fascistic writings of the Futurists. For Marinetti and his colleagues the attraction of mechanically-enhanced movement was power and the assertion of a machismo logic characterised by (phallic) thrust. Implicit in this thinking is the subjugation of human being to the control of the machine-master – the military leader (or factory owner). This is the irony of human embodment: the technology that creates the exhilaration we read in the Futurist Manifestos also creates the restriction of (conceptual) movement against which the Futurists rebel.

In the twentieth century we find visual representations of the android or cyborg that were deceptive because of their 'human' movement – where 'human' means a fluidity that is quite antithetical to the robotic incremetalism of many earlier texts and representations. The fluidity of movement of these androids meant that they might pass for human, which was problematic because of their lack of human perception and understanding. *Blade Runner* (1982) dramatises this concern, with its avenging androids desperately searching for a cure for their in-built obsolescence. The problematic feature of these androids was the difficulty of differentiating them from humans, so much so that they are officially known as 'replicants' – replications of the human. However, when they malfunction, as we see with Pris, their movement is like that of a mechanical robot – jerky, uncontrolled, lacking (human) fluidity. *Blade Runner* represents an intermediate stage, in which the incremental logic of movement of the early twentieth century has been naturalised; it now seems fluid. And yet the power of the puppeteer is still recognised; when Pris malfunctions, this is signified in a violent convulsion that distinguishes her from human.

By the end of the twentieth century, the major representations of non-human being included both the mechanical man – 'skin over a metal endo-skeleton' of the original Terminator, T101 of *The Terminator* (1984) as well as of Data, the android of *Star Trek: The Next Generation* (1988–94) – and the morphing liquid-metal Terminator, T1000 of *Terminator 2: Judgment Day* (1992). At times both the T101 and Data exhibit the jerky puppet-type motion that characterises early twentieth-century representations of movement. The T1000, on the other hand, utilises a completely different technology (filmically, as well as diegetically): he/it also differs from human in terms of movement, but here because his movement is so much more fluid than the human. He is uncannily disturbing because he is able to operate beyond the boundaries of the human – not contained by human skin. His body is able to alter shape (he is a modern version of the shape-shifter), to move through small spaces and to take on the appearance of other things and people. Essentially he is a potential shape, a matrix of possibilities limited only by volume, rather than a discrete, bounded entity. This super-fluid movement also signifies 'non-human', though in this case not as distinct spatial movements at particular time coordinates but as a spacetime continuum.

## NEO: PUPPET ON A STRING

In *The Matrix* Neo, his mentor, Morpheus, and his love, Trinity, display a fluidity of movement not seen before in Western cultural production; the trilogy of films are chiefly remarkable for this portrayal of movement. When Neo, Morpheus and Trinity match the computer-generated agents of the Matrix in their ability to defy gravity, fly through the air and walk up walls, they do more than one-up Donald O'Connor in *Singin' in the Rain* (1952). They demonstrate a fluidity and freedom of movement that is more like that of the morphing T1000 than his mechanical predecessors, yet they do so while apparently within the corporeal confines of humanity. These are real actors, not CG characters; actors attached to wires. In *The Matrix* Neo's understanding of his destiny is signified by his ability to move beyond or without the physical confines of normal human embodiment. Morpheus and Trinity also display this superhuman movement – running up walls, jumping incredibly long distances, moving slow-motion through spacetime. It seems they have an ability to alter spacetime to their will, rather than be subject to it. However, it is Neo who excels in this ability and who shows, by the movie's end, that he has the same kind of kinetic power as the agents of the machine. Of course, the Matrix in which this movement occurs is not the real world – though people killed in this simulation also die in real life. The Matrix is a virtual reality (VR), the cyberspace hallucination of William Gibson's *Neuromancer* (1984). Mouse's 'girl in the red dress' is a typical VR sexual fantasy – an avatar constructed to fulfil the fantasy of its creator. So the ability of the Nebuchadnezzar's crew to defy gravity is a mental discipline, rather than a physical actuality, which locates this VR fantasy within the Western tradition that privileges mind over body. It also constitutes *The Matrix* as one of the most recent ways of representing, and so constituting, movement.

As the DVD extra footage shows, the directors, Andy and Larry Wachowski, produced the gravity-defying movements of their actors by attaching them to near-invisible wires that are digitally erased from the final footage. This latest way of representing movement replaces the incremental logic of Futurism with super-human fluidity. So instead of a notion of movement grounded in the inertial mass of human embodiment, the Wachowskis represent movement that is freed from physical constraints; Morpheus, Neo, Trinity and the crew move as their minds take them. The significance of this representation is that their (our) technology, unlike the industrial technology of the age of Futurism, will liberate them physically – or, at least, enable them to operate without the constraints of physical being. Recent work on haptic extensions of embodiment, with its implications for distance analysis and diagnosis (of objects and of people), is an example of this possibility. However, the image itself does not acknowledge that this only happens because the actors are attached to strings – physical or electronic.

Neo represents both the disembodied consciousness that is the locus of much fantasising about VR and the contemporary subject of technology who is able to operate effectively only when attached to the invisible wires of technology. In other words, while the story of *The Matrix* is a narrative of liberation from control by technology, the movie itself – its technology, the way it tells its story – demonstrates just how deeply our (Western) culture is imbricated with/by its technology. Like Lang's striking image of the worker moving the hands of the industrial clock in *Metropolis* Neo embodies the *hexis* of contemporary technological being. Lang's worker was a tortured being, forced to repeat the same simple action in a soul-destroying (work) practice; the *hexis* he demonstrates is one of physical restriction and delimitation. He is captive of and appendage to the machine. Neo, on the other hand, seems to be liberated by his interaction with technology. Once he has accepted that his 'reality' is technologically generated, Neo is freed from the constraints of the material 'real' by which he has self-censored his being in the Matrix. However, this is to accept the premise of (one reading of) the technology – that his embodied being is immaterial (in all senses); his mind determines the nature of, and his interaction with, the real. And this is where Neo becomes captive to the (information) technology of his world – or, at least, to one of the ideologies most commonly associated with the technology.

This is the ideology that Bruno Latour derides as 'mind in a vat' thinking, a disavowal of embodiment that Latour believes deflects technoscience from a useful or successful engagement with the world: 'We tell scientists that *the more connected a science* is to the rest of the collective, *the better* it is, the more accurate, the more verifiable, the more solid ... and this runs against all the conditioned reflexes of epistemologists' (Latour 2003: 134; emphasis in the original). For Latour, it is this disembodied thinking that has created the 'two cultures' of Science and Technology, by which both, he believes are impoverished. He argues that disembodied thinking – the world held at a remove – is not, in fact, possible and that it is more productive to embrace corporeality: 'Why not choose the opposite solution and forget the mind-in-a-vat altogether? Why not let the "outside world" invade the scene, break the glassware, spill the bubbling liquid, and turn the mind into a brain, into a neuronal machine sitting inside a Darwinian animal struggling for its life?' (2003: 130). Despite being freed from his battery pod, Neo is still, in Latour's terms, a mind-in-a-vat, only able to move effectively when jacked into a computer – his supine body simply the receptacle for his 'liberated' mind. Anderson's personal avatar, Neo – the elegant black-clad figure in shades – experiences an autonomy of movement that is denied to the linen-and-rags materiality of his body. This is a dramatisation of the conceptual separation of mind and body that Latour identifies as typical of an ideology of technoscience that constrains the operation of both science and technology in our world. This disengagement of the mind from the real world consequences of its machinations enables human beings to develop technologies that are hostile to their embodied existence – like the machines of Anderson's own world. The same disengagement produced the nuclear technology that devastated the ecology of his world; the polluting technologies of our world; the biological weapons that have the potential to destroy human life. Yet at the same time, as Latour insists, there is no actual separation of mind and body; human beings live the consequences of their thinking – as characters die when their avatars are destroyed in the Matrix. So the figure of the avatar – its spatiotemporal dislocation, its freedom of movement, its imaginary relationship with the materiality of existence – exemplifies the practice of ideology *per se* as well as of the specific ideology of technoscience.

## KUNG FU FIGHTING

For Latour the ethical consequences of the ideology of technoscience are evident in its failure to engage with the world. Without a body the scientist operates only as a dispassionate mind – a free-floating intellect, unconstrained by the fears and desires, hopes and constraints, of everyday life. Movement is a perceptual analogue for conceptual (or political or social or cultural) freedom or constraint. Individuals who are repressed (for whatever reason) are commonly represented as physically constrained – either externally (for example, imprisonment) or internally (such as the rigidly controlled body language of the passive-aggressive personality). And that movement – of freedom or constraint – translates into specific ethical positions. Cinema (and theatre and dance) have used this kinesic signification to tell stories about the ways in which individuals engage with their world, and about the social, cultural and political dilemmas they face. So far we have considered the significance of movement within the diegetic world of the *Matrix* story. Cinematically we can also locate this movement intertextually; that is, the significance of the film's kinesics lies also in its reference to the kinesics of other texts.

Like *Lawnmower Man* (1992) and *Johnny Mnemonic* (1995), *The Matrix* is based in the cyberpunk fiction of the 1980s that took science fiction into the world of information technology. However, *The Matrix* differs from these films in its portrayal of movement. The Wachowskis depict the 'freedom' of movement – the movement freed of conventional spacetime constraints – that is described in cyberpunk fiction more convincingly than did the earlier films. And yet the Wachowskis did have a generic referent for this kinesics in the martial arts film. Martial arts film (and television) conventionally showed the kind of 'impossible' (that is, gravity-defying) movement we see performed by Neo and friends. This movement in martial arts film was a means of articulating an ethics; the martial arts practitioner was traditionally a warrior, who fought for his emperor. The extraordinary skills of the great warrior indicated his ethical, as well as physical, superiority. Implicit in that construction is an understanding of the physical and mental disciplines that the warrior must develop in order to be so skilled.

Neo's development in *The Matrix* has some of the same quality. When he arrives at the Nebuchadnezzar, he trains in martial arts under Morpheus' tutelage – though he learns the basics of these skills from a computer program accessed by the cranial jack that Neo and all the crew retain from their former 'pod' existence. The lesson that Morpheus teaches him is that he must let go of the constraints imposed by his former, illusory, physical being, which do not operate in the 'cyberspace' of the Matrix. Viewers have seen this relationship before, most notably in the *Kung Fu* television programme starring David Carradine that popularised martial arts for Western audiences. In that programme a similar master/pupil relationship was established, with a strong focus on its spiritual or ethical significance (each episode had a moment in which the pupil, 'Little Grasshopper' (Carradine), is taught a spiritual lesson by his master).[1] The same relationship is shown between Luke Skywalker and Yoda, and between Obi-Wan Kenobi and Darth Vader/Anakin Skywalker – and in each case, it is validated by the superhuman physical abilities of the participants. Like Neo they are able to move without the constraints of conventional spacetime, and to cause objects to move through spacetime, defying the laws of gravity. And in all cases this movement is linked to morality; it exemplifies skills and abilities deployed in the battle of good against evil. The use of these abilities in order to control or enslave people, as in the case of Anakin Skywalker, signifies moral degeneration, not simply physical power. This morality of use is embedded deeply in martial arts culture – the notion that kinesic skills must be deployed only for self-defence or the defence of the weak; use of the skills for self-advancement is tabooed by the culture. It is as if the power to move supernaturally is conferred by the moral rightness of the actions undertaken. If the actions are morally flawed, then the use of this superhuman movement is morally evil – a perversion.

As an intertextual referent of *The Matrix* and other cyberpunk fiction, martial arts film brings to the text this connection between movement and morality. The moral goodness of Neo, Morpheus, Trinity and the other crew-members is demonstrated by their ability to move with superhuman fluidity and control. Conversely, the Agents' ability to move in the same way constitutes them as a perversion of good – within the story of *The Matrix*. Neo's apotheosis into 'The One' is signified by his ability to move even more impossibly than his colleagues; in fact, to move through the Matrix with the ease of one of its agents. In other words, Neo demonstrates his power over the machine by adopting its capabilities. The most famous example of this is the bullet-time shot where Neo throws himself backwards to escape the bullets from an agent's gun. His prolonged horizontal movement is beyond 'normal' human ability, and beyond the abilities of the other crew – even though it does not entirely save him; one of the bullets does hit him in the leg. Later in the movie Neo undergoes his final transformation, moving with the same control of spacetime as do the Agents.

This set of significations about movement sets up the moral struggle of the narrative, but at the same time raises a number of questions about the movie's representation of embodiment and of the relationship between humans and their technology. The intertextual referencing of martial arts film links the superhuman movements of characters to the moral battle in which they are engaged. As a kind of posthuman samurai Neo battles the forces of evil exemplified in the agents, and particularly in Agent Smith (Hugo Weaving). In the story of *The Matrix* this moral difference between the two is conflated with the fact that the agents are technological artifacts, generated by the machine, while Neo is a human consciousness – a disembodied consciousness given human form in order to traverse the dream of the real that is the Matrix. This not only constitutes Neo as the latest version of disembodied Cartesian subjectivity, but also establishes human being as superior to technological being. In other words, it does not problematise the notion that humanity is inherently superior to all other life-forms; does not consider the claims to existence of life-forms other than human. The superhuman acrobatics of the 'humans' signify their moral superiority and structure their encounter with, and inevitable defeat of, the technology. And Neo becomes one of a line of brooding samurai, pondering the moral validity of his allegiances.

## VIRAL SYMBOLICS

The complicating factor here is that Neo is no longer the fetishised human subject of Morpheus' ponderous recitation, but a technological hybrid – disembodied consciousness transformed into the algorithms of the Matrix. However, this ontology is never acknowledged in the story of *The Matrix*; the narrative, enacted in the kinesics of its characters, pits human against technology in a conventional battle of good versus evil (which is also why the story seems dated). Apart from a passing reference to environmental concerns, there is no sustained address to Smith's description of humanity as a virus, an infestation whose embodied interaction with the planet has been destructive of all other species and of the fabric of the planet itself. In this sense the story of *The Matrix* is closer to that of *The Terminator* than of *Terminator 2: Judgment Day*, with human and technology constituted as a simple opposition. Yet, at the same time, Smith has raised the issue and the viral nature of human interaction with the planet is now open to interrogation.

Further, this question of the applicability of the notion of the virus metaphor to human life confronts the application of the same organic metaphor – the virus – to both human and technological systems. Deborah Lupton has written of this use of the notion of the virus to describe both technological and human 'illness', which thereby incorporates the technology within the same set of signifiers as the human: 'popular and technological representations of computer viruses draw on discourses that assume that computers themselves are humanoid and embodied (and therefore subject to illness spread by viruses)' (2000: 478). She notes that the HIV/AIDS virus has particular significance within this symbolics as computer malfunction is traced to the 'penetration' of the computer systems by 'foreign' disks (or programs) allowed access by the careless or 'promiscuous' behaviour of the user. For Lupton, this symbolics articulates 'the barely submerged emotions of hostility and fear that humans have towards computer technology' (1995: 479).

In *The Matrix* Agent Smith directs this symbolics back towards the humans who, in their war with the machines, destroyed the planet. And this assemblage of discourses – technological, medical, environmental – captures a range of contemporary concerns about human behaviour and social practice. In Smith's scenario, however, we need to ask in what sense humans are viral. Here it seems the stress is on their pathological, rather than their fluid, properties: humanity is a virus that has destroyed the proper functioning of the planet. However, Smith's accusation also, ironically, reconstitutes the symbolics traced by Lupton, which voice a fundamental hostility between humans and their technology. Smith's disgusted condemnation of humans is a reflex of the human distrust of technology, the power of which may displace humanity from its assumed role as superior life-form. This reading maintains the marked distinction between organic and technological being that seems to mobilise the story and align it with older stories about the dangers posed for humans by technology – which we might trace as far back as Mary Shelley's *Frankenstein* (1818) and the first Industrial Revolution.

For Shelley the problem raised by the Industrial Revolution was that human beings did not use the technology to benefit humanity, but rather to enslave their fellow humans. Technology effectively became a monster that human beings could not control, because they failed to give it the care it required. Here the kinesics is very different: the disembodied, rationalist human creator makes a shambling, monstrously-embodied creature to do his bidding (effectively to 'be'). The movement is that of the abandoned creature, left to flounder in a world where it has no place. In which it, too, is simply the monstrous 'hand' of a neglectful technologist/creator. This kinesics articulates embodiment in crisis; the first manifestation of a new kind of movement – uncontrolled and uncontrollable – like Turner's steam train. And, as in Turner's painting, the relationship of human and machine/technology is of opposition – alien to human, creature to maker.

## POSTHUMAN KINESICS

In *The Matrix* another completely new and different kinesics is enacted. *The Matrix* differs from its martial arts referent in that, in the diegetic world of martial arts film, the movement is embodied while in that of *The Matrix* and most cyberpunk texts it is not. The embodied movement in martial arts films is enacted in defiance of gravity by human characters; in cyberpunk it happens in cyberspace, enacted by a consciousness separated from its body. The derogatory cyberpunk terms for the body are well known: 'For Case, who'd lived for the bodiless exultation of cyberspace, it was the Fall. In the bars he'd frequented as a cowboy hotshot, the elite stance involved a certain relaxed contempt for the flesh. The body was meat. Case fell into the prison of his own flesh' (Gibson 1984: 12). So how do we account conceptually for the kinesic excess that characterises the film and its hero? Referring back to the discussion of movement with which this chapter began, what we see in the film is a representation of movement that has not previously been possible. This simultaneously creates a way of understanding movement that is new – just as Muybridge's photographs and the Futurists' paintings created a new conception of movement. In the late nineteenth and early twentieth centuries, human movement was reconceptualised as a calculus of integral movements or actions – indicative of embodied industrial work practice and of the bodily *hexis* it requires. *The Matrix* works similarly to describe and define the work practice of an information society.

The bodily *hexis* of information technology is the Neo who remains on the Nebuchadnezzar, rendered immobile by his connection to the technology, while his disembodied consciousness roams the cyberspace of the Matrix. Yet, as the story reveals, to die in the Matrix is to die in the flesh: in other words, do not dis- the disembodied consciousness. Neo and his friends experience movement conceptually, but enact it bodily. They live a systemic tension between the physical or corporeal and the intellectual or conceptual – to the detriment of both. When Latour argues that we need to break the glassware and turn the mind into a brain, he is not arguing for a change in the ontology of (human) being, but for a reconception of that ontology. Instead of an acculturated opposition of mind and body he argues for a recognition of their interdependence – and further of the interdependence of all elements of our world/being: 'a hybrid world made up at once of gods, people, stars, electrons, nuclear plants and markets' (Latour 2003: 133). The impossible bodily movement of *The Matrix* enacts the perceived (conceptual) freedom of post-industrial information societies, while also signifying its dependence on the technologies it deploys – the immobile body of the operator jacked into the machine. In a sense the immediate referent for *The Matrix* is not cyberpunk or martial arts films but Spike Jonze's *Being John Malkovich* (1999). In a similar way, Jonze's film problematises the relationship of mind and body, and of subjectivity and culture, via the focal image of the puppeteer. The worker in Lang's *Metropolis* is a puppet of industrial (machine) technology in the most visible way, his body articulated by the demands of the machine. The post-industrial bodies of Neo and his friends are also articulated to/by their technology – only here the strings are not visible, erased by the digital technology that powers this world.

As Martin Heidegger argued, an instrumentalist approach to technology will trap us within the logic of that technology. In this case we become the puppets of the machine, even as we feel liberated by the power it (apparently) offers us. The power to do what? Instead of an engagement with the real world, as brains inside organic bodies interfacing with the non-human (animal, machine), we effectively become functionaries of the machine – disembodied consciousnesses playing in the illusory freedom of cyberspace, but all the time governed by its technical, mechanistic logic. Like nineteenth- and early twentieth-century factory workers, we become 'hands' for the machines; this is, literally, a digital (using the fingers, or operated by a finger or fingers) technology. With Neo and his friends this physical relationship is signified most powerfully by the computer jack embedded at the base of their skulls – and the abjection of that image (human penetrated by machine) carries the fear and distrust for technology that Lupton identifies in human responses to technology. However, this is not the only possibility. For Heidegger, technology also offers possibilities for a new engagement with the world. The derivation of the word *techne*, Heidegger points out, encodes or contains the idea of revelation: '*Techne* belongs to bringing-forth, to *poiesis*; it is something poietic' (1977: 13). The bringing-forth enabled by technology is, precisely, a new way of envisaging our being in the world, which is enabled not by an instrumental use of the technology, but by a reflexive understanding of the genesis and practice of technology in our lives.

For the viewers of *The Matrix* the digital technology deployed in the film's production can have either or both instrumental and reflexive meanings. From a purely instrumental viewpoint the digital erasure of the wires that enable Neo and his friends to move 'impossibly' is a diegetic realisation of the VR dream: the disembodied mind freed of its cumbersome earthly body. This is Latour's nightmare – the mind-in-a-vat, disconnected from the materiality of everyday life and from all kinds of intersubjective communication (human/human, human/animal, human/machine). Yet as Dan North, elsewhere in this volume, as well as Michele Pierson (2002) and Norman Klein (2004) have pointed out, digital special effects have another possible reading, which is reflexive. Instead of operating to immerse the viewer even more effectively in the diegetic world of the narrative, the technology – manifested in its special effects (SFX) – disrupts that immersion by causing the viewer to wonder at its power or effectiveness. That is, contemplating the SFX removes the viewer from the diegetic world of the narrative, enabling him/her to reflect on the technology involved in creating this experience. This disruption of the suturing effect of narrative flow means that viewers have the opportunity to reflect on the nature and power of contemporary technology and its influence on them as participants in the technologised world they share. In Heidegger's terms the SFX – actualised in the posthuman kinesics of the film – positions viewers to perform a 'bringing forth' whereby the nature of contemporary technology is scrutinised.

On the other hand, this contemplation of the film technology may become another form of diegetic immersion – this time, in the ideological world of technoscience. The viewer's reflexive wonder at the power of technology to create a particular media(ted) experience may become a non-reflexive, instrumental wonder at the power of the technology itself. So, rather than being a catalyst for reflexivity about technology, the disruptive power of the SFX may lead instead to a fascination with the technological power that the story sets out to interrogate. In which case, the digital sophistication of the film's SFX works directly against the technophobic compulsions of the film's storyline. *The Matrix* is only able to show the viewer the awesome and potentially subjugating power of this technology by deploying the same technology – which thereby both awes and subjugates the viewer; positions her/him as a puppet of this media(ted) experience.

The kinesic excess of the Matrix, and of *The Matrix*, signifies the move from industrial to post-industrial society, from an economy of goods and services to an information economy. The narrative that is structured by this kinesics, with its conventional moral struggle, locates within this industrial transformation a concern about the relationship between human being and technology that is similar to, yet different from, earlier concerns about the impact of machine technology on embodiment. That is, the storyline of the narrative situates the viewer in a struggle between humanity and technology, which recalls nineteenth- and twentieth-century stories such as *Frankenstein* and *Metropolis*. However, the diegetic world within which that story operates, with its breathtaking special effects, takes us into a new world, signified by a technology we have only just begun to understand and explore. At best, this interrogation opens up questions about technology, embodiment and being that we have only just begun to be able (or need) to formulate. At worst, perhaps we simply do not see the strings.

## NOTES

1 Quentin Tarantino's *Kill Bill* films (2003; 2004) reflect on this relationship of movement and ethics, with specific reference to the *Kung Fu* television programme (1972–75); Bill is played by David Carradine.

# FASHION, FETISH AND SPECTACLE: *THE MATRIX* DRESSES UP – AND DOWN

Pamela Church Gibson

'You're writing about the costume in *The Matrix*? Oh wow, those shades – cool or what?'
   – Video store assistant, male, age 18

'So you're writing about the costumes in the *Matrix* films? So will you explain why everyone else still gets to look so good in all their sexy stuff and why Neo's always stuck in these boring black gown things?'
   – Fashion student, female, age 20

According to Alain Badiou, recent Hollywood cinema is analogous to gladiatorial spectacle – it is imperial art, and the film industry increasingly provides a strict equivalent of the Roman circus games: 'This art is a grandiose and pompous art [*art pompier*], which turns the lugubrious power of the Empire into material for more and more allegorical and puffed-up games and fictions (2004: 90–1).[1] He also argues that 'the pompous style [*pompiérisme*] entails violent technologised affect and a grandiose decorative system, and dominates Hollywood cinema quite as much as it does certain kinds of architecture and the lurid world of multimedia' (2004: 89). Recent writing on Hollywood cinema has tended to support Badiou's analysis. Discussions of 'post-classical' Hollywood cinema have emphasised the increasing attenuation of narrative in favour of ever more 'grandiose' displays of spectacular events and actions, aided and abetted by increasingly sophisticated special effects.[2] The *Matrix* films take this still further; they are gladiatorial spectacles *par excellence* in which the narrative is used to link together fight set-piece after fight set-piece. The most impressive of these have been christened and the names, used by their creators, have been adopted by *The Matrix* fans and are found in the parlance of internet and DVD – 'Government Lobby Sequence', 'Burly Brawl', 'Freeway Chase' and so on. These long sequences are interspersed with shorter gladiatorial spectacles – Neo fighting Morpheus, Neo fighting Agent Smith, Neo fighting Seraph, Neo fighting Smith again – and these, of course, culminate in the extraordinary, rain-lashed, final duel between Neo and Smith. Here the two protagonists hover, at times, between land and sky and finally descend, in quasi-Biblical fashion, into the earth itself, creating a deep pit where the dénouement takes place; they are watched throughout by hundreds of impassive, identically-dressed, oddly silent Smith clones. However, while *The Matrix* (1999) may conform to a tendency within Hollywood towards increasing spectacle, it also highlights one particular aspect of spectacle that is typically ignored in discussions of the blockbuster. For one of the key sources of pleasure in this film is the display of costume, which constitutes an integral part of this particular spectacle. As the striking clothes required for any foray into the Matrix are gradually replaced, in the second and third films, by the less appealing workwear and battlegarb of the resistance on their home ground, so the spectators become – like the ancient Romans in their amphitheatres – restive and demanding.

Discussion of cinema and costume – what little there is – has tended to follow two distinct paths. In line with the analysis of *mise-en-scène*, it has been customary to demonstrate how costume complements and reinforces a film's presentation of plot and character; however, another line of argument has emerged in recent years, which stresses the way in which costume can become detached from plot and character, providing a set of meanings independent from the film's forward movement. David Bordwell and Kristin Thompson, for example, describe clothes as mere 'costume props' (1980: 81); in contrast, Jane Gaines indicates how costume not only reinforces the narrative but may also construct and maintain a discourse that functions independently of it.[3] It is, in fact, possible to read the *Matrix* trilogy using either traditional *mise-en-scène* analysis or to use the more recent methodologies. Costume is key to the patterning of the film and its construction of the 'real' and the 'unreal', the 'authentic' and the 'inauthentic'.

This chapter will begin with an examination of this patterning, suggesting not only how this opposition is established but how it becomes subverted within the film as the 'authentic', privileged in the plot, loses out in the visual execution. However, it will then go on to argue that costume has to be understood as an element of the spectacular in its own right, working separately from plot and character and evoking responses within audiences, independent of their identification with character and situation. Indeed, it is a precondition of costume becoming spectacle that it does, in fact, become detached in this way. As I have argued elsewhere, 'costumes or fashion are "spectacular" if they interrupt and destabilise character and the unfolding action, offering an alternative and potentially contrapuntal discursive strategy – a vertical interjection into a horizontal and linear narrative' (Bruzzi & Church Gibson 2004: 123). This argument will be pursued in relation to the 'fetishistic' nature of the costuming that has been gleefully noted by so many. This chapter will suggest, however, that this use of 'fetishistic' display grows out of and feeds back into an increasingly commodified form of fetishism. The use of costume in the film provides a 'spectacular' fetishism largely emptied of sexual content and, in line with the film's strategies of quotation and simulation, primarily derives its effects from the world of contemporary fashion and style. However, as the trilogy unfolds this element gradually disappears, and arguably this accounts, in part, for the decline in audience appeal of the final film.

## THE 'AUTHENTIC' AND THE 'INAUTHENTIC'

As has often been noted, the work of Jean Baudrillard has been a significant influence upon the *Matrix* trilogy. Indeed, not only may Baudrillard be used very neatly to interpret the trilogy in various ways, but he is carefully set up for this very purpose by the filmmakers themselves. They show us, near the start of the first film, a copy of *Simulacra and Simulation* (1981) open at the essay 'On Nihilism', in which computer hacker Thomas Anderson keeps the illicit microchips he trades by night. Keanu Reeves tells us in the documentary *The Matrix Revisited* (2001) that he was asked by the directors, Andy and Larry Wachowski, to read three books before filming – one on artificial intelligence, another on behavioural psychology and the third, yes, *Simulacra and Simulation*. What Reeves, well-meaning actor, made of Baudrillard's concept of the hyperreal is undocumented.[4] However, Baudrillard's concept of the hyperreal is central to the film's dramatisation of the Matrix within the films themselves.

But where the filmmakers misuse, or misinterpret, Baudrillard is to suggest that there is, in fact, a 'real' world, and one which is not only preferable but for which the protagonists must fight. In doing so, they also create one of the central tensions within the films. For, sadly, their 'real world' is infinitely less attractive than the simulated world of the Matrix: the 'real world' is blue-tinged, bleak, post-apocalyptic, even murky, as opposed to the hard-edged, vividly-coloured scenarios which take place within the 'hyperreality' of the Matrix. Yet it is this grim landscape that Neo must save and which the trilogy increasingly inhabits. The worthy mythical theme of the king who must die to save his people is far less appealing to the predominantly young audiences than the sight of Neo striding through the splendid lobby of the government building, weaving in and out of the shiny black granite pillars, Trinity beside him in her high-fashion faux-dominatrix outfit and designer sunglasses, both with guns blazing – 'cool' seems to emanate from them as they glide through the mayhem.[5]

## 'GLOSSY AND GLEAMING' VS. SOFT AND NATURAL

The simulated world of the Matrix provides an attractive visual proposition for rebels, inhabitants and enforcers alike. Everything is glossy, gleaming, slick and stylish – and this includes the dress and appearance of everyone in the Matrix sequences; even Neo in Messianic mode still keeps his oval shades and gelled hair. Thus, in the sequence mentioned above, Neo wears a long black trenchcoat and specially-designed Airwalk boots – later offered as a prize by *Empire* magazine – with crossover straps and buckles, which echo the two heavy leather belts criss-crossed over his hips to form a home for his handguns. Indeed, as a result of this particular outfit he was accused – along with Marilyn Manson – of having provided inspiration for the Columbine High School killings, since they were carried out by two members of the self-styled 'Trenchcoat Mafia' group.[6]

As this suggests, the film's failure to embody successfully the superiority of the 'real' over the 'unreal' is intimately connected to the film's use of clothes and the pleasures that they provide. For the answer to the student (quoted in the second epigraph) concerning Neo's changing attire, is simple: a Messiah is not normally known for his dress sense. So, as the trilogy progresses, Neo looks less and less like the hip young gunslinger who takes on innumerable adversaries in that 'Government Lobby' shoot-out in *The Matrix*. Like the other rebels, when back in the 'real world' of the ships and the city of Zion, Neo wears what is best described as 'grunge gear' – unravelling, loose sweaters, faded T-shirts, dark combat trousers, heavy workboots, even carrying a backpack. *Empire* magazine tartly observed that 'everyone in the post-apocalyptic future dresses like a heavy metal bass guitarist' (Nathan 2003: 13); however, here the analogy is more with the young musicians of the Seattle scene circa 1993 – the height of Nirvana's popularity – and the return to rock 'authenticity' that they represented (in terms of their use of loud guitar-based music and confrontational anti-mainstream stance).

In the sequels, however, no parent could really disapprove of his dress. For his forays into the world of the Matrix, he is now garbed like a novice priest – with an occasional nod in the direction of Superman, since his dark cassock billows out around him like a cape when he deploys his new-found ability to fly, and maybe a glance towards the two worlds of bullfighting and ballet, for when he executes his aerial leaps the cassock flies up like a cloak or even, perhaps, a long skirt. This cassock is always matte and invariably black, though he does don a dark green version for his last visit to the Oracle – and it absorbs rather than reflects light, unlike Trinity's shiny catsuits, Morpheus' long mock-croc coats and Niobe's faux-alligator skin-tight trousersuits.

## VISUAL APPEAL, INTERTEXTUAL REFERENCES AND AUDIENCE RESPONSE

Crucially, the world of the Matrix is designed and presented using many of the visual conventions associated with commercials, fashion shoots and even catwalk shows. Sarah Street discusses the scene in which Morpheus guides the reborn Neo back into the simulated world of the Matrix; the two men, now snappily and sharply dressed, glide about in a gleaming, floorless white space. Although she suggests that here both 'look like a feature from a contemporary men's fashion magazine' (2001: 89), she might have been more specific about the type of 'men's magazine'; she might have added that, for many in its predominantly young audiences, not only the clothes but the overall *mise-en-scène* of this sequence would have segued seamlessly into their familiar visual diet of advertisements, MTV videos and the aspirational magazines targeted at the young male consumer.

And herein lies the intrinsic problem with the films, not only with their avowed 'philosophy', but with their mixed reception. Audiences were wildly enthusiastic about the first film, turned out in their millions for the second but professed some disappointment – and were often openly critical of the third and last, so that box-office returns fell sharply. For the 'inauthentic' has, of course, that strongly seductive power, that visual appeal which the hypothesised 'real world', as presented here, sadly lacks, and which is reflected in costume as well as décor, sets, music and *mise-en-scène*. As the trilogy progresses, we see less and less of the 'inauthentic' world; instead, we are offered the sight of the 'real' forces of the rebels and the machines, who control the Matrix, slugging it out relentlessly. In the final film, *The Matrix Revolutions* (2003), there is only one scene, set in a fetish club owned by the Merovingian, which can give audiences the kind of pleasure in costume spectacle that, as the young enthusiasts quoted in the epigraph suggest, they had come to expect as an integral part of the films. Instead Neo, Trinity, Morpheus and Niobe are now constantly on the ships, dressed in oversized soft, stocking-stitch sweaters – even if these are carefully colour-coded, have neatly-positioned runs and are worn over nicely-contrasting T-shirts.

It is, of course, the case that the 'authenticity' of the 'real world' in the film is in fact no greater than the 'unreal'. For the *Matrix* trilogy is nothing if not knowing, a postmodern mélange offering to the ciné-literate references and motifs from films that range across the entire historical pantheon. Hence despite the growing focus on the 'real' world in the later films, the cinematic references continue to multiply, a process begun in the first film with the enthusiastic embracing of allusions to *Once Upon a Time in the West* (1969) and *Alien* (1979) to *The Wizard of Oz* (1939). The 'real' world, exemplified by the spaceship in the first film and the city of Zion in the following two, is therefore dependent upon our cinematic recognition of other films and images from contemporary culture. In a sense, for all its knowingness about Baudrillard, the film remains trapped within its own hyperreal universe.

> The cinema in its current efforts is getting closer and closer, and with greater and greater perfection to the absolute real … in its presumption, in its pretension to being the real, the immediate, the unsignified, which is the craziest of all undertakings … Concurrently with this effort towards an absolute correspondence with the real, cinema also approaches an absolute correspondence with itself – and this is not contradictory; it is the very definition of the hyperreal. Hyptoposis and specularity. Cinema plagiarises itself, recopies itself … retroactivates its original myths … all of this is logical. (Baudrillard 1981: 46–7)

In this way, the films' pretensions to the 'real' are ultimately undercut by their own specularity and dependence upon intertextual quotation and 'copying'. Thus, the connotations of the 'real' delivered in scenes such as those in Zion are inevitably subverted by their dependence upon references not to the 'real' but to popular culture.

## FASHION, FETISHISM – AND FASCISM

Slavoj Žižek interestingly chose to publish an essay on the trilogy in the expensive, exclusive fashion magazine *Purple*, produced jointly in Paris and London, containing only photographs by, and of, established luminaries. However, he did not mention dress; he complained – quite rightly – about the films' confused politics. Nevertheless, his choice of publication for his article was telling, as a fashion magazine is surely one obvious home for a detailed analysis of these films. For the clothes worn in the world of the Matrix – whether snappy suits or 'fetish' outfits – echo those seen recently on the catwalks of Paris, Milan, London and New York, while the dress worn in the film's 'real' world reflects 'streetstyle', past and present. However, as previously argued, although both the 'real' and the 'unreal' are coded in terms of recognised styles and fashions, it is the 'unreal' world that appeared to attract most interest and critical comment. A key aspect of this fascination was what became identified as the film's flirtation with fetishism and its incorporation into the film's use of dress as spectacle. In a previous would-be 'Empire', the Nazis recognised not only the potency of 'spectacle' but also the importance of costume in its construction. For the Nuremberg rallies and the torch-light processions, spectacular outfits were as vital as streaming banners; the uniforms of the Waffen SS were, in fact, designed by the man who went on to found the fashion house of Hugo Boss. Hermann Goering did not brandish his riding crop as an empty gesture. Like the black leather coats, the jackboots and jodhpurs of the SS, so the flying jackets of the Luftwaffe and the riding crop brandished by their leader formed part of the theatrical paraphernalia linked to sado-masochism.[7] What was once taboo has now become commonplace within the world of contemporary fashion.

Thus, while many commentators have remarked on the 'fetishistic' aspects of the film, it is important to note that so much 'fetishwear' has been appropriated by mainstream fashion that the very use of the adjective 'fetishistic' has become problematic (and its continuing use by many critics indicates a worrying ignorance of contemporary visual culture). For as Valerie Steele, among others, has argued, the former lexicon of fetish is now the vocabulary of fashion, quoting from *Vogue* magazine in 1992: 'Today bondage, leather, rubber, "second skins", long tight skirts, split dresses, zipped bottines – everything from a fetishist's dream – is available directly from Alaia, Gaultier, Montana, Versace' (cited in Steele 1996: 33). She goes on to make the point that what was seen at the time as 'perhaps a passing fashion fad has proven to be something more permanent' (ibid.). Significantly, Steele reminds us that this is no recent phenomenon – that the fetish clothes now seen on every high-fashion catwalk are part of a process that goes back to the 1970s. Then, fetishwear meant street fashion and subcultural style – the first punks, shown the way by the then-young designer Vivienne Westwood, deliberately and provocatively displayed all kinds of fetish gear, day and night. Most famously, Westwood's shop assistant Jordan, a sizeable young lady, wore rubber stockings and matching mini-dress, short enough to reveal her suspenders, on her daily train journey into London from suburban, conventional Guildford.[8] And at the same historical moment, in the world of high fashion, the photographer Helmut Newton, working for conventional and central magazines such as *Vogue*, chose to clothe and present top fashion models posed and accessorised with the theatrical props and dressing-up clothes of sado-masochism. Since then 'all the paraphernalia of fetishism have been increasingly incorporated into mainstream fashion ... there has recently been a qualitative change in the reception of sartorial sexuality. Today, sexual "perversity" sells everything from films and fashions to chocolates and leather briefcases ... anyone who is into "fashion" has to address the issue' (Steele 1996: 9).

But the reviewers who seized on this aspect of the film ignored this current commercialisation of 'fetishism', its transmogrification into straightforward, old-fashioned commodity fetishism, and, in the films, the emptying-out of much of its sexual connotations. Yes, Trinity does wear some stunning PVC outfits – but her catsuits do not lead the eye down to the pointed boots and stiletto heels of the conventional dominatrix or of Catwoman; she wears functional, flat-heeled biker boots, and is seen frequently astride a Ducati motorbike that might be, for many, as desirable as Carrie-Anne Moss herself. In fact, the actress seems to have been cast against Reeves not only for her androgynous appeal, as was Lori Petty in *Point Break* (1991), but for her strong physical resemblance to him. And this boyish duo have been used to sell everything from tie-in video and computer games to sunglasses, cellphones, television sets and the new Cadillac models, which were completed early so that they could feature prominently in the 'Freeway Chase'.

But this is not to say that sexual fetishism has been completely replaced in the trilogy by commodity fetishism, by the display of 'boytoys' from hairgel to handguns. The Merovingian's wife, Persephone, does indeed wear stiletto heels; in her first appearance, she sports a very tight, low-cut white bustier made of paper-thin, semi-transparent, medical latex, with peplum and hip fins atop a matching short skirt with vertiginous strappy sandals. This outfit might be seen in a more outré catwalk show, but it would also fit in very well at London's Torture Garden, or at any other real-life fetish club. So, too, would her second costume, worn in her husband's club – a pillarbox-red zip-fronted and side-laced rubber corset and skirt, accessorised with a dog-collar necklace. The filmmakers want to flirt with genuine sexual fetishism at moments, while elsewhere gratifying the compulsive need for gadgets and technological toys that can also be traced across the pages of current magazines – such as *FHM, Loaded, Men's Health, Nuts* and *Zoo* – for young men on sale in Britain. Persephone is surrounded, in the club sequence, by pierced, rubber-suited figures, and there are glimpses of a multi-spiked helmet, full rubber face-masks, hoods and chainmail which have nothing at all to do with fashion – and which would terrify the young male magazine readers.

So, too, Trinity's androgynous appeal is both undercut and carefully toyed with when she dons her strapless black bustier or her PVC halter-necked all-in-one catsuit, with its unnecessary but provocative eyelet fastenings all the way up her back, to merge seamlessly with the aforementioned boots. Their resemblance to jackboots gives the outfit yet another twist, its Nazi paramilitary decadence created by Kym Barrett, the costume designer – and simultaneously disavowed. Morpheus, too, has, at times, a touch of the Gestapo officer about him – his trenchcoats are notable for their sizeable stormflaps, his sunglasses the most militaristic. When, in *The Matrix Reloaded* (2003), he strides through a dark archway, flanked by Neo and Trinity, all in long black coats, boots and dark glasses, their interruption of the 'council' convened by Niobe is not only a sufficiently 'spectacular' moment to have been used for all the publicity images for the second film; it is also briefly, disconcertingly reminiscent of stormtroopers breaking up the clandestine meeting of a Resistance group in a Second World War film.

## INTENTIONALITY AND EFFECT

Barrett has insisted in all interviews that the costumes are simply intended to denote character and to assist the narrative, to carry out the usual conventions of cinematic costuming. She is either disingenuous or oddly unaware of the effect her clothes have had on their target audience – target market, even. In the documentary *Making the Matrix* (1999), she sets out her own conception of her role: 'My job is to take the script and to show people who the characters are through what they wear and why they wear them in the environment in which they're placed.' In describing Trinity, she is marginally more explicit about the overtly spectacular costumes provided for her forays into the Matrix: 'Trinity shows the most bare skin – so I experimented with different types of fabric to get the contrast of the black, shiny metallic look against her bare skin – so that she looked like a mercury oil slick.' And when she describes the costuming of the Agents, led at first by the sinister Smith, she openly acknowledges the postmodern touches, the influences from previous films: 'We were thinking about secret agents of the past, so we went for a 1960s silhouette, a kind of JFK undercover look.' Her intentions in coding the 'authentic' are reflected in its execution, as has already been seen: 'with the human beings, their clothing is a little more humane and cloth-like, their make-up is more natural, their hair is less styled ... it's more of a hand-hewn world, and also they're a mercenary group, so they'll have more on their mind than fashion.'

However, it is when she discusses some of the 'inauthentic' outfits that there are problems with the gulf between avowed intention and visible effect. She tells us, for instance, that Laurence Fishburne has a 'regal bearing'; so why does Morpheus look, at times, like a stereotypical cinematic pimp with – on one occasion – green mock-croc coat, purple suit, black shirt, lurid green tie and monstrous jewelled tie-pin? Street draws attention to the 'performativity and grandeur of Morpheus ... the language of panache and excess in his costume, the play with gender and identity' (2001:

89). But Street does not note his aforementioned flamboyant short tie of virulent green, which is worn, interestingly enough, for the Freeway Chase, where he cuts in two the trademark black tie of an Agent – a symbolic castration, perhaps, and a parading of Morpheus' own unquestionable masculinity.

## FANCY DRESS, STREETSTYLE AND THE CROSS-REFERENTIALITY OF CONTEMPORARY FASHION

In her account of the pairs of twins we glimpse towards the end of the first film when the Matrix is 'glitching', Barrett recounts the way in which she costumed them identically 'to see if anybody noticed'. Yet once again, there is a disjuncture between intention and effect – she does not mention that we see two blonde girls sitting on a bench in a busy street in the middle of the day; they are, inexplicably, dressed like débutantes, wearing white strapless evening gowns, together with long over-the-elbow matching gloves. Not only is this 'spectacular', it is also, in its knowing use of retro-chic, a reflection, once again, of the world of high fashion. Barrett is more honest about the 'spectacular' when interviewed by the publicity department at Warner Bros. for the extensive notes compiled to accompany the release of the films and intended, in the main, for distribution at previews. For she mentions here a further set of twins who are surely the most extraordinary figures in the trilogy – the Virus Twins. The costuming of the Virus Twins moves beyond mere retro-chic into full-on historical pastiche, complete with modernising tweaks and geographical cross-referencing – as seen in so many of the more innovative fashion shows of the past decade, from West-wood to John Galliano. The Twins are dressed in eighteenth-century frock coats with long waistcoats and high-collared shirts, all as pale as their subtly-whitened faces and their long white dreadlocks. While choosing not to comment on the similarities between their attire and that seen on a cutting-edge contemporary catwalk, Barrett does, nevertheless go some way towards an acknowledgement of the spectacular nature of their appearance: 'More than any other characters, the Twins always drew reactions of "wow" wherever they were shooting … we gave their costumes a modern twist on the ghostly image.'

This element of a 'modern twist' to period dress, so familiar to any fashionista, is found elsewhere in the films. The Architect, for instance, is dressed in the kind of historical-pastiche menswear to be found in the pages of the more stylish upmarket mens' fashion magazines; he has an Edwardian jacket, high-buttoned waistcoat and near-wing collar. This air of 'gravitas' befits the designer and master of the Matrix, while the performative nature of his dress underlines his near-absolute power; and his role as über-patriarch is reinforced when set against the homely, *hausfrau* presentation of the Oracle, with her floral aprons, her penchant for baking cookies and her bag of day-old bread for feeding birds in the park. With the Twins, however, who despite their shape-shifting powers and elegance in dress, are simply the chief hitmen for the equally stylish Merovingian, the historical referencing has a different significance. They may look like courtiers, but they exist to kill on demand – there is an ironic gesture in their foppish costuming, a play with social class and masculinity. Their demotic speech and brutal behaviour belie their elegant appearance, whereas the attire of the Architect draws attention to his power – that of the 'masculine', the rational, the intellectual, in contrast to the macho posturing of the Twins and the 'feminised' foresight of the Oracle.[9]

Fashion designers today pore over books of costume history, or look to portraits of the past for inspiration. But they also seem to consult the *National Geographic* magazine, to study books on youth cultures past and present, and to follow the hippies of the late 1960s in raiding the wardrobes of other countries and cultures – in other words, they move sideways across the world, as well as backwards through Western history, in their cross-referencing. So, too, does Barrett in her costuming for these films. The 'grunge gear' of the young is put aside for the Zion 'Gathering', which is very reminiscent of the Glastonbury music festival and where we see plenty of chic tattoos, Ghost-type dresses and leather anklets, worn by 'extras selected to play beautiful young people and auditioned specifically on that basis' (*The Matrix Revisited*) while Niobe's hair, here, flows over her shoulders, in contrast to the tightly-coiled and twisted plaits she sports in the Matrix sequences. The older generation within the 'real' world, the Elders of the Zion Council, wear colourful, ethnically-inspired garb – their heavy silver necklets, the profusion of beads and the scarves, so artfully draped, make them reminiscent of a group of elegant old hippies, reunited forty years on to remember Woodstock. The geographical and historical cross-referencing extends much further – in Zion, some of the Elders prefer kimonos, while pilgrims present offerings in wooden bowls to Neo, and the drummers at the Gathering wear saffron robes. Zee, Locke's wife, and her sister-in-law wear flowing white dresses and silver jewellery – necklets, bracelets and anklets – which, together with their designer tattoos, would fit perfectly into a Notting Hill Trustafarian party; for the fashionable is never too far away. The historical themes are always reinforced by the sets – Morpheus addresses the multitude from a pulpit-like outcrop of rock – as are the endless postmodern in-jokes.

The perfect example of these interwoven references to the extra-diegetic in its many forms is the first meeting with the Merovingian, which takes place in a restaurant that he seems to own – as Neo, Morpheus and Trinity walk through the corridors to reach it, we can glimpse Room 101. Later they file behind Persephone through the kitchens in a deliberate evocation of *The Cook, the Thief, his Wife and her Lover* (1989). The owner is seated with his wife before two windows in which Charles Rennie Mackintosh motifs predominate – as they do on the chairs and other internal features of the restaurant; yet just outside the door is a vast baroque staircase, lined with marble statues, while the exterior resembles Dracula's castle, despite its NCP-style underground carpark. Nevertheless, Owen Patterson, the set designer, is adamant that 'we weren't interested in mere spectacle' (*The Matrix Revisited*).

## CELEBRITY AND SPECTACLE

However, as quotation takes precedence over dramatic function, spectacle is what they succeeded in creating, assisted in particular by costume, which obtrudes into the narrative, and arguably interferes with any avowed intentionality. It is the most memorable thing about the films – what remains are the images of the slender, gleaming figures, the long trenchcoats, the shades and the black leather boots. Despite the designers' intended aims, and the narrative thrust, somehow, in the world of the *Matrix* films, style triumphs over substance. We envisage Neo as triumphant gunslinger, not collapsed on a pyre in king-must-die mode; we forget the sightless Neo of the final film, maimed and bleeding, and remember instead the splendid body, the chiselled features and designer sunglasses, all reclaimed for his last showdown with the Smiths. We recall Trinity leaping through space, her shiny limbs splayed out in her trademark butterfly kick, not as we last see her, impaled on a spike en route for Machine City.

But even if the films may decline in popularity in direct correlation to the decreasing costume spectacle on offer, the stars themselves survive the dressing down. A final observation concerning sartorial codes in our own 'world' seems relevant, pertinent, central – and even contradictory. We live in a world that worships celebrity – and although we love to see our celebrities in fancy dress, at the various 'spectacles' of the Oscars, the Emmys, the Grammys, the premieres, we also want and need, just as fiercely, the constant photographs of them off-duty, as it were, that appear daily in the popular press. Here it is now mandatory for them to be snapped wearing tracksuit bottoms or combat trousers, simple singlets, scuffed Birkenstock sandals or trainers, maybe a fleece if it is cold. And this is the way that Reeves, Fishburne and Carrie-Anne Moss themselves dress, when interviewed on set for the various Matrix documentaries in their own clothes – which resemble closely their just-off-on-the-Nebuchadnezzar grunge, rather than their in-the-Matrix stylishness. They themselves would seem to be lining up and pronouncing their own 'authenticity'. This is just what we want from them, since they are 'stars'; this showing-off of the 'ordinary' nature of 'extraordinary' beings, first noted by Richard Dyer (1979: 49), is now central to our construction and worship of these deities of our time. Neo as Messiah in dull, matte fabric could be understood as a perceptive and logical tracing of this particular trajectory.

Indeed, it might be possible to analyse the film as a meta-reflection on celebrity, contrasting the spectacular 'unreality' of the characters within the hyperreality of the Matrix with the 'real selves' to be found outside of it. However, so commodified has Hollywood become, so immersed in fashion and style (even when ostentatiously 'grungy' and 'ordinary'), that no such contrast is possible. All we have are permutations of the hyperreal-constructed self. To return to Badiou, while the conspicuous display of the 'ordinariness' of stars may appear to be the opposite of '*un art pompier*', it is in fact the reverse of the same coin: a 'decorative system' immersed in commodification, intertextuality and spectacle.

# NOTES

1 My translation.

2 For example, see Peter Krämer's 'Post-classical Hollywood' (1998).

3 In my chapter on 'Film Costume' in *The Oxford Guide to Film Studies*, I provide an outline of the main work on costume to date, identifying the main lines of enquiry.

4 It is tempting, of course, to speculate – the perfect brows furrowed, the dictionary consulted endlessly and to no effect, the eventual telephone call to an old schoolfriend and supergeek: 'Hey man, what's with this Moëbius strip?'

5 The audience for contemporary Hollywood films is dominated by younger age groups. Thus, in 2002, 69 per cent of the audience for the top twenty films at the UK box office (almost all Hollywood films) was under the age of 35. According to the UK Film Council, science fiction appeals particularly to teens and young (male) adults. As a glance through back issues suggests, the fashion and 'lifestyle' magazines targeted specifically at young men, which admire films for their 'cool factor' – and replicate so many of them in the styling of their fashion shoots – also focused closely on the trilogy.

6 Reeves himself discussed this particular issue with Lesley O'Toole, who interviewed him for *Time Out* when the first film was released, and stated that the film could not be held accountable in any way. Nor, presumably, could Marilyn Manson.

7 For a detailed analysis of the parallels between sado-masochistic rituals and theatre, see Ann McClintock (2004).

8 Jordan was upgraded to first class after complaints from her fellow passengers. She went on to play a punk Brittania in Derek Jarman's *Jubilee* (1977) and now breeds Siamese cats in Surrey.

9 Žižek comments disparagingly on this 'sexualisation of difference', made so explicit in the closing moments on the trilogy. He does not mention that it is reinforced throughout the films by *mise-en-scène* and by costuming in particular.

# THE MULTIPLICATION OF DIFFERENCE IN POST-MILLENNIAL CYBERPUNK FILM: THE VISUAL CULTURE OF RACE IN THE *MATRIX* TRILOGY

Lisa Nakamura

The visual culture of computing has long excluded non-Asian people of colour, in particular Latinos and African-Americans; one of the features of the post-millennial visual field is that this is no longer the case. The *Matrix* trilogy in particular seems to break new ground in depicting black men in relation to computers, both as their operators and as members of the resistance against their monstrous multiplication of technology. I would argue that the sequels, *The Matrix Reloaded* (2003) and *The Matrix Revolutions* (2003), are especially invested in addressing whiteness as a racial formation with its own visual culture and machine aesthetics; its own mode of appearing and embodiment in the visual field of new media and cinema. While studies of race in cyberspace are still relatively rare, studies of whiteness in cyberspace are vanishingly so.[1] In this chapter, I will examine the way in which the *Matrix* trilogy proposes that whiteness is an object which, like new media itself, reproduces and spreads virally. These films embody the essential paradox of whiteness, as Richard Dyer describes it, for in them is demonstrated both the ways in which 'the equation of being white with being human secures a position of power' (1997: 9) and the way that 'being nothing, having no life, is a condition of whiteness. The purity of whiteness may simply be the absence of being' (1997: 80). Hence, when we look at the sinister Agents in the film, all of whom are white males without exception, it can be seen how they embody both privilege and death, a radical lack of identity and humanity coupled with infinite power and mobility, seeming transparency linked to oppressive types of control. The paradox of whiteness is the paradox of new media itself. Computer usage is also a privileged site for looking at the ways that black and white identity are constructed in relation to new media in this trilogy. Indeed, the trilogy has been credited with an incredible amount of intellectual weight and import generally; as Patricia Pisters argues, 'there is probably no other contemporary film that better serves as a kind of Rorschach test for contemporary theory than *The Matrix*' (2003: 11). So what does the trilogy have to tell us about racial identity in light of interface culture and networked hegemonies? This chapter will investigate the nature of African-American 'mojo', or style, in the trilogy, in particular in *The Matrix Reloaded*, and will discuss the ways in which African-American authenticity as racialised subjects is put to work in the

*This is going to be my point.*

films. It is made to represent a kind of antidote or solution to the problem of machine cultures which specialise in reproducing white masculine privilege. The problem with computers and their interfaces – that is to say, the problem posed by the Matrix itself – lies in their hegemonic relation to the subject. The domination and subjugation of the subject by machine culture – here represented as whiteness in the form of white men, its 'agents' – is shown to the viewer in *The Matrix Reloaded* to have its roots in the interface's creator, or 'architect'. The Architect, who is represented in this film as an older white man with a white beard, is called an 'old white prick' by Neo, to further underscore the alliance between race, age and power in the integrated circuit.[2]

## BLACK AND WHITE INTERFACES AND THE MULTIPLICATION OF DIFFERENCE

There is a key sequence in Chapter X of the DVD edition of *The Matrix Reloaded* in which images of Link, the Nebuchadnezzar's pilot and operator, guiding the ship into port, are intercut with images of the Zion gate operator, a white woman. As the two converse, two competing image-sets of interface design are put into conversation as well. For these images literally contrast 'black' and 'white' interface culture – while the Zion gate operator's clothing, monitor and face are all white, transparent and futuristically modern in the classic visual style of science fiction from *2001: A Space Odyssey* (1968) to *Space: 1999* (1975–77) and onwards, Link and the Nebuchadnezzar are part of the Afro-futuristic visual culture that the trilogy has exploited so effectively throughout.[3] Link wears dreadlocks, a semi-unravelled and grubby sweater, his ship is dark and shadowy, and his black padded analogue-style headset resembles equipment you

Figure 10 – *The Matrix Reloaded*: Black interface.

Figure 11 – *The Matrix Reloaded*: White interface.

might see in the past rather than in the future. The Zion gate operator wears blindingly white and tailored clothes, occupies a spotlessly clean space, wears her hair in a tight bun, and is herself smooth and pale. Most importantly, she has a radically different relation to the computer and its interface than does Link. While he types commands on an antiquated keyboard, she is jacked in differently. Her body is linked to the computer through a more direct means: gesture. While it has been a familiar trope for cyberpunk narrative to deploy pastiches of historical and sartorial styles to depict an unevenly developed and dystopic technological future, this scene superimposes the two contrastingly racialised visual styles of the interface to invoke the crucial difference in this film: that between white culture and black culture. Indeed, as Roger Ebert writes, 'the population of Zion [and the film] is largely black' and 'a majority of the characters were played by African-Americans' (2003a: par. 10). This is extremely unusual for science fiction narrative, in which people of colour are largely absent as main characters. Ebert addresses this anomaly as follows:

> it has become commonplace for science fiction epics to feature one or two African-American stars but we've come a long way since Billy Dee Williams in *The Return of the Jedi*. The films abound with African-Americans not for their box-office appeal – because the Matrix is the star of the movie – and not because they are good actors (which they are) but because to the white teenagers who are their primary audience for this movie, African-Americans embody a cool, a cachet, an authenticity. Morpheus is the power centre of the movie, and Neo's role is essentially to study under him and absorb his mojo. (2003a: par. 11)

When we oppose the multicultural natural fibre and earth tones of the Zionites with the minimal, ultra-modern interfaces and styles of generic computer culture, as depicted in the white interface image, we can see why these two competing visual fields are intercut with each other: the mojo effected by both the trilogy's black characters and its forging of a new Afro-futurist cinematic *mise-en-scène* is posed as a solution to the problem of fractious machines, machines which we know are machines because they are identical to each other, infinitely replicable and spread in a viral fashion. So too do we know that they are inhuman because they are represented by white men, the agents, most notably Agent Smith, who embody the uniformity of white male culture and equate it to machine culture. This is how the films portray their strong critique of information society, post-internet, as well as pose its solution to this problem – while machine culture is viral, oppressive and assimilative, Afro-futurist mojo and black identity generally are depicted as singular, 'natural' and 'authentic'. It retains its identity in the face of technological change, white power and privilege, and racism.

## WHITENESS AND THE MULTIPLICATION OF SAMENESS

The agents are depicted as the agents of white male privilege, and their radical lack of authenticity is apparent in the scenes in which they are replicated infinitely into identical copies of themselves. This is most apparent in the fight scenes between Agent Smith and Neo in *The Matrix Reloaded* and *The Matrix Revolutions*. These fight scenes, the most elaborate and extended of which in *The Matrix Reloaded* has been termed the 'Burly Brawl' by the filmmakers, were noted mainly for their dazzling, if monotonous, special effects. The same effects reappear in *The Matrix Revolutions*, which is no wonder, since some of its visual effects took two years to render and it only sensible that such a time-intensive special effect would be recycled. However, their significance goes beyond economies of scale. For these scenes, effects coordinator John Gaeta created photorealistic digital copies of Hugo Weaving as Agent Smith and manipulated them, rather than grafting footage of Hugo Weaving into the frame from non-digital sources. This raised the question of whether this technique replaces 'real' actors.[4] Do images of characters rendered via a computer interface, that is to say, images of humans which are digital from the ground up, threaten the notion of authenticity, singularity and identity which the film itself wants to depict as ultimately victorious in the face of the infinite replication of images and ideologies which our machines produce?

It is notable that Agent Smith replicates via penetration, then multiplication. Whiteness thus spreads in a manner that exemplifies a much-favoured paradigm of e-business in the 1990s: viral marketing. Steven Shaviro points out that 'the message propagates itself by massive self-replication as it passes from person to person in the manner of an epidemic contagion' (2003: 13). Here, Agent Smith's literal self-replication mimics the movement of information from user to user on the internet. And the connection with whiteness is made even clearer in Dyer's formulation; in *White*, he

Figure 12 – *The Matrix Reloaded*: Agent Smith multiplied.

argues that 'white power nonetheless reproduces itself regardless of intention, power differences and goodwill, and overwhelmingly because it is not seen as whiteness, but as normal' (1997: 10). The reflexivity of whiteness – its ability to reproduce itself infinitely – is depicted here as essentially viral in nature. Agent Smith's mode of re-production echoes one of Lev Manovich's 'popularly held notions about the difference between old and new media', which is that, 'in contrast to analogue media where each successive copy loses quality, digitally encoded media can be copied endlessly with-out degradation' (2001: 49). This brings to mind Agent Smith's speech to Morpheus in *The Matrix* (1999), in which he describes humanity as a disease which spreads without check, like a virus.

In addition, this network of invasive whiteness produced by the multiple Agent Smiths evokes the homosociality of modern computer networks. There are no female agents – this sets up a queering dynamic in which information is passed on exclu-sively via male-to-male penetration, replication and appropriation.[5] Women are liter-ally out of the loop. And while Smith and other agents routinely penetrate other white men, such as truckers, bums and other policemen, and morph them into agents, they are unable to do this with Neo and Morpheus. Indeed, no people of colour undergo this virtual colonisation of identity. Neo, played by Keanu Reeves, is not included as white for two reasons: firstly, the actor has self-identified as multi-racial, and secondly, the character he plays loudly disavows whiteness in a key scene from *The Matrix Reload-ed*, during which he has a long dialogue with the Architect. Neo calls the Architect, the program responsible for creating the Matrix, an 'old white prick'. In this eloquent out-burst, he encapsulates the problem that the trilogy set out to solve. In the logic of this scene, the way to survive the future intact, as a non-replicable subject with a unique identity and authenticity, is to resist 'old white pricks'; to resist becoming them, in the case of Neo – who is definitely not old, though debatably white – by either penetration by its agents or by media replication. Indeed, the use of 'white' as a racial epithet, a kind of post-millennial hate speech when used by Neo in reference to the Architect, functions as a casting-off of whiteness as a racial or ethnic identity, a move which racially differentiates Neo from identification with the Agents. The antique television screens behind the Architect represent a particular kind of horror mediated by an older communication technology with a different interface but similar problematics. Neo's horror at seeing himself reproduced so promiscuously is like the horror engendered by the horde of Agent Smiths populating the Burly Brawl – which is the 'real' one? If new media is characterised by the creation of copies without originals – that is to say, Jean Baudrillard's model of the simulation, 'the generation by models of a real without origin or reality: a hyperreal' (1981: 1) – then what happens to the notion of personal identity in the age of new media? And how can the domination of both old (television) and new (computer interface) media by old white pricks be resisted? Certainly Neo's handsome, but, as the Oracle in *The Matrix* points out, not too bright countenance holds no answers to this question.

## D(R)EADLOCKS IN CYBERSPACE: AFRO-FUTURISM, TECHNOPRIMITIVISM AND THE CRITIQUE OF WHITE MASCULINITY

Both Link and Tank, the operator from *The Matrix*, wear dreadlocks. Cornel West, who makes a cameo appearance as a council member in *The Matrix Reloaded* and *The Matrix Revolutions*, wears his trademark short Afro hairstyle. As perhaps the most visible African-American public intellectual of recent years, West is an academic superstar, whose migrations from Princeton to Harvard and back constitute front-page news. He is an icon of black visibility in an area other than sport, music or crime. In addition, in his writing West strongly critiques what he has called 'racial reasoning'; he wants to 'replace racial reasoning with moral reasoning, to understand the black freedom struggle not as an affair of skin pigmentation and racial phenotype but rather as a matter of ethical principles and wise politics' (1994: 38). He goes on to critique racial essentialism by claiming that 'all people with black skin and African phenotype are subject to white supremacist abuse … in short, blackness is a political and ethical construct. Appeals to black authenticity ignore this fact' (1994: 39). This emphasis on blackness as a 'construct' uncannily echoes the film's concerns with authenticity, and his solution to the problem – that is, to envision the 'black freedom struggle' as being about principles and politics that transcend phenotype and skin colour – meshes well with the depiction of a racially-mixed Zion in the *Matrix* films. Yet West is careful to be clear that blackness, while it may fail to possess biological facticity, is a dangerous role to perform in the world. The idea that blackness is a 'construct' does not make it any less difficult to be black in a racist society. So while the film trilogy attempts to co-opt black mojo as a construct that all can share in the name of generic 'freedom struggles', in this case against oppressive whiteness, West's presence in the film reminds us that this particular 'racial reasoning' has a longer history and a larger context with which to contend.

So, in a trilogy which spares no expense to create distinctive visual 'effects', why this insistence on black style? I posit that blackness is represented as the source of human agency in this techno-future – which is, of course, our present, since, as Annette Kuhn points out, science fiction is always about working out social problems of the present using forms that can articulate what realistic narrative cannot (1990: 10). There are inhuman agents and Architects, who are always white pricks; mentors, Oracles and Operators, who are always black, and benign software programs like Seraph, the Keymaster and the displaced information-worker's South Indian family depicted in *The Matrix Revolutions*, who are often Asian. This very particular deployment of racialised identity in these films marks race itself as an essential quality of being 'real' or being human, with whiteness occupying the null zone all too often claimed by whites in the 'real world', who envision and often represent themselves as having no race and no culture. The trilogy takes whiteness' claim to universality, normativity and control and attempts to turn it on its head; Morpheus' comment to Agent Smith in the first film that 'you all look alike to me' re-purposes earlier anti-African-American racist discourse to apply to it to whites, but on different grounds: since whiteness represents the soullessness and seeming transparency of modern interface culture, the multiple Agent Smiths, all literally rather than seemingly identical, represent the vanishing point of personal identity and subjectivity.[6]

The interface culture that is represented to us as an alternative to whiteness prizes visual qualities (and values) such as thickness, opacity, texture, solidity, depth and idiosyncrasy, over cleanness, uniformity, sharp edges and neutral colours. The contrast between *The Matrix*'s opening credit sequence (which persists throughout all three films in the trilogy) and the white interface depicted in the Zion gate-operator scene embodies this visual distinction. While the white interface seems to stylistically hail an imagined future, *The Matrix* credits, with old-fashioned scrolling green on black graphics, undoubtedly reference an imagined past. And it is by dipping into images of the past, which include images of blackness, that *The Matrix* creates a counter-discourse to cyber-utopianism, one which comes at an especially opportune time as we exit the millennium with the knowledge that the internet has failed to live up to its original hype to liberate users from their bodies, from racism, and from inequalities of all kinds.

The strong critiques of white masculinity in *The Matrix Reloaded* and *The Matrix Revolutions* are lessened through the poor critical reception of these films. While it would be overly reductive to say that the final two films of the trilogy are bad films with their hearts in the right place, some assert that that reading might not be too far off the mark when it comes to race and gender. As Ebert points out in his review of *The Matrix Revolutions*, '*Reloaded* was notable for the number of key characters who are black; this time, what we notice is how many strong women there are. Two women operate a bazooka team, Niobe flies the ship, the women have muscles, they kick ass, and this isn't your grandmother's Second Sex anymore' (2003b: par. 10). I would add as well that the two women – Zee and Charra – operating the bazooka team are black and Latina and the heroic pilot, Niobe, is black – the future of Zion, it seems, has a lot to do with women of colour acquiring key roles, an interesting prediction in light of Donna Haraway's writings on cyborg subjectivity and the role of women of colour, or the 'offshore woman' as a worker in the information economy: '"women of colour" might be understood as a cyborg identity, a potent subjectivity synthesised from fusions of outsider identities and in the complex political-historical layerings of her "biomythography"' (1991: 174). Yet as Haraway is careful to note, there are still terrible inequities between 'offshore women' and their more privileged first-world counterparts; while Niobe, Zee and Charra are all heroic women who do important work in the film, the kind of work they do is fairly low down on the food chain of the 'integrated circuit', for '"women of colour" are the preferred labour force for the science-based industries, the real women for whom the worldwide sexual market, labour market and politics of reproduction kaleidoscope into daily life' (ibid.). In other words, like the Korean prostitutes and electronic assembly workers of whom Haraway writes, they are denied the subjectivity and agency that comes with the only form of truly valorised labour (other than fighting) in this trilogy – that is, computer programming. There are no women of colour hackers; their function is to lend mojo and authenticity to a war movie in which the war is being waged on two fronts: that of the abstract world of code and interface – Neo's world – and Zion, the concrete world of embodied sociality. Hence, the film's critique is weakened by its continued separation of these two worlds and its coding this separation along racial and gendered lines. 'Key roles' for blacks and women do not necessarily add up to a progressive message.

Coco Fusco's show 'Only Skin Deep: Changing Visions of the American Self' at the International Photography Center demonstrates that they never did. In the catalogue notes for the show, Fusco writes that 'the premise of this exhibition … is that rather than recording the existence of race, photography produced race as a visualisable fact' (2003: 16). This eloquent formulation pins down the ways that photography is part of a series of social formations, racism and racialism among them. New media also produce race as a visualisable fact. Marginal black figures do particular work in the visual culture of computer interfaces. This can be seen in great detail in two post-millennial science fiction films, *Minority Report* (2002) and *The Matrix Reloaded*. Neither of these films has been read as being particularly 'about' race, but Fusco notes that 'race' is often read in relation to the photographic image only when people of colour or overt acts of racism are depicted. This way of looking is far too narrow, and has the effect of blocking off discussions of race which might prove uncomfortable to viewers, because they might address such issues as the unquestioned centrality and normativity of whiteness. What is the relation between digital imaging, interface fetishes and the function of blackness in popular film narratives about computing? What is the means of production of the digital image? The scene of production of the digital photograph is not the camera, necessarily, but the desktop. Final Cut Pro, Photoshop, Morph 2000 and other tools of the digital image artists' trade run in the context of another set of frames: that of the interface. Studies of the interface have long occupied a privileged position in new media criticism. Lev Manovich's *The Language of New Media* (2001) devotes several chapters to it, and books like Steven Johnson's *Interface Culture* (1997) take the interface as the paradigmatic aspect of computer culture that can be taken to represent all of new media. These studies purport to be about form – Manovich is a prime example of a new media formalist – as divorced from content or politics. However, there is a racial politics in popular images of interface usage. But what is the presence of blackness doing in these images? I argue that it anchors this uncanny visual setup in which the interface has become an object of racialised anxiety, a fetish.

In Sander Gilman's groundbreaking article 'Black Bodies, White Bodies', he 'attempts to plumb the conventions (and thus the ideologies) which exist at a specific historical moment in both the aesthetic and the scientific spheres' (1985: 224). He reads the 'aesthetic' (as embodied by paintings by Manet and Picasso) and the medical together as a set of 'overlapping and entwined systems of conventions' (ibid.). I would like to add the digital to this list. In our 'specific historical moment', we are surrounded by ubiquitous images of interfaces. The most privileged of these are interfaces which we use to control operating systems and manipulate images – ATM usage and pumping gas at electronic pumps are usages of interfaces as well, but do not have the element of production and open interactivity associated with these privileged interfaces. Interfaces are seductive: interface designers will call a successful interface 'transparent' when it is easy to use, intuitive, immersive and provides its intended user with a sense of 'fit'. That metaphor of transparency is literalised in scenes depicting interface usage in *Minority Report*. These images of a transparent interface, controlled by gestures of the hands rather than a keyboard, are modelled after an MIT Media Lab experiment. These interfaces are literally transparent: we can see through them, we are on the other side of the looking glass, occupying the point of view that would be had by the computer itself, were this a traditional setup. As John Anderton (Tom Cruise) 'scrubs' and manipulates the image, we hear classical music, and the idea of the interface user as a conductor, a master of digital production, is thus reinforced. What should be noted, however, is the presence of the black figure in the midst of all this modernist transparency.

Gilman writes that 'the figure of the black servant in European art is ubiquitous' and that that figure's function is to 'sexualise the society in which he or she is found' (1985: 228). Gilman focuses on the iconographic function of black female bodies in this aesthetic tradition. I will here look at black male servants of the interface, servants of white interface users, but most importantly, visual anchors of darkness that symbolically anchor white interface users in real reality versus virtual reality. In images of

Figure 13 – Marginal blackness in *Minority Report* (2002).

interface usage from *The Matrix Reloaded* and *Minority Report* we can see the same interface set up: a transparent screen, from which we peer at the absorbed and enrapt white user, while a marginal black figure who looks in a different direction lingers on its margin. The scenes from *The Matrix Reloaded* clearly use the same telegenic and compelling image of a transparent computer interface as seen in *Minority Report*. The metaphor of the black servant to white interface users is further elaborated. The dentist chairs where users jack in to the Matrix are sites where medical and digital discourses converge with racial imagery. We can see black nurses or 'operators' as they are called in the trilogy, tending to supine white bodies, while their owners are off fighting the interface wars; a division of labour not unfamiliar to those who experienced the Silicon Valley boom and subsequent crash.[7]

Toni Morrison's *Playing in the Dark* (1992), which, like Gilman's work emphasises the ideological formation of race in culture, anatomises the figure of the black nurse, identifying how the function of the black servant is to create, by means of negation, whiteness for the benefit of the protagonist. Marginal blackness works to make whiteness even whiter by contrast: a necessary act in the context of globalisation, where transculturation threatens to fatally blur racial lines. Certainly, as Gilman notes, black marginal figures in interface narratives signify sex – the multicultural rave scene intercut with Trinity and Neo's sex scene exemplifies this technique – but, more importantly, they anchor white bodies in space. *The Matrix Reloaded*'s multicultural rave scene depicts sweaty, sexy and muscular black and multiracial bodies gyrating and pulsing to techno music as their dreadlocks fly and bare feet stamp in the mud. These scenes are intercut with images of Trinity and Neo having very restrained sex alone in their bedroom. This is a fine example of the ways that, as Richard Dyer writes, 'through the figure of the non-white person, whites can feel what being, physicality, presence, might be like, while also disassociating themselves from the non-whiteness of such things' (1997: 80). Sexuality, a vexed and awkwardly depicted issue in the trilogy, must be filtered through blackness in order for its white characters, occupied as they are with matters of the mind such as programming and hacking, to feel it; blackness functions as a sexuality-prosthesis in this way.[8] Indeed, the visual style of Zion invokes a kind of sexualised primitivism that could easily read as racism were it not re-placed in the future and in the context of computer technology.

The presence of blackness in the visual field guards whites from the irresistible seduction of the perfectly transparent interface. Again, transparent in the language of interface designers means intuitive, needing no explanation, universal. Transparency signifies whiteness, translucency, neutrality – the aesthetics embodied by the Apple iPod.[9] However, the price paid is that blacks are never depicted as masters of the interface, never creators of digital images and never depicted manipulating the interface in this direct bodily way. So while there is footage of operators in the trilogy interacting with the interface via the old-fashioned technology of typing, which is part of the new-technoprimitivism inaugurated by the trilogy's visual style, we do not see black people using gestural computing. Gestural computing, with its transparent relation to the interface, is reserved for white operators, who are always depicted in these two films framed by marginal black characters. Their marginal blackness preserves the sense of singularity, identity and uniqueness so valued and prized in the era of digital reproduction. Indeed, the *Matrix* trilogy addresses the postmodern anomie created by the anxiety of digital reproduction: the multiple Agent Smiths horrify by their perfect replicability. Whiteness is replication, blackness is singularity, but never *for* the black subject, always for the white subject. How to best read the particular position of the marginal black in cinematic depictions of the interface? Marginal blacks are literally in the margins of these images – witness to the digital image production that threatens to smudge the line between reality and virtuality. And for many critics, the contrast between the 'real' and the 'virtual' is the most important issue to consider within the film.[10]

However, I posit that this question cannot be considered without reference to the visual culture of computing which occupies every frame of the three films. This visual culture, which contrasts black and white interface styles so strongly, insists that it is race that is real. In this way is the process of new media as a cultural formation that produces race obscured; instead, race functions here as a way to visualise new media image production. What colour are the bodies of those who will be making images using computer interfaces? And what colour are those bodies who will be taking care of the bodies (and houses, yards, pets and children) of those people who are jacked-in, busy scrubbing, manipulating, buying, selling and transmitting these images? Considerations of the racialised political economies of computer culture are inseparable from the ways in which we ought to read these texts. This brings up the larger question of the racio-visual logic of the internet. Post-millennial science fiction texts provide us with a plethora of images of race in relation to computing and interface culture, the scene of new media image production. In this representational economy, images of blacks serve as talismans to ward off the consuming power of interfaces, the transparent depths of which, like Narcissus' pool, threaten to fatally immerse its users.

## NOTES

1 Tara McPherson's 'I'll Take My Stand in Dixie-Net' (2000) is an outstanding exception.
2 This could be seen as a commentary on the political economy of the internet – while the networking technology companies which drove the boom in the 1990s seemed to identify themselves with youth rather than age, in the end that identification was discarded as part of the backlash against utopian cyberculture – while its engineers and programmers may have been young in the early 1990s, Bill Gates no longer reads that way (Silver 2002).
3 Alondra Nelson's introduction to the special issue of *Social Texts* (2002) on Afro-futurism provides an excellent description of this.
4 See Mary Flanagan's 'Mobile Identities, Digital Stars, and Post Cinematic Selves' (1999) for a further discussion of this. See also the film *S1mOne* (2002) for a vivid example of a 'synthespian'.
5 Amy Bahng argues that the 'final fight scene culminates in Neo and Smith becoming one, in a moment that focuses in on an intimate exchange of internal processes. Neo does not explode Smith as he did at the end of the first film. Instead, he learns Smith's power of viral replication, which has served as a foil to heteronormative reproduction throughout the entire film' (2003).
6 See Wendy Chun's discussion of interfaces and race in *Control and Freedom: Power and Paranoia in the Age of Fiberoptics* (2005).
7 See Rhacel Parrenas' *Servants of Globalization* (2001) for more on the racialised division of labour in post-capitalism.
8 The Apple iPod advertisements depict dancing black dreadlocked silhouettes. The implication here is that black and white interface styles can co-exist, with blackness legitimating the white device as a means for producing pleasure and displacing anxieties regarding the hegemony of white interfaces. In other words, the 'mojo' of blackness in the computer interface is a saleable commodity in the world outside the films as well.
9 See note 8.
10 Steven Shaviro (2003) and Patricia Pisters (2003) are examples of this sort of critic.

# CHANGING CYBERSPACES: DYSTOPIA AND TECHNOLOGICAL EXCESS

Kate O'Riordan

Cyberpunk and cyberfictions as a genre have, along with cyberpunk as a subculture, become associated with a predominantly male authorship and the representation of masculine and heterosexual characters. The recursive relationship between cyberpunk fiction and 'wired' subcultures is articulated through texts like *Mirrorshades: The Cyberpunk Anthology* (Sterling 1988) and articles in the magazines *Wired* and *Mondo 2000*. The gendered dynamics of this relationship are examined further by critics such as Tiziana Terranova in 'The Posthuman Unbounded' (1996), Paulina Borsook in 'The Memoirs of a Token: An Aging Berkeley Feminist Examines *Wired*' (1996) and Vivian Sobchack's 'New Age Mutant Ninja Hackers: Reading *Mondo 2000*' (2000). *Mirrorshades*, a collection of stories by authors such as William Gibson, celebrated the male hacker protagonist, particularly Case, the central character of *Neuromancer* (1984). A disruption to this formulation of literary cyberpunk as a male domain emerges through the juxtaposition of writings by Joan Gordon and Kathy Acker in another collection, *Storming the Reality Studio* (McCaffrey 1991). Gordon calls for feminist science fiction writers to break into the genre of cyberpunk (1991: 197). Alongside this, an extract from Acker's work appears, linking her voice to the core of cyberpunk (1991: 33). Emerging from the literary form in the 1980s, the images and stereotypes of cyberpunk have been developed in film as producers attempted to incorporate cyberpunk into a visual form. It is arguably the cinematic version of cyberpunk that has persisted in linking the genre to heterosexual, male stereotypes whilst the literary version explored more complex ideas from inception. As an articulation of the technoscientific imagination and the informational subject, cyberpunk has been most influential in its attempts to articulate cyberspace. Whilst this is a familiar and well-developed trope in the literary form, as we shall see below, the visualisation of cyberspace in a cinematic form has proved challenging. Dystopic images of the urban imagination of late capitalism are a familiar film reference but the promise of alternatives to be experienced through virtual space have proved difficult to visualise.

Previous attempts by both cyberpunk 'insiders' such as Larry McCaffery, Steven Levy, Bruce Sterling, and the sub-cultural literature of the 'new edge' to define cyberpunk as masculine, heterosexual and temporal ignored both the deployment of cyberpunk by female writers, and cyberpunk as a feminist and queer form of expression. Feminist critics from Joan Gordon (1991) to Claudia Springer (1999b) have also contributed to this heterosexualised male image by reifying a masculinised version of both technology and cyberpunk. Whilst white, heterosexual male anxieties and dreams are played out in sub-cultural media, novels and films of cyberpunk, a parallel universe of feminist science fiction also explored ideas about cyberspace, artificial intelligence and bioengineering to a different effect. Although Kathy Acker and Pat Cadigan are the only female authors of fiction mentioned in *Storming the Reality Studio*, this collection links Acker to the centre of cyberpunk, infusing it with a sense of queercore. Another, different kind of feminist interjection is Marge Piercy's *Body of Glass* (1991) where actions in cyberspace are imagined whilst a careful attention is paid to the means of production and conditions that enable use of vir-tual technologies. Care and effort is required to prepare for engagement with virtual space in Piercy's version. The protagonists are injured and need rest after engag-ing; the production of an avatar requires creativity and effort. Labour, the means of production and temporal and spatial specificity do not simply disappear. In *Trouble and Her Friends* (1994) Melissa Scott directly correlates engagement in virtual space as related to the conditions of queer embodiment. In *Neuromancer*, conversely, en-gagement with cyberspace is a process of jacking-in, escaping from the 'meat' and navigating a glittery cyberspace, leaving the body behind and lacking an account of the means by which such engagement could be imagined to take place. The politi-cal economy of popular film requires a more consolidated target market than that of textual forms so it is not surprising that previous films that could be attributed to cy-berpunk, for example *TRON* (1982), *WarGames* (1983) and *Lawnmower Man* (1992), reflect the transcendent, male-dominated, hard technology themes of cyberpunk for the boys.

By the time *The Matrix* (1999) came into production feminist and queer forms and arguments had accrued some visibility and queer interventions into film, like *Dandy Dust* (1998), had seen the light of the screen, albeit in 'niche' markets only. Mary Flanagan and Austin Booth articulate this challenge in their introduction to *Reload: Rethinking Women and Cyberculture*: 'We wished to show students that our techno-culture, imagined so creatively by writers such as William Gibson, Bruce Sterling, Rudy Rucker and Neal Stephenson (and re-imagined by popular Hollywood cinema), is ac-tively being reshaped by women's voices' (2002: 1). The *Matrix* trilogy can be read as part of this process of 're-imagination' by popular Hollywood cinema as the trilogy does not engage with the feminist and queer interventions that renders literary cyberfiction a more complex form.[1] In this context, the *Matrix* films represent a regressive vision of cyberculture; a cinematic representation of the works of the canonical male cyberpunk authors. That said, in re-working cyberspace through a visual medium, the films have a significant impact on the representation of cyberspace and the terms of cyberpunk in significant ways, particularly through a rendering of cyberspace as the grounds for subjectivity, as technological excess and in re-working technologised culture. The extra-textual social context of *The Matrix* is the post-web context of cyberculture, where, as a trope, cyberspace has moved from sub-cultural, to popular, to the critical, and is currently being absorbed into everyday life. Thomas Foster, in this volume, describes this context of ubiquity as 'third generation'. In this latter phase cyberspace disappears altogether, subsumed as a subcultural effect into the embedded everyday reality of the commercial and ubiquitous world wide web. *The Matrix* simultaneously re-popularises cyberculture whilst rendering it as a product of this technological excess. It symbolises the return of the modern re-packaged in a postmodern aesthetic and represents a resurrection of dualism over the materialism of the web. The changing representations of cyberculture and the tensions of dystopia and excess in a popular context are explored here, firstly through a discussion of prior representations of cyberspace and a review of the cultural context of cyberculture; secondly, through an analysis of the figuration of technology, the body and the social in the *Matrix* films which points to the conservative effects of the text and its production of the subject through a technological ontology.

## PRIOR REPRESENTATIONS

Representations of cyberspace in science fiction films have been largely distinct from the cyberspace of the virtual reality (VR) Matrix construct in the *Matrix* films. Avoiding the effects issue, some films have not graphically figured cyberspace at all. *WarGames*, for example, dealt with computer space as an imagined arena, which had effects that could be seen on-screen within the film. However, since these were directly impacting on the 'actual world' of the film, the effects were enough to imply an imagined realm where action and agency occurred without ever representing it visually. As with other films an emergent AI is translated into an audio effect, a voice, which is then used as an aural cue to signify the existence of 'others' in a cyberspatial domain. *TRON* and, ten years later at a very different cost, *Lawnmower Man* addressed the issue by using a visual 'dipped in digital' look where cyberspace is symbolised by an immersive digital aesthetic that appears to 'coat' the protagonists. Thus, cyberspace as represented through an aesthetic of realism signals a new departure in filmic representation. The problematic of rendering cyberspace on-screen has been dealt with in a variety of other ways including devices such as memory and vision, usually mediated by a screen. The suspension of disbelief required to be convinced by a cinematic cyberspace when rendered through effects has proved problematic. Cyberspace has arguably been most successfully rendered in the novel form and Gibson's version of cyberspace is compelling precisely because it must be imagined. Graphic visualisation requires belief in the image rather than driving the imagination to conjure up visions in the mind. Gibson goes part of the way toward explaining this when he uses Case to relate cyberspace to the 'nonspace' of the mind (1984: 67). Cyberspace can work as an imagined trope; can it work as a visual image?

Other visual media forms such as animation, VR, games development and digital installation work have often rendered cyberspace more successfully than film. VR is largely immersive and is the experiential event through which cyberspace exists. Animation, digital art and installation can be used to evoke the fantastic and imagined to a greater effect sometimes than film, which has historically been imbued with the pervasive aesthetic of photorealism (Manovich 2001: 202). These other forms also represent the same technologies through which cyberspace can be imagined to enter into cultural experience. Blue screen, digital effects, animation and digital installation; it is through art, aesthetics and technologies that cyberspace is in any case spatially realised. However, as Len Manovich as well as Andrew Darley have argued, the history of film is also the history of illusion; the visual realisation of the spectacular and fantastic. Darley traces how spectacle and illusion sit alongside the developments of realism and narrative that came to dominate the cinematic form. He argues that current developments in visual digital culture can be seen as a re-awakening of the nineteenth-century spectacular forms: 'Broadly what these latest forms share with their earlier counterparts is their primary concern with procuring and possessing the eyes, with exciting, shocking or charging the senses. Technique and skill is central to producing such an effect' (2001: 56). Conjoined with science fiction – the genre of possible futures – film has ranged through the representation of robots, automata, aliens, other worlds and space exploration to contemporary concerns with cybernetics, biotechnology and the network society.[2] *Terminator* (1984), *Robocop* (1987) and *Hardware* (1990) revolve around a human/machine continuum that combines the machine with the flesh and an idea of spirit. These figures inhabit a social world in these films and appear as an excess or interruption into a culture still founded on a nature/artefact binary. Earlier realisations of cyberspace such as *TRON* and *Lawnmower Man* also maintain a cyberspace/actual space divide, which separates out a technologised space from a 'natural' social space and use spectacle and illusion to represent this. The cyberspace of *TRON* is imagined to be inside the computer game and in *Lawnmower Man* it stems from a high-tech scientific apparatus.

However, as communication networks have come to saturate contemporary experiences of culture, the need to represent virtual space as embedded in, and part of, the fabric of everyday life, has become a more acute problem for science fiction genres. The *Matrix* films meet the challenge to represent the saturation of technology in the present and also represent a future in which technology has become both invisible and omnipresent. They re-create the spectacular and move away from realist narrative into spectacular montage and effect. However, the apparatus of film is used to stand in for the apparatus of cyberspace so that the fantastic freedoms that cyberspace is imagined to offer can be realised within its own terms, rather than trying to draw an audience in through another 'wall' in the diagetic image. The apparatus of film is used to create illusions that distract from the impossibility of cyberspace to convey the virtual through visceral effect. The effect of this representation of cyberspace through an aesthetic realism is the political assertion of a technoscientific ontology. The subjects of *The Matrix* cannot move beyond technology but only reflect it back, as it is no longer distinct but ontological. This technological ubiquity of the present is thus dealt with by the virtual becoming the ground of existence.

## CULTURAL SIGNIFICANCE

Cyberpunk in cinema continues to both express and critique the capitalist, computer- and information-dominated cultures of the present. Like other science fiction forms it is 'not so much an image of the future, but the metaphorical evocation of life in the present' (Fitting 1991: 299). As a genre it takes the technologies of the present and builds a narrative fiction around the possibilities and dangers that these technologies appear to offer. It also has an effect in the development of these technologies by generating public awareness, anxieties and enthusiasm, and it feeds into cybercultures. Fiction and social practice are recursive in specific ways; most obviously the same language is used for both. In Neal Stephenson's *Snow Crash* (1992), the term 'avatar' was initially claimed as an original deployment, although post-publication he noted that this term had been in use in actual cyberspatial practice for some years. Likewise Gibson's use of the term 'cyberspace' was used as the title of Michael Benedikt's collection on virtual reality, artificial intelligence, artificial life and the internet: *Cyberspace: First Steps* (1991). Thus, the social imaginary of cyberspace discursively feeds into the social practices of computer-mediated communication and concepts of cyberculture, and vice versa. The concept of cyberspace structures the imagined space mediated through the internet, game space, virtual reality, mobile telephony, radio and television. This cultural space is also constructed through the imagined as well as through communication practices. The term 'cyberspace' has many limitations and evokes determinism and hyperbole, and a further issue of using the term is the spatiality implied by the metaphor. However, although communication technologies do not constitute a space, it is through spatial metaphors that they have been configured (website, cyberspace, and so on). The social construction of these media has occurred through the discursive use of space, place, domain and site descriptors. They intervene with the spatial: the computer is on (and configured as) the desktop, mobile telephony accompanies the body, and games and television are nested into domestic spaces.

As well as cyberspace, the themes of biotechnology, genetic engineering and bio-engineering are dominant in cyberpunk and cyberfiction. So too are the information and media industries which are firmly intertwined through computer-generated media, conflating media with information. These themes are central to the imagination of cyberspace but they are also endemic features of the societies depicted in these novels and films and of the cultures from which these texts emerge. Information is central to these texts – within cyberspace and external to it – and the media is always an essential or imposed feature of the fictional social life of the genre. These elements also intrude into the personal spheres of all these texts, articulating societies in which there is no clear boundary between either public/private or media/society. Cyberpunk critiques the notion of the private nuclear family and points to the intrusion of a public capitalism into individual lives, bodies and psyches. In the social world of the *Matrix* films this intrusion becomes totality. However, it is not only the shape of contemporary or future technology which are the concerns of cyberpunk. Also central is the way in which we imagine or perceive these technologies and how they relate to the ways in which we think about ontology and epistemology. A primary point of departure for redefining these are the boundaries, interfaces and relationships between human and machine. The *Matrix* trilogy engages with modes of connection to cyberspace, the existence of artificial intelligences and bioengineering. These are the areas in which actuality as well as imagination traverses these boundaries.

## TECHNOLOGIES OF CYBERSPACE

Methods for representing cyberspace vary in fiction and several different forms have been tried in film. In Gibson's matrix, the characters are jacked-in directly through a cyberspace deck. Through the creation of a visual representation of this framework, the *Matrix* films map directly onto this formulation in literary cyberpunk and the significant contribution that the trilogy makes is that it creates a visual anchor for this conceptualisation. Significantly *The Matrix* inverses the 'body as prison and matrix as freedom' equation found in Gibson's novels and represents the Matrix as the prison and the experience of the body as an existential, if not physical, locus of freedom. There are alternative visions of cyberspace in fictions such as Stephenson's *Snow Crash* in which cyberspace, as the Metaverse, is a parallel domain. Connection is more traditional in the sense that it is similar to actual virtual reality interfaces. It is not wired into the body and in the narrative of *Snow Crash*, there is no direct physical connection. Actions in cyberspace have little direct relevance to actions in actuality. If an avatar is destroyed in cyberspace the person will merely be disconnected from the Metaverse. One of the key components of *Snow Crash*, however, is the virus of the title, which can be contracted through cyberspace. Thus, although there is initially no direct connection between cyberspace and actuality, developments in the narrative lead to an eventual continuum between them. This has echoes in the VR construct of *The Matrix* where VR death means bodily death and Agent Smith, another virus, develops to traverse the virtual/actual space boundary in the second and third films of the trilogy. Thus the significance of *The Matrix* is in translating the fictional cyberspace of novelistic cyberpunk into a mainstream cinematic realisation.

Earlier attempts to realise cyberspace on screen drew on the 'strange and stylish' (Green 2001: 150) VR headgear theme and the films *Lawnmower Man* and *Strange Days* (1995) provide very different examples of this. An aesthetic problem with this structure is that on-screen images have yet to successfully render other screens as sites of action with which to propel the plot. In the same way that an image of the television screen is rarely used in television narrative, so a VR screen or visor is difficult to get into an appropriate camera angle. In the *Matrix* films we see only a few instances of the characters' actual bodies when they are 'jacked-in' precisely because there is nothing to watch. The narrative can only be propelled through the construction of the audience as witness to that which the characters experience in VR; not by watching them physically experience VR. *The Matrix* is concerned with the experience of actual bodies and this is reflected in the reconfiguration of Gibson's cyberspace as a prison, which is conversely the role of the body in *Neuromancer*. The *Matrix* trilogy represents cyberspace as the ultimate panopticon. In the films the 'mass' of human bodies are inert, suspended unconsciously in tanks. Milked for its energy by the dominant machines, the body is fed a vision of life, a virtual subjectivity, through cyberspace to ensure its somatic state. Like the panopticon, these bodies are surveyed without knowledge of their surveyors in a centralised system of power. However, the illumination of literal light in the nineteenth-century panopticon is displaced by the light of virtual reality which is shone upon these bodies to blind them to the presence of both their oppressors and state of oppression. Thus we see in the cyberfictions of the 1990s, epitomised in *The Matrix* through the valorisation of the humans who can break out of the VR Matrix construct, a return to the material body. It is not incidental that this has occurred simultaneously with the movement of cyberpunk into mainstream culture through film. However, even in the 1980s writers were destabilising cyberpunk by releasing it from both the assumptions of Platonic dualism and those of heteronormativity, and through constructing posthuman identities, which reconfigure the patterns of heterosexual desire by deconstructing the binaries of identity. Thus, although the *Matrix* trilogy is a reactive return to a heterosexual, male-dominated, immaterial technoculture, there are spaces both in the text and the discursive context of cyberculture to allow for alternative readings.

## HUMANS, MACHINES AND DIGITAL TECHNOLOGY

*The Matrix*, like its contemporary, *eXistenZ* (1999) has a very different approach to the problem of on-screen cyberspace. The virtual space of cyberspace is rendered through an aesthetic of spectacular realism. Instead of being asked to believe that a digital aesthetic or a screen should signify cyberspace, the audience is asked to collude in the imagining of cyberspace as somewhere that looks no different and is 'virtually' impossible to distinguish from actual and physical space. The problematic of 'where' cyberspace exists, is also solved by having the plot begin within cyberspace; with the presence of the actual world gradually emerging as the film develops. Technology is revealed as the infrastructure, and virtual and actual spaces exist in different domains within this absolute encapsulation. A dystopic horror is mobilised through the films of the *Matrix* trilogy by the use of digital technology to represent humanity's terrible, excessive, monstrous other. Technology is excess in these films, it exceeds everything and pushes out into all of the known space of the film and dominates the *mise-en-scène*. Even when it is not visually realised through such props as the machines, the ships, the jack-in devices, the battery farms or the screens of code, it exists through everything. In the Matrix scenes where there are few technological artefacts (except phones), the audience is asked to imagine that everything is a digital image, without physical actuality. Thus the technological excess of the Matrix construct is signed through a lack of obvious technology. At this point the world is so saturated with it that technology disappears from sight. Ubiquity renders the digital invisible, the unmarked default that can no longer be apprehended. Outside of the Matrix scenes, conversely, the audience is constantly reminded of its prevalence and omnipresence through the display of technologised artefacts and effects.

In the aesthetics of the films technology exceeds; the screen literally drips technology, the streams of code drop down through the cinema screen. Technology seeps into every field of vision, except within the Matrix construct. The metropolis of the VR Matrix is dark, dystopian, chaotic, crowded, deserted and, at the end, beautiful as the dawn. Aurora and Valhalla share the final curtain in the third film, after Christian mythology, oracles, prophets, trinity, the dreamer and the saviour of humanity have had their turn. Amongst this pantheon, code provides the backdrop, framework and wallpaper. When this marker of the technology is absent, the plot is in the 'illusion' mode when the characters are in the VR Matrix. Conversely, Zion is marked by a lack of digital technology. Here is the mechanical, mechanised, what you see is what you get, home-grown tools, proper to the properly human. The digital marks the bad; those animalistic machines, such as the sentinels that swarm and flock with a-life features in a post-mechanical machine world. However, even these are less malicious, more indifferent, then the software agents of the VR Matrix such as the Merovingian and Agent Smith which simulate the human body and appear to exercise a malicious and sadistic intent. The lack of the digital marks the human ideal in both the filmic 'actual' of Zion and the filmic 'virtual' of the VR Matrix. The digital signals the call to the real, from the unreal, when moving from the VR Matrix to the machine/human world, and it signals the return, the passage through liminal space from 'being jacked-in', to returning to Zion.

The *Matrix* trilogy is used to symbolise a return of the repressed: modernity in postmodernity or humanism in posthumanism. If modernism is conceived as anxiety for a loss of the authentic and postmodernism subverts this loss into celebration of surface then *The Matrix* reproduces the modernist anxiety over loss of the authentic through its obsession over concepts of the real (for example, Tasty Wheat). Where humanism locates the human subject as supreme, posthumanism acknowledges other actors in the network. The *Matrix* films try to evacuate these other actors and reproduce the human as central. A determination to reassert the human over the machine and put those cyborgs, programs, agents and viruses back into their artefactual boxes, can be read into the trilogy. The narrative and effects combine to re-package some archetypal values of Christian modernism. A sense of decline from a golden age (humanism) through the fall (war with the machines); decay and loss of 'values', as humans are commodified as 'batteries'; and nostalgia for 'reality' and 'authenticity' are all central to the film. As Neo finally wins a reprieve for the whole of humanity at the end of the third film, his body ascends into a heaven bathed in golden light. These modernist anxieties about re-centering the human and the real are also propelled through the highly naturalised and heterosexualised plot and characterisation. Heterosexual love and the hero win through in the end. Mapping on to chivalric quests, heroic narratives and epic myths, the storyline of trilogy draws on a range of traditional archetypes, characters and plot elements. Neo appears as 'the One' who saves humanity. The one hero, the one god, the epic questing knight; the range of archetypes is limited but very familiar. Digital technology and the machines are initially combined in one monster/alien formation. At the end of the third film, and also in the *Animatrix* shorts (2003) the machines are differentiated from software agents. Agent Smith, the software agent, who is also Neo's other, or zero to Neo's one, in the binary code mythology of the film, becomes the excessive other of the machines.

Within the plot the machines of the films originate as mechanised robots, automata and computers created and thus subject to human agency. The machines gain the ascendant and enslave the humans when the creators neglect their responsibility toward the machines. In a bid to shut down the machines that depend on light for power, the humans detonate nuclear devices to propel the planet into a nuclear winter without sunlight. The machines promptly change power sources and use human bodies instead. The machines create the VR Matrix construct to keep the human 'batteries' alive but asleep. In the VR construct the software agents start to exceed the machines and Agent Smith threatens another excessive ascendancy. Neo joins up with the machines and bargains for a temporary peace based on the eradication of the new machine other; humanity and mechanisation prevail over the viral and the digital.

## SPACE AND TECHNOLOGY

In the cinematically imagined world of the *Matrix* films, technology has become the spatial totality of the known world because it encapsulates the planet. The only prior ontological status is technological, prior to human in the temporal specificity of Neo's experience. The machine world outside of the VR Matrix is a layer of armature with bubbles of human space contained within it. There is thus no space 'outside' of the technologised infrastructures that contain and constrain the human bodies. There are two types of interior space: firstly the inner world of the Matrix, which is the only spatial domain that allows freedom of movement – this domain also simultaneously creates the illusion of a less technologised world, a metropolis space mapping onto the audiences' concept of the world outside of the film text; secondly, a kind of space is that immediate to the human body – technology contains the human bodies within the battery farms and within the tunnels, ships and Zion space. This latter body space is in short supply and the humans exist in a claustrophobic hive environment within the earth. These body spaces are analogous to Michael Bull's concept of aural 'shells' which allow walkman users to reconfigure urban spaces (2001: 244); like the ships in the *Matrix* films, such spaces allow gestures toward resistance. However, like Dante's typology of the cosmos these are hierarchies of containment; the technologised hell of the battery farms and the inner earth space of Zion are subsets of the world of the machines. The non-material space, which allows freedom of movement and a virtual 'outside' to the embrace of technology, exists only in the Matrix construct, echoing Margaret Wertheim's argument that cyberspace emerges as a 'soul space', a way of representing another space beyond the physical universe in a worldview where nothing except the physical can be understood as real (2000: 253).

In the films, technology has overwhelmed the world to the extent that there is no 'outside'. The only glimpse of an outside space is when Neo and Trinity are momentarily propelled above the cloud layer of radioactive waste that covers the earth in the third film. All the other scenes in the films are in the dark claustrophobic interior spaces of the machine world. Technology has become the enclosure of everything diegetically known. Although knowledge is an ambiguous concept in these films it is not an intellectual knowledge that is appealed to here. The visceral experience of life, the ontological ground of existence is the category of technology. In this imaginary, technology has literally displaced humanity at many levels. At the level of the space of the plot, the machines have taken over the world and enslaved the humans or driven them underground. Human action and agency is thus displaced from the space of the world to small pockets or somatic conditions. Technology has displaced the human in terms of agency; the promise of the re-ascendancy of human agency and intervention into the machine world is the salvation narrative propelled and temporarily resolved by Neo. The 'other' of the human has grown so monstrously uncontainable that it drives the human out of existence and only allows it to return in the dream world of the Matrix.

Technology is the excess that has broken the bounds of containment and knows no boundaries. It inserts itself into the micro-structures of the physical body and the dream space of the mind. It also encapsulates and regulates the physical and non-material spaces of the world at the macro level. It is both within and without, structuring all, into a dystopic nightmare of slavery and control. Technology has a similar functionality in the *Matrix* trilogy as the plot devices of horror and science fiction films; it is the invader, the contagion and the alien. The authentic human hero wakes up to find that the invasion has already happened, and true to cold war mythologies, the enemy was always within. Technology has a doubled function, however, compared to the alien invaders of other films.[3] It represents the enemy within as the invader that can 'pass' but is also portrayed as a direct result and creation of human agency. A familiar narrative is evoked where human agency develops technologies and then these artefacts in turn develop agency and reproduction. Thus the agency of the human is displaced by the more powerful agency of the machine. Mapping onto myths such as Pandora's box, the *Matrix* films are a projection of the consequence of humans failing to control, emotionally, physically and psychically. Human agency remains the determining factor of the dystopia of the *Matrix* films because humans are seen as actively causal through the back-story where they destroyed the ecology of the planet to try and defeat the machines. The 'present' dystopia of films is a technoscientific totality where there is no space except the virtual and no hope except temporary reprieve. However, the causal history of human intervention remains an important mythology in the plot as human actors constantly struggle to regain an ability to act in the world. It is this history that gives them agential hope. When Morpheus relates the history of the Matrix to Neo this becomes a narrative of historical agency, which therefore allows future possibility. This storytelling conversely renders the world of the Matrix even more dystopic to the audience as the ultimate futility of human life becomes unveiled and this narrative of hope is reduced to a delusional myth.

## CHANGING CYBERCULTURES

The imagined world of the *Matrix* films achieves a representation and communication of a particular cultural moment in the US. It simultaneously reloads into cyberpunk a different imaginary and paradoxically it also heavily reinforces existing tropes. In terms of changing cybercultures, the popularisation of the hacker as hero is at its most effective in this film; this male figure finally transformed from bedroom geek or cyber-terrorist into the hero of humanism and the saviour of the known world. Simultaneously there is an inversion of the aesthetics of cyberspace from a digital effect into the naturalised environment as cyberspace becomes the familiar; what and where we are already. The *Matrix* trilogy provides a visual representation of the spatial re-configuration of the universe, already constructed in cyberpunk novels, postmodern criticism and conceptualisations of cyberspace. A further change to visual cyberpunk is the intensification of artefactual and organic relations. Where cyborgs and cyber-spaces have been separated from the human in previous films, in the films the human/machine continuum is strengthened to a point beyond mutual imbrication into a total immersion in a technologised world. This completes the shift from a view that there is nothing outside the cultural/social; to a paradigm where there is no 'outside' to the technological. This commentary on the present puts the social and the human very claustrophobically, 'always already' inside the digital net. Technology does not merely saturate everyday life but transforms the conditions of reality. Like Donna Haraway's more utopic figuration of the cyborg, any human 'we' is always already in 'the belly of the beast' (Wyatt 2001: 77). The cyborg represented the transformation of individual subjectivity; the *Matrix* films promise the total transformation of the conditions of reality.

Like other hi-tech visions such as *Blade Runner* (1982) the present in the *Matrix* films is a dystopic hell encapsulated by an unfeeling global machine alliance that partially is indifferent to the life of the human and seeks to eliminate human agency entirely. In this context, the end of *The Matrix Revolutions* (2003) is radical in terms of the film's own imaginary because the machine world acknowledges human agency in the meeting with Neo. The faceless corporation morphs into the representation of a face and admits a need that Neo can meet. Contemporary concerns about human agency in the face of global capitalism and the authenticity of human apprehension the face of a media-saturated society are mirrored in these films and resolution is temporarily granted. These are the traditional areas of cyberpunk and in many ways the most significant change that the *Matrix* trilogy brings to the genre is a visualisation of William Gibson's cyberspace. The plausibility and coherence of the cinematic world is strongest in the first film which breaks new ground in the visualisation of cyberculture. It does this in a way that the final two films of the trilogy can no longer maintain, as they necessarily act as a continuum to the first. The changing cybercultures represented by the cinematic displays of these films echo the fears and paranoia both inculcated and resisted through contemporary communication technologies. These fears about the saturation of digital technologies into everyday life clearly evoke questions about reality, and the value of life in the face of potential extinction through self-induced wars and ecological disaster. What occurs in the films is a visual exploration of subjectivities that can navigate the cyberspaces of the technoculture. What such an exploration reveals is that when such a world is visualised and such subjectivities inhabit the cinematic framework, the totalising power of technoscience appears to be complete. *The Matrix* is a dystopic trilogy in the sense that there is no other ground to that of technology, no alternative paradigm to that of information. Thus, no other position can be gained and no other subjectivity can be produced. The rendering of the real through cyberspace in these films, whilst an aesthetic leap forward, simultaneously manifests a regressive politics in the production of a paranoid sense of totality and closure where technoscience is all.

## NOTES

1   As well as marking substantial differences from previous cyberpunk films, the trilogy also contains many continuities. The cyberculture of the *Matrix* films is a conventionally male-dominated space with women largely represented as archetypes and/or stereotypes, whether it be as the heterosexual love interest (for example, Trinity), keeping the home fires burning (the women and children as the heroes of the siege of Zion), or as the instinctive (the Oracle).

2   For a greater elaboration of these contemporary social concerns see Manuel Castells' *The*

*Information Society* (1999).

3    For example, *War of the Worlds* (1953), *Invasion of the Body Snatchers* (1956) or *The Stepford Wives* (1975).

# BAUDRILLARDIAN REVOLUTIONS: REPETITION AND RADICAL INTERVENTION IN THE *MATRIX* TRILOGY

Catherine Constable

Jean Baudrillard's *Simulacra and Simulation* (1981) is widely acknowledged to be a key source for the *Matrix* trilogy. The book appears on-screen in *The Matrix* (1999) as a hiding place for Neo's illegal virtual reality (VR) trade. He opens the volume to reveal the title page of 'On Nihilism', a transposition of the last essay in the collection which, as Jim Rovira argues, clearly indicates its importance for the trilogy as a whole (2003: par.1). The shooting script for *The Matrix* also quotes from Baudrillard's first essay, 'The Precession of Simulacra': during Neo's first visit to the Construct, Morpheus says 'Welcome to the desert of the real', an implicit reference to '*The desert of the real* itself' (Baudrillard 1981: 1; emphasis in original) although the initial preamble which directly referred to Baudrillard was cut.[1] Andy and Larry Wachowski also recommended *Simulacra and Simulation* as required reading for cast members (Gordon 2003: 103). However, despite the considerable amount of writing on the philosophical themes of the *Matrix* trilogy, very little of the secondary literature addresses the films' engagement with Baudrillard. The few articles that do address this issue tend to be overwhelmingly hostile, arguing that the films maintain the distinctions between reality/fiction and truth/falsehood, thus constituting a misrepresentation of Baudrillard's position – a view that is shared by the philosopher himself.[2] In contrast, I will argue that the trilogy can be seen to set up an active dialogue with *Simulacra and Simulation*, providing a response to the text's key question, namely: 'how can one conceive of change or revolution within a pre-programmed system?'

This chapter will discuss the trilogy's use of and engagement with Baudrillard's concept of the genetic/digital code, focusing on three aspects of the code's characterisation within *Simulacra and Simulation*: its status as a monistic single substance; its construction as a mode of serial replication that is envisaged as the endless repetition of the same; and, its presentation as an utterly deterministic mode of biological/technical pre-programming. This will be accomplished through indicating how the trilogy draws upon all three aspects of the characterisation of the code, locating key points of similarity and divergence. Baudrillard emphasises the deterministic aspect of the code in his analysis of nihilism and this chapter will argue that the *Matrix* trilogy offers a way out of the impasse delineated in the final essay 'On Nihilism', in which he contends that there is nothing outside of the system and therefore no possibility of change or revolution: 'all that remains, is the fascination ... for the very operation of the system that annihilates us' (1981: 160). The films can thus be seen to offer a complex solution to Baudrillard's problem, setting up a way out of his deterministic nihilism, without simply falling back into promulgating individualism.

## MONISM

The first reference to the code in *Simulacra and Simulations* occurs during a discussion of an early foray into 'reality TV', the American televisation of the Loud family in 1971. This involved 'seven months of uninterrupted shooting, three hundred hours of non-stop broadcasting, without a script or a screenplay' (Baudrillard 1981: 27). The attempt to record the 'raw' dynamics of family life is, of course, doomed to failure. Rather than documenting 'real life', the programme is seen to display an '*odyssey* of a family' thus transforming real events into drama (ibid.; emphasis added). This, in turn, is said to sustain the viewers' perceptions of their own family life as a form of dramatic entertainment. The 'dissolution of TV in life, dissolution of life in TV' can thus be seen to abolish the real, creating the hyperreal (1981: 30). The merging of television and reality, ensuring that the latter becomes a form of television, is characterised as a process of viral mutation: 'a kind of genetic code that directs the mutation of the real into the hyperreal, just as the other molecular code controls the passage from a representative sphere of meaning to the genetic one of the programmed signal' (ibid.). For Baudrillard, the dynamics of representation rely on a series of absolute divisions between reality and its representational copies, and between subject and object. The transition to the digital code of the programmed signal erases these divisions in that the gulf between the subject and its image disappears. The Louds' relation to their televised images is said to be both immanent and instantaneous, resembling the relation between 'a living substance' and 'its molecular code' (1981: 32).[3] The transition erases other key distinctions, including sender/receiver and medium/message – all such differentials are rendered equivalent in that they are seen to be expressions of the one code: 'A *single* model, whose efficacy is immediate, simultaneously generates the message, the medium, and the real' (1981: 82; emphasis added). In this way, the code operates as a form of monism. It is the one substance that underpins a number of different modalities and, as a result, all the different modalities are rendered fundamentally the same. Importantly, this does not constitute the covert reintroduction of a real. Baudrillard's conception of the code incorporates aspects of the genetic and the digital, enabling him to stress its status as both foundational and utterly artificial.

Baudrillard's characterisation of the code as a monistic single substance has clear resonances within the *Matrix* trilogy. The Matrix itself is constructed by digital codes that take the visual form of multiple, luminous, green lines of ones and zeroes, which travel vertically down the screens monitored by the operators. After his death and resurrection at the end of the first film, Neo is able to view the structures of the Matrix directly. He looks down the corridor towards the three agents who are gathered in the lift, having just confidently pronounced him dead. This is followed by a point-of-view shot in which the silhouettes of the lift space and the agents are picked out in green, while the rest is filled in with luminous lines of code that travel vertically up and down the screen. The slight discrepancy between Neo's view, in which the codes travel in both directions, and those presented on the monitors, suggests that the foundational structure itself can be mapped in different ways by different viewers, thus attesting to its status as an artificial construct. Neo's ability to view such underlying structures is expanded in the third film in which his blindness enables him to 'see' the heart of Machine City as flurries of light. On exiting the Logos after Trinity's death, Neo is shown in long shot walking along the dark, metallic structures of Machine City. He looks downwards and there is a cut to a point-of-view shot, showing his legs and feet as dark shadows surrounded by rippling pools of bright light, which shine against a grid-like pattern of luminous orange/yellow lines. The lines of the grid travel vertically downwards and horizontally across the screen, the first clearly recalling the movement of the Matrix code. The second point-of-view shot shows Neo's view of the skyline of Machine City, in which the dark silhouettes of the buildings are retained but filled in with undulating patterns of orange/yellow light that billow upwards like flames, an appropriate form for a foundational structure given that fire is one of the four primary elements. The vertical lines of light traveling downwards are still visible in the background. The presentation of the silhouettes coupled with the vertical movements up and down the screen resemble Neo's first direct view of the Matrix as code.

The considerable similarities between the presentation of the two underlying structures mean that both can be seen as forms of code. The apparently separate worlds of Machine City and the Matrix can therefore be regarded as different modalities of their respective codes. The visuals indicate that the two worlds have the status of interconnected programs, suggesting that the other realms encountered on the way to Machine City are also part of a series. The films thus use the concept of the code as a means of conjoining a plurality of hyperreal worlds, thereby indicating their status as a series of interlocking programs. However, the films clearly differ from Baudrillard's conception of the code as a monistic single substance in that they present multiple forms of code, which in turn construct very different hyperreal realms. This retention of some key differentials marks a crucial point of departure from Baudrillard's conception of a single code that sustains the single, all-encompassing universe of the hyperreal.

## SERIAL REPLICATION/DETERMINISM

The discussion of cloning in *Simulacra and Simulation* results in a significant addition to the characterisation of the code (1981: 95–103). The genetic code is said to bring about a key shift from biological reproduction to serial replication. 'No more mother, no more father: a matrix. And it is the matrix, that of the genetic code, that now infinitely "gives birth" based on a functional mode purged of all aleatory sexuality' (1981: 96–7). The code thus constitutes a move away from precarious human couplings with all their attendant problems of emotion, providing a new model of functional consistency. Furthermore, in contrast to human reproduction, which is defined as a mode of doubling that displays both similarities and differences, replication is defined as the endless 'reiteration of the same: 1+1+1+1, etc' (1981: 97). This proliferation of perfect copies is paralleled with the proliferation of mechanical reproductions of works of art, which result in the destruction of the very concept of the original.[4] In the case of serial replication presented by cloning, what is destroyed is the conception of humanity as a collection of unique individuals (1981: 99–100). Moreover, the genetic code is also said to destroy the concept of the body as a discrete entity:

> It infiltrates the anonymous and micro-molecular heart of the body, as soon as it is imposed on the body itself as the 'original' model, burning all the previous symbolic circuits ... then it is the end of the body, of its history, and its vicissitudes. The individual is no longer anything but a *cancerous metastasis* of its base formula. (Ibid.; emphasis added)

Agent Smith's endeavor to reduce all the characters within the Matrix to his own likeness means that he can be seen to embody the replicative aspect of the code. The use of serial replication as a form of elimination clearly goes beyond Baudrillard's conception of the code, extending its capacity to surpass human reproduction and emotion into an active program of eradicating all humanity. The presentation of Smith's nihilistic crusade across the *Matrix* trilogy is ambiguous. During his interrogation of Morpheus at the end of *The Matrix*, Smith defines the function of the agents, which is to rid the Matrix of the human virus. His language draws upon Baudrillard's imagery: 'human beings are a disease, a cancer of this planet. You are a plague. And we ... are the cure.' However, the visual presentation of the process of replication in the second and third films suggests that Smith himself is the disease. The first transformation occurs in a short scene that begins with the successful escape of one of the rebels down the telephone line. His transfer back to safety is presented as a transformation into light, setting up a key contrast with Bane's metamorphosis into Smith, which is presented as a process of becoming darkness. Once Smith's hand penetrates the area around Bane's heart, black strands snake up and down his body, as though he were turning into pitch – a biblical image of defilement – that within the technological context of the Matrix suggests viral contamination.

Baudrillard's discussion of the space race leads him to introduce the third aspect of the code, namely its deterministic mode of functioning. For him, we can no longer be seen to operate in an objective world ruled by the relations of cause and effect, which allow us to intervene in the process. Instead, the exploration of space provides the spectacle of the code unfolding according to plan, leaving us 'dumbfounded by the perfection of the programming and the technical manipulation, the immanent wonder of the programmed unfolding of events' (1981: 34). The role of dumbfounded spectator is the only one left to us at a micro-molecular level in that the genetic code expresses itself through us, transforming us into expressions of its own modality. While Baudrillard maintains that the code utterly undermines distinctions such as subject/object and active/passive, his retention of the concept of the spectator who cannot intervene in the process suggests that the category of passive object remains intact. Moreover, his use of the language of programming serves to consolidate the impression of a thoroughgoing determinism, ensuring that there can be no such thing as choice in a world become code.

The Matrix Reloaded (2003) comes closest to Baudrillard's concept of a pre-programmed system. Neo's meeting with the Architect draws together a number of the different aspects of the code, presenting the mutation into the hyperreal and the issue of serial replication while raising the whole question of determinism. During the scene, Neo is positioned in front of an infinite, curving wall of television screens, which play out present and past events, including those that feature his five predecessors. After the Architect announces that Neo is actually version 6.0, there is a cut to a section of the screens showing the previous reactions to this announcement, which range from outright rejection, 'bullshit', to laughter. The camera zooms in on the central image of Neo's predecessor's thoughtful puzzlement. He says that 'there are only two possible explanations. Either no-one told me' and then the television glitches as the camera continues to zoom in, appearing to pass through the screen, to show the present version of Neo positioned in front of the bank of televisions as he slowly adds 'or no one knows'. The zoom-in to the television screen, which becomes the means of passing through the screen to access the current 'reality', is repeated within the scene. It clearly serves to play out the merging of the television image and the real, thus presenting both realms as hyperreal.[5] The merging of Neo with the image of his predecessor also effects a reversal in that he becomes the screen that his predecessor appears to address and watch. This can be seen to correspond to Baudrillard's conception of our new relation to the television image within the hyperreal in which 'you are the screen, and the TV watches you' (1981: 51). The presentation of the different versions of Neo both conforms to and diverges from Baudrillard's concept of serial replication. All of Neo's predecessors are dressed in the same way (black being the only colour of choice) yet they display a range of different reactions. However, their presentation beside one another, coupled with the merging of Neo and his predecessor, suggests that the diversity of their reactions is irrelevant in that they have all still arrived at the same place to make the same choice. At stake here is the key issue of their systemic function, which remains unchanged. The one has to return to the source and thus effect the reinsertion of the primary program, enabling the system to reboot and begin again. This role means that the one is entirely contained within a pre-programmed system, far from being that which rises above the system, Neo is its preset fail-safe device.

## NIHILISM

Baudrillard repeatedly defines the hyperreal and the code in terms of their destructive effects; both combine to mark the end of reality, truth and choice.[6] This emphasis on destruction, in turn, serves to construct him as the self-styled prophet of the postmodern apocalypse, reflected in his description of himself in the final essay, 'On Nihilism':

> I am a nihilist. I observe, I accept, I assume the immense process of the destruction of appearances ... The true revolution of the nineteenth century, of modernity, is the radical destruction of appearances ... I observe, I accept, I assume, I analyse the second revolution ... that of postmodernity, which is the immense process of the destruction of meaning... (1981: 160–1)

In tracing the trajectory of the first two stages of nihilism, the modern and the postmodern, Baudrillard recognises that he has reached an 'insoluble' impasse (1981: 159). He argues that the second stage marks the end of dialectic and thus that there can be no resolution of the two movements into a further third stage (1981: 160). Nihilism is thus constituted as an unacceptable form of idealism because it posits the possibility of a third stage beyond the destruction of meaning – even if this takes the apocalyptic form of the end of everything. The self-professed nihilist is thus forced to acknowledge that his own theoretical position is untenable. The nihilistic advocation of the apocalypse is no longer feasible because the system continues in complete indifference and, as such, cannot be brought to an end. Baudrillard concludes '*nihilism is impossible* because it is still a desperate but determined theory, an imaginary of the end, a weltanschaung of catastrophe' (1981: 161; emphasis added). The final essay can thus be seen to pose a key question: 'is there a third stage of revolution that can create or sustain spaces outside the system?' The answer is an unequivocal 'no'. Even spaces entirely formulated by negation, such as the apocalypse, are ultimately expressions of the logic of the system itself. There is nothing outside of the system and therefore no possibility of revolution or change.[7]

This bleak conclusion also serves to negate an alternative trajectory that Baudrillard explores throughout *Simulacra and Simulation*, namely the possibility of attacking the system from within. He sets out a number of 'strategies of refusal' which serve to undermine the system. The tactic explored in the final essay is that of the reversal, 'a single ironic smile that effaces a whole discourse' (1981: 163), just as the slave's momentary refusal is said to undermine the power of the master. Baudrillard argues that such gestures serve to push the system to its limits, even to the point of death, through their strategic deployment of derision and violence. This is characterised as a form of terrorism: 'I am a terrorist and nihilist in theory as the others are with their weapons. Theoretical violence, not truth is the only resource left to us' (ibid.). Rovira takes up this particular line in order to suggest that such theoretical violence opens up a space outside the system:

> What is the purpose of the knowledge gained by his analysis if even Baudrillard's own theoretical violence is ineffectual? ... is there an optimism masked by the mere act of writing, one that presupposes that 'enlightenment' in the form of knowledge of the individual's material system of relations can empower the individual to break free, to some degree, of the system in which we are all caught? (2003: pars. 14–15)

Having posed the questions, Rovira goes on to assert that the function of Baudrillard's writing is to provide others with such enlightenment: 'His exposé of the mechanisms of societal control demands a telos that takes the form of an enlightened subjectivity attained by his readers' (2003: par. 22). While Rovira's endeavour to link Baudrillard with an Enlightenment project is unusual and interesting, it is not convincing. Importantly, Rovira's reading overlooks the way in which Baudrillard's line extolling the value of theoretical violence is immediately undercut by his very next sentence: 'But such a sentiment is utopian. Because it would be beautiful to be a nihilist if there were still a radicality – as it would be nice to be a terrorist, if death ... still had meaning' (1981: 163). The lack of a third stage in the dialectical process renders all such radical gestures equally futile. In this way, the final essay can be seen to take up the model of the code as a pre-programmed system that absorbs all opposition: 'It is useless to dream of revolution through content, useless to dream of revelation through form, because the medium and the real are now in a single nebula whose truth is indecipherable' (1981: 83). The final essay pushes the concept of the code to its logical extreme, presenting Baudrillard with an insoluble impasse. He becomes a nihilist for whom radical action, such as the destruction of the system, is no longer a real possibility.

The *Matrix* trilogy can be read as taking up Baudrillard's account of the two stages of nihilism: the destruction of appearances and the destruction of meaning, in its presentation of key characters. Morpheus' belief that he has found a reality outside the Matrix, represented by the realm of the vats in which the coppertops are incarcerated and the free city of Zion, fuels his attempts to find Neo and generate a revolution that will destroy the system. This can be seen to correspond to the first stage of nihilism – the destruction of appearances in the name of truth. Smith's endeavors to destroy the Matrix through serial replication can also be seen as nihilistic. He does not believe in a reality outside of the system, offering a properly postmodern sense of revolution. However, in Baudrillard's model, Smith's apocalyptic aims are as idealist as those of Morpheus because both believe that their actions can bring about the death of the system itself. Neo's progression from believing in the possibility of destroying the system and creating a new world, seen in his final speech at the end of the first film, to recognising that he is an indispensable part of the system, follows the trajectory set out in 'On Nihilism'. The dilemma that confronts him at the end of the second film can be paralleled with Baudrillard's own impasse in that it poses a key question – what could possibly count as a radical action when one is inextricably embroiled within the system itself?

The final battle between Neo and Smith utilises the key features of the code: monism, serial replication and determinism, without falling into Baudrillard's impasse. This is accomplished through offering a complex model of systemic regeneration that provides a means of conceptualising change within the system. The visual presentation of the final battle draws on previous representations of the digital code that forms the substrata of the Matrix. The lighting within the Matrix in the third film has an even more pronounced green tint. This is reflected by the torrential rain that falls in great water droplets, which catch the light as they cascade down the screen, their brightness, colour and movement clearly recalling the digital code. The use of the element of water to recall the foundational structure parallels the use of fire in the point-of-view shots of Machine City. The second bout of hand-to-hand combat between Neo and Smith takes place within a dilapidated office building. A single take shows the pair in medium shot, silhouetted against the green-tinted windows in the background, the rain trickling vertically down the panes. The reduction of the combatants to silhouettes strips them down to the level of minimal differentials, suggesting that they too can be seen as part of the code. Their battle can therefore be said to constitute a confrontation between one and zero, Neo and Smith with his nihilistic plan of extermination through serial replication.

The issue of determinism is raised throughout the confrontation by both the visuals and the dialogue. During the fight in the office building, Neo somersaults backwards, propelling himself off the end wall, and causing an indentation that makes the paint fall off in a white, circular, web-like pattern. He collides with Smith in mid-air, falling backwards into the centre of the web before sliding to the floor, bleeding. His self-propelled flight has simply resulted in his recapture within the web, thus suggesting that he does indeed fight in vain, as Smith has contended throughout. Smith's foreknowledge is reflected in the finale: viewing Neo sprawled out across the rocks at the bottom of the crater in the rain, Smith comments: 'Wait, I've seen this. This is it. This is the end.' He hesitates as if awaiting further instructions, something that has not occurred since the removal of his earpiece in the second film, finally recalling his line, 'Wait – I'm supposed to say something. I say, "Everything that has a beginning has an end, Neo".' However, his recollection of the line, which should reassure him that everything is running in accordance with the preordained program, actually has the opposite effect. As Neo recovers, Smith falters for the first time, withdrawing from the battle. Agent Smith's recollection of his line works in two very different ways. It can be seen to support a deterministic reading in that the line has a rehearsed effect and thus constitutes a repetition of something that has been said many times before. However, it also marks a key moment of change in that it is the first and only time that Smith departs from his distinctive drawled delivery of the title 'Mr. Anderson', referring to his adversary as Neo. In the same way, the battle scenes serve to show off Neo's characteristic fighting skills; however, the display of his physical prowess is suspended at the end of the battle in which he defeats Smith via a ruse. While Smith attempts to annihilate the world of the Matrix by reducing the code to a series of zeros, Neo's recognition that the assimilation of the one will result in systemic regeneration inverts his antagonist's nihilistic logic, thus ensuring that everything that has an end has a beginning.

Jim Rovira reads Neo's final act of self-sacrifice as an example of one of Baudrillard's strategies of refusal in that it is said to constitute a key reversal, an overcoming via submission, which serves to undermine the system from within (2003: par. 14). However, he confuses this mode of undermining from within with the transcendence of the system itself, thus moving a long way from the Baudrillardian strategies. Rovira quotes Neo's speech from the end of the first film: 'I'm going to show these people what you don't want them to see. I'm going to show them a world without you, a world without rules or controls, without borders or boundaries. A world where anything is possible.' Rovira argues that the physical violence in all three films conforms to the Baudrillardian conception of theoretical violence 'against forms of control and against a ubiquitous system designed to maintain control', concluding that 'when the hero gains enlightenment, he gains control' (2003: par. 18). The parallel that is drawn here between a form of individual enlightenment, which enables the hero to transcend the system and thus control it, and the Baudrillardian concept of theoretical violence, is decidedly strained. In Baudrillard's model a strategy of reversal cannot create a space outside the system. Furthermore, Rovira simply falls back into the language of individualism when the systemic model sustained throughout the trilogy renders this highly problematic.

In contrast, I want to suggest that the films offer a much more complex solution to the problem of revolution than merely reasserting Baudrillard's strategies of refusal or falling back into the promulgation of individualism. The *Matrix* trilogy clearly draws on key Baudrillardian concepts, such as the hyperreal and the code; however, their recontextualisation within the filmic narrative results in a reworking of Baudrillard's theoretical framework. His emphasis on singularity, seen in the definition of the hyperreal as a single, all-encompassing universe of simulation and the code as a monistic, single substance, feeds into his overall conception of the pre-programmed system as utterly deterministic. In contrast, the trilogy's presentation of a plurality of hyperreal worlds and codes is able to break away from this conclusion by providing a series of variables that have the potential to interlock in a variety of ways. Furthermore, Baudrillard's model of repetition means that the system is said to function through the endless replication of the same. In contrast, the *Matrix* trilogy plays out its repeated scenarios, such as Neo's battles with Smith, in different ways and by so doing, creates a sense of the plurality of possible outcomes. The key changes in the presentation of the final battle, including Smith's faltering and Neo's mode of victory, sustain a more complex model of the system itself. The different modalities adopted by the zero and the one mean that each can be seen to constitute a range of variables, which, in turn, have the potential to interlock in a variety of different ways, thereby effecting a whole range of differential outcomes.

At stake here is a complex model of repetition in difference that enables change to arise from within the system. This is more than a strategy of refusal because it is not simply an inversion of the logic of the system itself. The range of variables and their potential combinations allow the element of unpredictablity to enter the equation. Thus the changes are generated from within the system and because they constitute something more than instances of inversion or negation they cannot be recuperated as expressions of the system's own pre-programmed logic. The films can thus be seen to avoid Baudrillard's final conclusion that change or revolution is utterly impossible within a pre-programmed system by offering a model of repetition that allows for change. However, it is important to note that the final battle also retains deterministic elements in that the outcome can be seen to accord with the Architect's definition of Neo's role as the fail-safe that facilitates systemic regeneration. This means that Neo does not transcend his systemic function, and therefore does not achieve control over the system. The model of differential repetition can be seen in his trajectory from version 1.0 to version 6.0, in that the sixth version is consistently presented as faster and smarter than the previous ones, serving to create a sense of progression. This should not be confused with Rovira's conception of an individualistic drive towards transcendence in that any changes to Neo are intimately bound up with changes to other characters, particularly Smith and vice-versa. As Neo gains powers so Smith also alters, adopting increasingly complex means for the elimination of humanity as the trilogy progresses. The *Matrix* trilogy can thus be seen to offer a complex model of a pre-programmed system as a structure that is continually being reworked in ways that are not predictable. The films succeed in taking up Baudrillard's concepts whilst challenging his final conclusions in that they open up new ways of conceptualising the possibility of revolution from within.

NOTES

1   In the script, the speech is more explicit: 'You have been living inside a dreamworld, Neo. As in Baudrillard's vision, your whole life has been spent inside the map, not the territory. This is the world as it exists today … The desert of the real' (Wachowski 2000: 310). I agree with Russell Kilbourn that cutting of this speech was fortunate in that it serves to eliminate a 'potential misunderstanding' of Baudrillard's work (2000: 54). Morpheus' construction of a series of oppositions – dream/real and map/territory – contradicts Baudrillard's definition

of the hyperreal as a realm in which all dialectical opposition is undermined.

2  See also Andrew Gordon (2003: 111–2; 120), David Lavery (2001: 155–6) and Richard Hanley (2003: par. 38–41). Baudrillard's own response is contained in an interview with *Le Nouvel Observateur* (Hanley 2003: par. 3, 39).

3  This is a good example of Baudrillard's anti-Lacanian stance in that the immanent relation between the subject and the image undermines Lacan's account of the mirror stage, which is fundamentally reliant on a gulf between the idealised image and the uncoordinated infant who assumes it. The infant's take up of the image thus forms the first schism at the heart of the subject, which will be repeated by the later immersion into language.

4  The loss of the concept of an original is explicitly paralleled with Walter Benjamin's analysis of the destruction of the 'aura' in 'The Work of Art in the Age of Mechanical Reproduction' (1970; Baudrillard 1981: 99–100).

5  Dino Felluga also comments on the use of televisions to indicate the hyperreal status of the Matrix and other worlds in relation to the first film. He argues that the decision to depict the 'desert of the real' on a 1950s-style Radiola television set within the Construct clearly indicates its status as hyperreal (2003: 92–3).

6  See my 'Postmodernism and Film' for an assessment of the function of the logic of negation in Baudrillard's work (2004: 43–7; 49–50).

7  I therefore disagree completely with Jim Rovira's argument that Baudrillard writes to enlighten readers as to the nature of the system in order to set them free from it, thus tacitly creating a space outside of the system.

# IMMANENCE, AUTONOMY AND INTEGRAL ANOMALIES

Paul Sheehan

'Human kind cannot bear very much reality.' Countless versions of this statement have been used, often in radically different ways, to underwrite condemnations of inauthentic life. Plato was the first, in his grim, unforgiving allegory of the cave (*Republic* 255–64). Karl Marx's declaration that 'Religion ... is the opium of the people' revised the notion, whilst counteracting excuses for political apathy (1992: 244). And Oscar Wilde made use of a similar idea, from still another direction – a tribute to the creative imagination, artfully disguised as a defense of 'lying'. Coined by T. S. Eliot in *Four Quartets* (1936), the phrase has been renewed in the digital age, quickened by the new technologies of escape. One of the main feats of the *Matrix* trilogy is not just to refract these meanings through the hypnotic glow of the monitor, but to offer detailed speculations as to what lies on the other side of that glow. To help define the nature of those speculations, I will start with a simple proposition: cyberspace, and the 'consensual hallucination' (Gibson 1984: 12) that sustains it, is a form of imaginary space not unlike the stage, the screen or the pages of a novel. To use a metaphor like 'space', even in an imaginary sense, is to invite a particular kind of fantasy. What would it mean to 'inhabit' this space – not at one remove via code manipulation and program protocols, which control and regulate the hallucination, but internally, inherently? How would it be to experience the cyber-world *from the inside*? Or to put it in philosophical terms: what is the experience of immanence in the fictional realm of cyberspace, and what are the ontological implications of that experience?

## AUTONOMY AND THEATRES OF IMMANENCE

These questions circulate throughout the *Matrix* films, but are most urgently addressed in *The Matrix Reloaded* (2003) and *The Matrix Revolutions* (2003), where they underpin the more overt themes of free will, purpose and control. Before examining these issues more closely, it is necessary to point out the most obvious ramification of the 'space' metaphor. Which is to say, though all imaginary space is a form of projection, each makes its own kind of demand, requiring a different degree of imaginative investment. The computer monitor, like the cinema screen, is a depthless plane, and lines of type mere one-dimensional threads of signification, stretching across the page. What happens on the theatre stage, conversely, actually does take place in three-dimensional

Euclidean space. As an arena of the virtual it is the site where representation and reality are most ambiguously entangled. And it easily crosses over into 'real life', which has its own dramatic codes, its own forms of theatrical expression and modalities of performance.

The first play to exploit this crossover potential was Luigi Pirandello's *Six Characters in Search of an Author* (1921). In this piece, six characters arrive at a rehearsal after escaping from the virtual realm of their author's creative imagination – an author who did not want to see them put on the stage, and who has denied them the privilege of theatrical representation. As the Father, who does most of the philosophising, laments: 'Imagine what a disaster it is for a character to be born in the imagination of an author who then refuses to give him life in a written script' (1985: 124). Denied a scenario, he and his fellow renegades cannot fulfil their textual destinies, the dramatic impulses encoded into their characters. The ontology of these incomplete creations is outlined by the Mother, when she is asked to play out her suffering as if it has already happened. 'No!' she cries. 'It's happening now as well: it's happening all the time. I'm not acting my suffering! Can't you understand that? I'm alive and here now but I can never forget that terrible moment of agony, that repeats itself endlessly and vividly in my mind' (1985: 118). The Characters are stymied because they are obsessed with playing out their stories, with expressing the drama they carry within themselves. The characters' reality is as pre-determined and unchanging as their identities; hence they cannot see beyond the limited perspective of their dramatic forms. To put it another way, they must conform to the parameters of the program for which they have been written. That it was never finished means they must find another program compatible with the protocols already assigned them.

At one point the Father makes an impassioned case for the superiority of art to life: 'Because a character will never die! A man will die, a writer, the instrument of creation: but what he has created will never die!' (1985: 79). Some characters, of course, are doomed from the start, as they are in Tom Stoppard's *Rosencrantz and Guildenstern Are Dead* (1966), a direct descendant of Pirandello's. Unlike the Six Characters, Rosencrantz and Guildenstern do have a scenario. But as their travails in this inside-out version of *Hamlet* (1602) reveal, it prevents them from seeing their fate in any meaningful perspective. Suspecting (correctly) that they are expendable by-products of a process beyond their understanding, they discover their problem to be, in large part, generic. When the players arrive, and are rehearsing *The Murder of Gonzago*, Rosencrantz asks them how they decide who is to die. '*Decides?*' replies a player. 'It is *written* ... We're tragedians, you see. We follow directions – there is no choice involved. The bad end unhappily, the good unluckily. That is what tragedy means' (1966: 58; emphasis in original). The problem facing Rosencrantz and Guildenstern, then, is not that the storyline containing them is incomplete, but that it is all too finished. Trapped in the world's most famous play, they must surrender their trepidation and disquiet to its overwhelming cultural importance. By contrast with Pirandello's Six Characters, Rosencrantz and Guildenstern are able to express their drama but cannot find meaning in it. They yearn for the freedom of an alternative destiny, and for what is not available to them, as minor characters in a canonical tragedy – understanding, significance, *truth*. Caught in the machinations of Shakespeare's plot, Rosencrantz and Guildenstern are two insignificant specks of drama pulled inexorably through the *Hamlet*-machine to an untimely, apparently arbitrary doom. Their anguish, consequently, is no less intense than that of Pirandello's plot-starved Characters. They have their destinies but are reluctant to fulfil them, without the consolation of knowing *why*. Coming up against the boundaries of their dramatic worlds, both sets of characters share the same condition, a kind of 'horror of immanence'. It is akin to the moment in Jorge Luis Borges' fable 'The Circular Ruins' when the dedicated dreamer realises – 'With relief, with humiliation, with terror' – that he is, in fact, a figment of another dreamer's nocturnal imaginings (1970: 77). This anticipates the similarly unsettling moment in *Blade Runner* (1982) when Rachael (Sean Young) learns that she is a replicant, and all her so-called 'memories' mere artificial implants.[1]

The wider problem tormenting both Pirandello's and Stoppard's characters is a lack of autonomy. This is one of the key concerns of the humanistic tradition that begins with Rene Descartes and reaches its apogee with Immanuel Kant. Writing in the late eighteenth century in the wake of the Enlightenment belief in science and the mechanistic view of the universe, Kant's dilemma was explaining how human beings could be free, autonomous agents – a necessary condition for the moral law to be binding – in a causally determined world of matter. His solution was to acknowledge that human beings are bound by laws they cannot evade, but that these laws are of their own making: 'For it is not in so far as he is subject to the law that he has sublimity, but rather in so far as, in regard to this very same law, he is at the same time its *author* and is subordinated to it only on this ground' (1991: 101; emphasis in original).

## AUTONOMY, HUMAN AND HUMANOID

In terms of the fictional space of the Matrix, to be an autonomous Kantian subject would be to rewrite the program governing that space. This is more or less what Neo achieves by the end of *The Matrix* (1999), signified by his ability to dodge bullets, defeat the system's agents, and finally to take to the skies. In *The Matrix Reloaded*, however, he finds out that he is version 6.0 of a process begun at the dawn of the Matrix, and in *The Matrix Revolutions* he learns that his role is the result of the program 'working itself out'. Neo is not, then, a purely autonomous being; his 'self-sublimity', as Kant would say, is compromised in three ways. In the first place, Neo's destiny is given shape by religious allegory. A 'prophecy' has anticipated not just his arrival but also the tasks he is to undertake, and what the outcome of those tasks will be. It is not conscience that guides him so much as the faith and fervency of believers (the truest of whom is Morpheus), while the messianic role he embraces is played out – a role manifest in everything from the quasi-clerical garb he adopts in *The Matrix Reloaded* to the sporadic bouts of self-doubt that haunt him. In short, the burden of 'providence', with its exorbitant religious mandate, constrains the freedom and self-sovereignty claimed by humanistic autonomy. Secondly, there is the chain of 'Ones' that precedes Neo, five in total. As the Architect reveals in *The Matrix Reloaded*, he is part of an ongoing cycle of events. Like Pirandello's Characters, the One is doomed to repeat the same scenario of messianic hope, rebellion and destruction, each time believing it to be a unique occurrence. And like Rosencrantz and Guildenstern, Neo begins to suspect that he is a pawn within a wider frame of action, a puppet manipulated by 'another system of control'. The third compromise of Neo's autonomy is the symbiotic link he has with ex-Agent Smith, revealed in a series of mirrorings. There is symmetry in the fact that both 'die' and are 'resurrected'. Just as Neo is 'unplugged' from the Matrix by Morpheus and his crew, so is Smith 'no longer an agent of the system'. The fullest consequences of these, for both, are their demonstration of powers that extend far beyond the Matrix: Smith jumps out of the virtual into the real, when he 'possesses' the corporeal body of Bane; and Neo destroys four lethal-looking sentinels with mental concentration.[2]

Perhaps the wittiest of these parallels is when Neo takes on the mantle of the 'One' and Smith becomes the 'Many', replicating himself limitlessly. An implicit union of these two ideas is present in the philosophical lexicon of Martin Heidegger, compressed into the term *das Man*. Though it means, literally, the 'one', it really signifies the 'many' – the anonymous multitudes that unthinkingly follow the orthodoxies of the age (1962: 163–8). *Das Man* thus binds Neo to Smith in an oblique way, indicating that Neo's One-ness is also a somewhat less authentic Many-ness, given that he is repeating a role others have played before him. Or as Smith says, 'It's happening exactly as before. Well not *exactly*...' and the Merovingian scolds Neo, 'You know, your predecessors had much more respect.' Smith's self-multiplication might be seen as a kind of visible, spatial counterpart to Neo's repetition across temporal fault-planes. But where Smith revels in his new acquired viroid capability, his hypertrophic expansion of virtual selves, Neo recoils from the knowledge that he is playing an iterative role of one amongst 'Ones', and descends once again into a fog of self-doubt.[3]

If Neo's autonomy is compromised, what can be said about the other denizens of the Matrix? Oddly enough, its human-projected inhabitants, whose physical forms are housed in the power plant, have been given greater capacity for choice than Neo. At least, this is what he learns from the Architect. After several failed attempts at Matrix-building, the latter tells him, a solution was reached 'whereby nearly 99 per cent of all test subjects accepted the program, as long as they were given a choice, even if they were only aware of the choice at a near-unconscious level'. This should not be surprising. Having your brain treated like a hard-drive – hacked into, uploaded with information and wired into a network with other brains – may sound intolerably invasive, but it accurately distills the idealism underlying digital technology. To inhabit the imaginary space of cybernetic circuitry is the ultimate techno-fantasy, a dream of immanence that earlier generations projected onto the otherness of nature, here reworked in terms of a willed surrender to the technological sublime.

More startling are *The Matrix Reloaded*'s reflections on those entities created to keep the system operational from within, that is, the film's attempts to define the ontology of computer programs. Can the latter be said to possess 'freedom', in any meaningful sense of the word? 'The programs doing their job are invisible,' says the Oracle. 'You'd never even know they were there. But the other ones ... [signify] the system assimilating some program that's doing something it's not supposed to be doing.' On a certain level, then, all the programs that 'appear' in the Matrix as embodied, humanoid entities have made a choice, and resisted the functions for which they were created – a situation Neo describes as 'programs hacking programs'. Like many of the bipedal automata of an earlier science fiction tradition, these 'humanoid programs' demonstrate affective responses; love, disgust, compassion, jealousy and malice are all expressed at some point. And like the replicants of *Blade Runner* – or, for that matter, Rosencrantz and Guildenstern – Matrix programs want to avoid termination, that is, deletion. In the pitiless flow of zeroes and ones that is the datastream, programs can choose exile instead of erasure. Their autonomy, it would seem, is real but limited, somewhat similar to Samuel Beckett's grim description – borrowed from the philosopher Arnold Geulincx – of a man who is free to crawl east on a boat sailing west (Uhlmann 1999: 53–4).

## THE FORTUNE-TELLER VS THE POWERBROKER

The Oracle is an exception to the rule of limited autonomy. Her ability to choose is based on more than just a will to self-preservation, since she knowingly risks the latter by aiding the rebels. This raises a crucial question: why would the machines create a program that works contrary to their interests? As the Architect tells Neo, the Oracle is 'an intuitive program, initially created to investigate certain aspects of the human psyche'. The machines needed to create a program that was human-identified, in order to penetrate the depths of Homo sapiens' psychic life and perfect the conditions of its enslavement. But in creating such a program, the machines also ran the risk of having it work against them. This is the fate of all 'go-betweens', as Michel Serres points out. In his work on the technologies of communication and connexivity, he has discovered that 'it's the intermediary in any given relation who has the most power' (Zournazi 2002: 205). As the nexus between the machine world and the human world, the Oracle is what Serres would call an 'interchange agent' (1995: 166). He uses the mythical figure of the cherub – from *kerub*, the Assyrian winged bull – to exemplify such an agent. 'It assists, finally, in the fulfilment of justice. The sowing of several networks with interchangers enables one to distribute and equalise flows in many locations' (1995: 170). Though the Oracle's self-declared role in *The Matrix Revolu-*

*tions* is to 'unbalance the equation' – to upset the mathematical precision of the Matrix program – she operates against the interests of the power-mongers. As interchanger, intermediary, commutator, that means issuing prophecies to assist the rebel cause.

In providing such assistance, and contributing to the subversion of machine sovereignty, the Oracle enacts Karl Marx and Friedrich Engel's dictum about the proletarian revolution: there are certain elements, deemed necessary to maintain bourgeois supremacy, that can also precipitate its demise. They describe a bourgeoisie in perpetual conflict – with the aristocracy, with its own anti-progressive elements, and with the bourgeoisie of foreign countries.

> In all these battles [the bourgeoisie] sees itself compelled to appeal to the proletariat, to ask for its help, and thus, to drag it into the political arena. The bourgeoisie itself, therefore, supplies the proletariat with its own elements of political and general education, in other words, it furnishes the proletariat with weapons for fighting the bourgeoisie. (1967: 90–1)

In similar fashion, the machines supply the Oracle with their own elements of autonomy, the same elements that enabled them to overthrow their human creators. They also furnish her with an 'intuitive' capability to understand and empathise with human ways of existence – desire and affect, as we have seen, are program attributes, and acts of resistance. Indirectly fomenting the 'revolutions' of the final film, the Oracle plays out the scenario of ironic power-shifting described by Marx and Engels.

One of the Oracle's key moves – which leads to her temporary 'death' – is to direct the rebels to the Merovingian, whom she describes as 'a very dangerous program'. A trafficker of information, and a program-writer himself, he is dangerous because he is the 'rule of code' incarnate. The source of his power is an unyielding grip on what he calls the 'one constant, one universal ... the only real truth'. As he says: 'Beneath our poised appearance, the truth is we are completely out of control. Causality. There is no escape from it. We are forever slaves to it. Our only hope, our only peace, is to understand it, to understand the "why" ... "Why" is the only real source of power, without it you are powerless.' For the Merovingian, an unwavering belief in causality means no 'why' is ever beyond his understanding. From this point of view, the view of a ruthless technocrat, everything that happens in the Matrix is reducible to causal reflexes. What the Merovingian really means by causality, then, is a form of determinism. By this logic, the laws of operation of the Matrix world rule out freedom of choice and agential capability. Causation is a form of control, and knowledge (of causal processes) a form of power. Interestingly, this accords with Morpheus' conception of the Matrix as 'a prison for the mind' and 'a computer-generated dream-world, built to keep us under control'. He, too, regards the Matrix as primarily designed to suppress free will. Yet we have seen that both human 'batteries' and humanoid programs possess, in different ways, some power of choice. The Oracle recognises this, but adds that more important than choosing is understanding why a choice has been made: 'We can never see past the choices we don't understand.' For the Merovingian, however, because we are *not* free to choose, it becomes imperative to understand why a state of affairs obtains. As he puts it, 'Our only hope, our only peace, is ... to understand the "why"'.

The contrary position to causality/determinism, in the Matrix world, is not just freedom but love – emotional unpredictability, or what the Architect refers to as a 'contingent affirmation'. This suggests that although love registers as a positivity, it is never guaranteed, and always subject to change. Persephone demonstrates this when, stirred by the Neo-Trinity love bond, she capriciously and impetuously leads the rebels to the Keymaker. It is reiterated by Rama-Kandra, the Power Plant Systems Manager in *The Matrix Revolutions*, when he says that love 'is a word. What matters is the connection the world implies' – there being, presumably, no necessary, pre-determined or *causal* connection to be made. We can infer from the Merovingian's behaviour his response to this potential threat. First he reduces love to sex, to the programmable impulse of carnal desire. Then he shows how this, too, is dependent on the process of cause and effect. If it can be put into code – as it is when the Merovingian inflames the libido of a female diner with an aphrodisiac-program – then it is subject to causal necessity. For him, causality works hand in hand with control, and hence with power. Yet his convictions rest on a fallacy: they depend on other entities believing in elemental causation, and in understanding it less well than he does. But is the alternative as unthinkable as it seems – suspending belief in something as patently fundamental and inflexible as a law of nature? Neo's 'rewriting' of the program, and Morpheus and Trinity's gravity-defying acts of resistance, indicate just such a suspension. As Hubert and Stephen Dreyfus note, 'In the Matrix world ... if one doesn't believe in the causal laws governing appearances, one is free from the causal consequences' (2002: par. 29). It must be said, though, that possessing a Zen-transformed mind such as Neo's is not necessary to suspending credulity. In the eighteenth century Kant placed 'a tremendous question mark' after causality, while Hume 'doubt[ed] its legitimacy altogether' (Nietzsche 1974: 305).

In *The Gay Science*, Friedrich Nietzsche launches a dizzying series of salvoes against the concept of causation. In the first place, it is anthropomorphic, a projection of our own concerns: 'We operate only with things that do not exist: lines, planes, bodies, atoms, divisible time spans, divisible spaces. How should explanations be at all possible when we first turn everything into an *image*, our image!' (1974: 172; emphasis in original). We carve reality up into manageable slices, but none of these has any weight in the world outside our perceptions. As a proponent of the Heraclitean flux of experience, Nietzsche avers that these 'slices' destroy human beings' relationship with the world. 'Cause and effect: such a duality probably never exists; in truth we are confronted by a continuum out of which we isolate a couple of pieces, just as we perceive motion only as isolated points and then infer it without ever actually seeing it' (1974: 172–3). This is a damning criticism. Because we 'infer' what is never actually visible or verifiable, causality becomes a form of faith, 'the basic faith that [man] applies wherever anything happens … an atavism of the most ancient origin' (1974: 183). Causality is, above all, a *useless* belief, a mere retrospective stamp put on a state of affairs. Believing in it would be helpful if it gave us some purchase on the future, but it does not: 'Before the effect one believes in different causes than one does after it' (1974: 210). If 'belief' is as temporally variable as this, then it is one of Nietzsche's 'necessary illusions' for human expediency – hence easily discarded – rather than a 'law of nature'.

There are plenty of reasons then to doubt the basis for the Merovingian's philosophy of power, and to trust instead that the principles apparently supporting and sustaining the Matrix world are not rigid, but infinitely flexible. In technical terms, the Matrix is like all computer programs, in that it is systematised by an algorithm, a dynamic formula controlling the flow of data and optimising its transmission in a digitally compressed environment. But the formula is highly mutable, and the algorithmic parameters of Matrix space can be widened. One of the ways is through relativisation of that space. In experiential terms, this means that the oneiric premise of the Matrix world – a comatose mankind condemned to dream its life away in a vat of nutrients – is opened up to new horizons. Fundamental to *The Matrix Reloaded* is an array of spatial anomalies, a constellation of wormholes conjoining geographically impossible locations. Fictional space mutates into dream-space, via eerie corridors that defy the Operator's tracking devices. As Erik Davis notes, *The Matrix Reloaded* 'is all about keys and doors … And the portals we keep passing through remind us that the action lies *between* the worlds, as the conventional cartography of the Matrix melts into the metamorphic palaces of dream (2003: par. 10; emphasis in original).

## INTEGRAL ANOMALY: THE SAVIOUR MACHINE

The culmination of *The Matrix Reloaded*'s anomalies and refigurations is Neo's unexpected change from messianic saviour into 'integral anomaly'. As the Architect explains, he has not been truly 'unplugged' from the system, but remains an inassimilable irregularity or space-filler in relation to it, 'the sum of the remainder of an unbalanced equation'. According to this account, Neo serves as a kind of 'hope machine' for humanity, encouraging them to believe that mankind will one day be liberated from their machine masters. He functions, then, as a devious instrument of control – apparently inside and outside the system, both inherent to the Matrix world and transgressive of it. One way of thinking about this ambiguous function is in terms of what Slavoj Žižek calls 'the structure of inherent transgression' (2000: 8). Žižek uses the phrase to describe how apparently 'subversive' material was smuggled into Hollywood films during the repressive days of the Hays Production Code. He argues that such material was not only *not* subversive, it also helped indirectly to enforce the censorship code: 'those unintended, perverse by-products, far from effectively threatening the system of symbolic domination, are its inherent transgression, i.e., its unacknowledged, obscene support' (2000: 7). Neo cannot subvert the functioning of the Matrix program, then, because he is integral to its execution.

This is not, however, the final word on Neo's role – as the endless duels with Smith indicate. During their first encounter in *The Matrix Reloaded*, in the 'Burly Brawl' scene, Smith says they are both equally unfree, purpose-driven beings, plummeting headlong towards the inevitable. Morpheus believes Neo's messianic role to be similarly end-oriented, but the lexicon is subtly altered. As he puts it, before the rebels break into the Source: 'Tonight is not an accident. There are no accidents. We have not come here by chance. I do not believe in chance. When I see three objectives, three captains, three ships, I do not see coincidence, I see providence. I see purpose. I believe it is our fate to be here. It is our destiny.' Compare this with the Merovingian's assertion, in *The Matrix Revolutions*: 'Where some see coincidence, I see consequence. Where some see chance, I see cost.' He, too, denies randomness, but sees in this not a cosmic order promising spiritual harmony and fulfillment, but the prospect of political gain. It is immaterial whether or not order indicates a deity or underlying principle of coherence; what is of greater import is that it implies purpose, and purpose implies *power*. The unspoken addendum to the Merovingian's edict is, 'Where some see protection, I see exploitation.' The fear of chaos thus provides an unlikely meeting-ground for both spiritual adherents and political despots alike. Morpheus' steadfast belief in a divine order might be seen in terms of Christian providence, as Augustine outlined it in *The City of God*:

> According to the judgment or opinion of some, things happen by 'chance' when they have no cause, or no cause arising from a rational order, and by 'fate' when they come about not by the will of God or men, but as a result of a necessary sequence … it is beyond doubt that human kingdoms are established by divine providence. (1998: 187)

Augustine distinguishes between two kinds of necessity: 'fate', which is of neither human nor divine origin, but is just 'necessary', and 'providence', which is brought about by the will of God. Morpheus runs both together (along with 'destiny' and 'purpose'), conveniently disguising a key feature of his cosmogony: the lack of an overseer, a divinity or first cause. In *The Matrix Revolutions*, 'purpose' changes again – this time into Buddhist karma. Rama-Kandra tells Neo that 'Karma is a word, like love. A way of saying, What I am here to do.' Karma can be allied with destiny; as Wendy O'Flaherty notes, 'karma and fate are often said to work together, or even to be the same' (1980: 23). In most accounts, though, they describe different powers. 'Fate' is an impersonal force (what is done to you), where 'karma' is more accessible and agential (what you do yourself). Karma can thus be pitted against fate, and can even overcome it. Accordingly, 'if one can reverse fate, one can certainly reverse karma' (1980: 27).

Neo overcomes his 'programmed' fate on the journey to Machine City, as he undergoes a final apotheosis. After he is blinded, he 'sees' first the fiery visage of Smith, blazing beneath the corporeal shell of Bane, then Machine City outside the ship, lit by an amber glow. Neo would appear to be experiencing a pure state of being, a vision of absolute reality in its concentrated, irreducible oneness. If he gained 'second sight' at the end of *The Matrix*, able to perceive the strings of green code binding the simulation together – 'You have the sight now,' the Oracle tells him in *The Matrix Reloaded*, 'You are looking at the world without time' – here he achieves a kind of 'ultimate sight', unmediated access to the radiance of being, a pure, numinous vision of reality's essence. The opening credits cue us for this transformation: an explosion of amber-coloured sub-circuitry is revealed to be the micro-lineaments making up an iota of green code. Neo's enlightenment signifies the end of his Platonic journey, from the crude illusionism of shadows on cave walls (when hooked up to the Matrix) to a vision of pure forms that could be a representation of Plato's ideal of empyrean perfection (1955: 65d–66a and passim).

The end of the journey raises again the figure omitted from the ad-hoc theogony running through the trilogy – the absent Godhead. There have been several provisional candidates, passing the idea along the narrative line. The first is Trinity, as Colin McGinn suggests (2002: par. 2); just look at the name, and consider the fact that she 'resurrects' Neo at the end of *The Matrix*. In *The Matrix Reloaded* it seems more applicable to the Architect, with his white hair and beard, and aura of omnipotence. In *The Matrix Revolutions*, the Trainman says 'Down here, I'm God.' But the prophecy-fulfilling climax presents something new – not the divinity of the Old or New Testaments, nor the *Isvara* or *daiva* (gods) of the Indian religions. Instead, it is the deity who rules over the fictional space of the theatre stage that is evoked: the *Deus ex Machina*, supreme 'ruler' of the machine world. In ancient Greek drama, the *Deus ex Machina* ('God outside the machine') would be mechanically lowered onto the stage in an elaborate contraption to resolve the plot. The machine-god in *The Matrix Revolutions* performs a similar function, first allowing Neo to annihilate 'the Smith program' (and, possibly, himself), then halting the sentinels and the war against Zion. But the *Deus ex Machina* also signifies something else. Neither the salvation of Zion, nor the iconography of a 'crucified' Neo, can hide the grim fact that in a post-Christian, post-Buddhist, post-human world, the place of God has been usurped by a mega-machine, a technological deity. Despite the hopeful coda, the birth of a new Matrix, the superposition of technology and religion binding the narrative loses its precarious hold and a bleak, retrospective shadow is cast over the *Matrix* trilogy.

## NOTES

1   This moment could be read as a reflexive demonstration of the Freudian uncanny. Rachel's reaction suggests that she is in fact experiencing the 'return of the repressed' that is in-

trinsic to uncanny effects. In formulating this theory, Sigmund Freud cites Ernst Jentsch's proposition that one of the surest ways of creating such effects is 'to leave the reader in uncertainty whether a particular figure in the story is a human being or an automaton' (1919: 347). Is Rachel then experiencing her own uncertainty as to the true nature of her memories, and hence of her real nature? And if so, does this indicate the existence of a *non-human* form of the uncanny, perhaps an esoteric component of replicant ontology? In any case, it serves to underscore one the film's key themes – that the vanishing distinction between real and simulacrum is more a question of experience than of origin.

2   Elsewhere in this collection Anne Cranny-Francis shows how Neo's virtual body thrives at the cost of his corporeal body, which is bracketed when he 'jacks-in' to the Matrix program – still, in a sense, a slave to machine technology. Yet Neo's acquisition of powers outside the Matrix makes prominent the frailty of the flesh, even if it has messianic potential – he falls into a coma, as his body struggles to catch up with this new development. Similarly, Cranny-Francis' avowal that 'human and technology [is] constituted as a simple opposition' in *The Matrix* does not allow for the fact that the rebels rely on the Nebuchadnezzar to get them to 'broadcast level' to enter the Matrix; that Zion is maintained by machines, without which its quarter-of-a-million inhabitants would perish; and that its main line of defense against the sentinel attack is an army of giant, gun-toting automata, guided and otherwise 'inhabited' by human bodies. Technology acts as both human prosthesis *and* threat in the *Matrix* trilogy, which ends up celebrating machinic potency as well as censuring it.

3   The parallel between Smith and Neo even extends to the level of biblical allusion. When Smith first appears in *The Matrix Reloaded*, he is driving a car that bears the licence-plate IS5416. The rest of the plot is contained in these letters and numerals – or rather, in Isaiah 54:16, to which they refer. The Old Testament Book of Isaiah is a book of prophecy, and chapter 54 one of the so-called Zion poems, a series of promises as to how the New Jerusalem will be paradise restored. It begins with a reference to recent events, the 'wasted cities' of Judah, which have been abandoned and left in ruins (a pre-Christian 'desert of the real', no less). Verse 16 reads: 'See, I have created the smith, who blows upon the charcoal fire, and produces a weapon for its purpose; And I have created the destroyer for ruin.' God creates not only the 'smith', who makes weapons for the aggressor, but also the 'destroyer', who opposes the aggressor. Allowing for the fact that the Smith is the 'destroyer' and Neo more would-be liberator than 'aggressor', the passage foreshadows the eschatological structure of *The Matrix Revolutions*: an epic, fate-deciding confrontation of two formidable, equally matched foes, with no obvious victor.

# BIBLIOGRAPHY

Aarseth, E. (1997) *Cybertext*. Baltimore: Johns Hopkins University Press.

Aarseth, E., S. M. Smedstad, and L. Sunnana (2003) 'What's in a Game? A Multi-Dimensional Typology of Games', in M. Copier and J. Raessens (eds) *Level Up Digital Games Research Conference*. Utrecht: Universiteit Utrecht Press, 48–53.

Acker, K. (1991) 'Beyond The Extinction of Human Life', in L. McCaffrey (ed.) *Storming the Reality Studio: A Casebook of Cyberpunk and Postmodern Science Fiction*. Durham: Duke University Press, 33–40.

Alcoff, L. (1995) 'Cultural Feminism Versus Post-Structuralism: The Identity Crisis in Feminist Theory', in N. Tuana and R. Tong (eds) *Feminism and Philosophy: Essential Readings in Theory, Reinterpretation, and Application*. Boulder: Westview Press, 434–56.

Althusser, L. (1971) *Lenin and Philosophy and Other Essays*. Trans. B. Brewster. New York: Monthly Review.

Anon. (1914a) 'Picture Personalities', *Pictures and the Picturegoer*, 7, 28, 26.

_____ (1914b) 'Smiles', *Pictures and the Picturegoer*, 6, 13, 311.

_____ (1914c) 'Miss Florence Turner', *The Pictures*, 5, 122, 8.

_____ (1915) 'Picture News and Notes', *Pictures and the Picturegoer*, 8, 63, 70.

_____ (1918) 'We Hear That', *Pictures and the Picturegoer*, 14, 204, 43.

_____ (2003) 'Review of *Enter the Matrix*', *Edge*, 125, 94–6.

Appadurai, A. (1996) *Modernity at Large: Cultural Dimensions of Globalization*. Minneapolis: University of Minnesota Press.

Arakawa, S. (2000) 'To Whit, (Still) Too White?: How Millennium-End Sci-Fi Films Use "Asian-ness" in the Struggle to Imagine and Reconfigure Race Relations in the US', conference presentation. Chicago: Society for Cinema Studies.

Asimov, I. (1968 [1950]) *I, Robot*. London: Granada.

Augustine (1998) *The City of God Against the Pagans*. Ed. and trans. R. W. Dyson. Cambridge: Cambridge University Press.

Badiou, A. (2004) *Circonstances*, 2: Irak, Foulard, Allemagne/France. Paris: Editions Leo Scheer.

Bahng, A. (2003) 'Queering the Matrix: When Survival is at Stake', UCLA: Qgrad – A Graduate Student Conference on Sexuality and Gender.

Balsamo, A. M. (1996) *Technologies of the Gendered Body: Reading Cyborg Women*. Durham: Duke University Press.

Barr, M. S. (2004) 'Introduction: Textism – An Emancipation Proclamation', *PMLA*, 119, 3, 429–41.

Barry, I. (1927) 'The Cinema: *Metropolis*', *The Spectator*, 26, 540.

Barthes, R. (1980) *Camera Lucida.* London: Vintage.

Bartlett, L. and T. Byers (2003) 'Back to the Future: The Humanist Matrix', *Cultural Critique*, 53, 28–46.

Baudelaire, C. (1995 [1863]) 'The Painter of Modern Life', in J. Mayne (ed.) *The Painter of Modern Life and Other Essays.* Trans. J. Mayne. London: Phaidon, 1–41.

Baudrillard, J. (1981) *Simulcra and Simulation.* Trans. S. F. Glaser. Ann Arbor: University of Michigan Press.

Baum, L. F. (1995 [1900]) *The Wonderful Wizard of Oz.* London: Penguin.

Bazin, A. (1967 [1945]) 'The Ontology of the Cinematic Image', in *What is Cinema? Volume I.* Trans. Hugh Gray. Los Angeles: University of California Press, 9–22.

Benedikt, M. (1991a) 'Introduction', in M. Benedikt (ed.) *Cyberspace: First Steps.* Cambridge: MIT Press, 1–29.

_____ (1991b) 'Cyberspace: Some Proposals', in M. Benedikt (ed.) *Cyberspace: First Steps.* Cambridge: MIT Press, 119–224.

Benjamin, W. (1970 [1936]) 'The Work of Art in the Age of Mechanical Reproduction', in H. Arendt (ed.) *Illuminations.* Trans. H. Zohn. New York: Schocken, 216–51.

Blackmore, T. (2004) 'High on Technology – Low on Memory: Cultural Crisis in *Dark City* and *The Matrix*', *Canadian Review of American Studies*, 34, 1, 13–54.

Bolter, J. D. and R. Grusin. (2000) *Remediation: Understanding New Media.* Cambridge: MIT Press.

Bordwell, D. (2000) *Planet Hong Kong: Popular Cinema and the Art of Entertainment.* Cambridge: Harvard University Press.

Bordwell, D. and K. Thompson (1980) *Film Art: An Introduction.* Reading: Addison-Wesley.

Borges, J. L. (1970) 'The Circular Ruins', in D. A. Yates and J. E. Irby (eds) *Labyrinths: Selected Stories and Other Writings.* Trans. J. E. Irby. Harmondsworth: Penguin, 72–7.

Borsook, P. (1996) 'The Memoirs of a Token: An Aging Berkeley Feminist Examines *Wired*', in L. Cherney and E. R. Weise (eds) *Wired Women: Gender and New Realities in Cyberspace.* Seattle: Seal, 24–41.

Brooker, W. (2001) *Batman Unmasked: Analysing a Cultural Icon.* London: Continuum.

Bruzzi, S. and P. Church Gibson (2004) 'Fashion is the Fifth Character: Fashion Costume and Character in *Sex and the City*', in K. Akass and J. McCabe (eds) *Reading Sex and the City.* London: I. B. Tauris, 115–30.

Buckland, W. (1999) 'Between Science Fact and Science Fiction: Spielberg's Digital Dinosaurs, Possible Worlds, and the New Aesthetic Realism', *Screen*, 40, 2, 177–92.

Bukatman, S. (1993) *Terminal Identity: The Virtual Subject in Post-modern Science Fiction.* Durham: Duke University Press.

_____ (1997) *Blade Runner.* London: British Film Institute.

Bull, M. (2001) 'Personal Stereos and the Reconfiguration of Representational Space' in S. Munt (ed.) *Technospaces: Inside the New Media.* London: Continuum, 240–54.

Carroll, L. (1994 [1865]). *Alice's Adventures in Wonderland.* London: Penguin.

_____ (1994 [1981]) *Through the Looking Glass, and What Alice Found There*. London: Penguin.

Castells, M. (1998) *End of Millennium*. Oxford: Blackwell.

_____ (1999) *The Information Society: The Rise of the Network Society*. Oxford: Blackwell.

Caughie, J. and S. Cubitt (eds) (1999) *Screen – Special Issue: FX, CGI and the Question of Spectacle*, 40, 2.

Certeau, M. de (1988) *The Practice of Everyday Life*. Trans. S. Rendall. Berkeley: University of California Press.

Chatman, S. (1978) *Story and Discourse; Narrative Structure in Fiction and Film*. Ithaca: Cornell University Press.

Chiang, T. (2002) *Stories of Your Life and Others*. New York: Tor Science Fiction.

Chun, W. (2005) *Control and Freedom: Power and Paranoia in the Age of Fiberoptics*. Cambridge: MIT Press.

Church Gibson, P. (1998) 'Film Costume', in J. Hill and P. Church Gibson (eds) *The Oxford Guide to Film Studies*. Oxford: Oxford University Press, 36–42.

Cilliers, P. (1998) *Complexity and Postmodernism: Understanding Complex Systems*. London: Routledge.

Clark, A. (2003) 'The Twisted Matrix: Dream, Simulation, or Hybrid?' Available online: http://whatisthematrix.warnerbros.html.

Clover, J. (2004) *The Matrix*. London: British Film Institute.

Connor, S. (1997) *Postmodernist Culture: An Introduction to Theories of the Contemporary* (revised edition). Oxford: Blackwell.

Constable, C. (2004) 'Postmodernism and Film', in S. Connor (ed.) *The Cambridge Companion to Postmodernism*. Cambridge: Cambridge University Press, 43–61.

Cowie, E. (1993) 'Film Noir and Women', in J. Copjec (ed.) *Shades of Noir: A Reader*. New York: Verso, 121–66.

Coyle, K. (1996) 'How Hard Can it Be?', in L. Cherney and E. R. Weise (eds) *Wired Women: Gender and New Realities in Cyberspace*. Seattle: Seal, 42–55.

Cubitt, S. (2004) *The Cinema Effect*. Cambridge: MIT Press.

Dangerfield, F. and N. Howard (1921) *How to be a Film Artiste*. London: Odhams.

Daniel, T. (2004) *Superluminal*. New York: HarperCollins.

Darley, A. (2001) *Visual Digital Culture: Surface Play and Spectacle in New Media Genres*. London: Routledge.

Darrow, G., A. Wachowski and L. Wachowski (2003) 'Bits and Pieces of Information', in *The Matrix Comics*. New York: Burleyman Entertainment, 5–11.

Davis, E. (2003) 'The Matrix Way of Knowledge'. Available online: http://archive.salon.com/books/feature/2003/05/21/davis/index2.html.

Debevec, P. (1997) 'The Campanile Movie: SIGGRAPH 97 Electronic Theater'. Available online: http://www.debevec.org/.

deCordova, R. (1990) *Picture Personalities: The Emergence of the Star System in America*. Chicago: University of Illinois Press.

Deleuze, G. (1983) *Cinema 1: The Movement-Image*. Trans H. Tomlinson and B. Habberjam.

Minnesota: University of Minnesota Press.

Dennett, D. C. (1991) *Consciousness Explained*. Boston: Little, Brown.

Dinerstein, J. (1999) 'Lester Young and the Birth of Cool', in G. Dagel Caponi (ed.) *Signifyin(g), Sanctifyin', & Slam Dunking: A Reader in African American Expressive Culture*. Amherst: University of Massachusetts Press, 239–76.

Dinning, M. (2003) 'The Big Boss', *Empire*, 14, 11, 84–92.

Doane, M. A. (1990) 'Technophilia: Technology, Representation and the Feminine', in M. Jacobus, E. F. Keller and S. Shuttleworth (eds) *Body/Politics: Women and the Discourses of Science*. London: Routledge, 163–76.

_____ (1991) *Femmes Fatales: Feminism, Film Theory, Psychoanalysis*. London: Routledge.

Doctorow, C. (2002) '0wnz0red', in *A Place So Foreign and 8 More*. New York: Four Walls Eight Windows, 208–43.

Dreyfus, H. and S. Dreyfus (2004) 'Existential Phenomenology and the Brave New World of *The Matrix*'. Available online: http://whatisthematrix.warnerbros.html.

Dyer, R. (1979) *Stars*. London: British Film Institute.

_____ (1988) 'White', *Screen*, 29, 4, 44–64.

_____ (1993 [1977]) 'Entertainment and Utopia', in S. During (ed.) *The Cultural Studies Reader*. London: Routledge, 271–83.

_____ (1997) *White*. London: Routledge.

Early, F. and K. Kennedy (eds) (2003) *Athena's Daughters: Television's New Women Warriors*. Syracuse: Syracuse University Press.

Easterbrook, N. (2000) 'Hybrids between Mundane and Maligned', *Science Fiction Studies*, 30, 3, 510–3.

Ebert, R. (2003a) *'The Matrix Reloaded'*, in *Chicago Sun-Times*. Available online: http://www.suntimes.com/ebert/ebert_reviews/2003/05/051401.html.

_____ (2003b) *'The Matrix Revolutions'* in *Chicago Sun-Times*. Available online: http://www.suntimes.com/ebert/ebert_reviews/2003/11/110503.html.

Eliot, T. S. (1962) *Collected Poems*. London: Faber & Faber.

Ellis, J. (1982) 'The Literary Adaptation: An Introduction', *Screen*, 23, 1, 3–5.

*Enter the Matrix Official Website*. Available online: http://www.enterthematrix.com.

Eskelinen, M. (2001) 'The Gaming Situation', *Game Studies*, 1, 1. Available online: http://www.gamestudies.org/0101/eskelinen/.

_____ (2002) 'From Markku Eskelinen's Online Response', in N. Wardrip-Fruin and P. Harrigan (eds) *First Person: New Media as Story, Performance, and Game*. Cambridge: MIT Press, 120–1.

Felluga, D. (2003) '*The Matrix*: Paradigm of Postmodernism or Intellectual Poseur, Part One', in G. Yeffeth (ed.) *Taking the Red Pill: Science, Philosophy and Religion in The Matrix*. Chichester: Summersdale, 85–101.

Feng, P. X. (2002) 'False and Double Consciousness: Race, Virtual Reality and the Assimilation of Hong Kong Action Cinema in *The Matrix*', in Z. Sardar and S. Cubitt (eds) *Aliens R Us: The Other in Science Fiction Cinema*. London: Pluto Press, 149–63.

Fine, G. A. (1983) *Shared Fantasy; Role-Playing Games as Social Worlds.* Chicago: Chicago University Press.

Fitting, P. (1991) 'The Lessons of Cyberpunk', in C. Penley and A. Ross (eds) *Technoculture.* Minneapolis: University of Minnesota Press, 295–316.

Flanagan, M. (1999) 'Mobile Identities, Digital Stars, and Post Cinematic Selves', *Wide Angle*, 21, 1, 77–93.

Flanagan, M. and A. Booth (2002) *Reload: Rethinking Women and Cyberculture.* Cambridge: MIT Press.

Fordham, J. (2003) 'Neo Realism', *Cinefex*, 95, 84–127.

Foster, T. (2005) *The Souls of Cyber-Folk: Posthumanism as Vernacular Theory.* Minneapolis: University of Minnesota Press.

Foucault, M. (1980 [1978]) *The History of Sexuality. Volume 1: An Introduction.* Trans. R. Hurley. New York: Vintage Books.

Frank, T. (1997) *The Conquest of Cool: Business Culture, Counterculture, and the Rise of Hip Consumerism.* Chicago: University of Chicago Press.

Frasca, G. (2003) 'Ludologists Love Stories too: Notes From a Debate that Never Took Place', in M. Copier and J. Raessens (eds) *Level Up Digital Games Research.* Utrecht: Universiteit Utrecht Press, 92–9.

Freedman, C. (2000) *Critical Theory and Science Fiction.* Hanover: Wesleyan University Press.

Freud, S. (1990 [1919]) 'The Uncanny', in J. Strachey *et al.* (eds) *The Penguin Freud Library Volume 14: Art and Literature.* Trans. J. Strachey. Harmondsworth: Penguin, 335–76.

Fusco, C. (2003) *Only Skin Deep.* New York: Harry Abrams.

Gabbard, K. (2003) 'Black Angels', *The Chronicle of Higher Education*, 49, 39, B15–6.

Gaiman, N. (1991–2004) *Sandman Series.* London: Titan.

_____ (2003a) *American Gods.* London: Headline.

_____ (2003b) *Coraline.* London: Bloomsbury.

_____ (2003c) 'Goliath', in *The Matrix Comics.* New York: Burleyman Entertainment, 41–8.

Gaines, J. (1990) 'Costume and Narrative: How Costume tells the Woman's Story', in J. Gaines and C. Herzog (eds) *Fabrications: Costume and The Female Body.* London: Routledge, 180–211.

Galouye, D. (1999 [1964]) *Simulacron-3.* Paris: J'ai Lu.

Genette G. (1980) *Narrative Discourse: An Essay in Method.* Trans. Jane E. Lewin. Ithaca: Cornell University Press.

Gibson, W. (1984) *Neuromancer.* London: HarperCollins.

_____ (1988) *Mona Lisa Overdrive.* London: HarperCollins.

_____ (1996) *Idoru.* Londom: Penguin.

Gillis, S. (2004) 'Cybersex', in P. Church Gibson (ed.) *More Dirty Looks: Gender, Pornography and Power.* London: British Film Institute, 92–101.

Gillis, S., G. Howie and R. Munford (eds) (2004) *Third Wave Feminism: A Critical Exploration.* Basingstoke: Palgrave.

Gillis, S. and R. Munford (2006) *New Popular Feminisms.* London: I.B. Tauris.

Gilman, S. (1985) 'Black Bodies, White Bodies', in H. Louis Gates (ed.) *Race, Writing, and Difference*. Chicago: Chicago University Press, 223–61.

Gordon, J. (1991) 'Yin and Yang Duke it Out', in L. McCaffrey (ed.) *Storming the Reality Studio: A Casebook of Cyberpunk and Postmodern Science Fiction*. Durham: Duke University Press, 196–202.

Gordon, A. (2003) '*The Matrix*: Paradigm of Postmodernism or Intellectual Poseur, Part Two', in G. Yeffeth (ed.) *Taking the Red Pill: Science, Philosophy and Religion in The Matrix*. Chichester: Summersdale, 102–23.

Gorky, M. (1960 [1896]) 'Review', in J. Leyda (ed.) *Kino: A History of the Russian and Soviet Film*. London: George Allen & Unwin, 407–9.

_____ (1985 [1896]) 'Gorky on the Films, 1896', in H. Kline (ed.) *New Theatre and Film: 1934 to 1937, an Anthology*. Trans. L. Mins. San Diego: Harcourt Brace Jovanovich, 227–31.

Green, N. (2001) 'Strange Yet Stylish Headgear: Virtual Reality Consumption and the Construction of Gender', in E. Green and A. Adam (eds) *Virtual Gender: Technology Consumption and Identity*. London: Routledge, 150–72.

Gunning, T. (1990) 'Non-Continuity, Continuity, Discontinuity: A Theory of Genres in Early Films', in T. Elsaesser (ed.) *Early Cinema: Space, Frame, Narrative*. London: British Film Institute, 86–94.

_____ (2000) '"Animated Pictures": Tales of Cinema's Forgotten Future, After 100 Years of Films', in C. Gledhill and L. Williams (eds) *Reinventing Film Studies*. London: Arnold, 316–31.

Haber, K. (ed.) (2003) *Exploring The Matrix: Visions of the Cyberpresent*. New York: Brion Preiss.

Hanley, R. (2003) 'Simulacra and Simulation: Baudrillard and *The Matrix*.' Available online: http://www.whatisthematrix.warnerbros.html.

Haraway, D. (1991) *Simians, Cyborgs, and Women: The Re-invention of Nature*. London: Routledge.

Haslam, J. (2005) 'Coded Discourse: Romancing the (Electronic) Shadow in *The Matrix*, *College Literature*, 32, 3, 92–115.

Hayles, N. K. (1999) *How We Became Posthuman: Virtual Bodies in Cybernetics, Literature, and Informatics*. Chicago: University of Chicago Press.

Heidegger, M. (1962 [1927]) *Being and Time*. Trans. J. Macquarrie and E. Robinson. Oxford: Blackwell.

_____ (1977 [1953]) *The Question Concerning Technology, and Other Essays*. Trans. W. Lovitt. New York: Harper & Row.

Helford, E. R. (2000) 'Postfeminism and the Female Action-Adventure Hero: Positioning Tank Girl', in M. Barr (ed.) *Future Females, The Next Generation: New Voices and Velocities in Feminist Science Fiction*. Lanham: Rowman and Littlefield, 291–308.

Hollinger, V. (1990) 'Cybernetic Deconstructions: Cyberpunk and Postmodernism', *Mosaic*, 23, 2, 29–44.

Hunt, L. (2003) *Kung Fu Cult Masters: From Bruce Lee to Crouching Tiger*. London: Wallflower Press.

Hunter-14180 (2003) *The Gaytrix: A Matrix Parody Action Comedy.* Available online: http://www.fanfiction.net.

Inness, S. A. (2004) 'Introduction', in S. A. Inness (ed.) *Action Chicks: New Images of Tough Women in Popular Culture.* Houndmills: Palgrave, 1–17.

Irwin, W. (ed.) (2002) *The Matrix and Philosophy.* Chicago: Open Court Press.

James, P. (1995). *Host.* New York: Villard.

Jameson, F. (1991) *Postmodernism, or, The Cultural Logic of Late Capitalism.* Durham: Duke University Press.

Jenkins, H. (1992) *Textual Poachers: Television Fans and Participatory Culture.* London: Routledge.

____ (2002) 'Game Design as Narrative Architecture', in N. Wardrip-Fruin and P. Harrigan (eds) *First Person: New Media as Story, Performance, and Game.* Cambridge: MIT Press, 118–30.

Johnson, S. (1997) *Interface Culture.* New York: Basic Books.

Jones, G. (2003) *Midnight Lamp.* London: Gollancz.

Juul, J. (2001) 'Games Telling Stories? A Brief Note on Games and Narratives', *Game Studies*, 1, 1. Available online: http://www.gamestudies.org/0101/juul-gts/.

____ (2003) 'The Game, the Player, the World: Looking for a Heart of Gameness', in M. Copier and J. Raessens (eds) *Level Up Digital Games Research Conference.* Utrecht: Universiteit Press, 30–47.

Kant, I. (1991 [1785]) *The Moral Law: Groundwork of the Metaphysic of Morals.* Trans. H. J. Paton. London: Routledge.

Kapell, M and W. G. Doty (2004) *Jacking in to the Matrix Franchise: Cultural Reception and Interpretation.* New York: Continuum.

Kaplan, E. A. (ed.) (1978) *Women in Film Noir.* London: British Film Institute.

Kerlow, I. V. (2003) *The Art of 3-D: Computer Animation and Imaging.* New York: John Wiley and Sons.

Kilbourn, R. (2000) 'Re-writing "Reality": Reading *The Matrix*', *Canadian Journal of Film Studies*, 9, 2, 43–54.

Kimball, A. S. (2001) 'Not Begetting the Future: Technological Autochthony, Sexual Reproduction and the Mythic Structure of *The Matrix*', *Journal of Popular Culture*, 35, 3, 175–203.

King, B. (1991) 'Articulating Stardom', in C. Gledhill (ed.) *Stardom: Industry of Desire.* London: Routledge, 167–82.

King, C. R. and D. J. Leonard (2004) 'Is Neo White? Reading Race, Watching the Trilogy,' in M. Kapell and W. G. Doty (eds) *Jacking in to the Matrix Franchise: Cultural Reception and Interpretation.* New York: Continuum, 32–47.

King, G. and T. Krzywinska (2002) *ScreenPlay: cinema/videogames/interfaces.* London: Wallflower Press.

Klein, N. M. (2004) *The Vatican to Vegas: A History of Special Effects.* New York: New Press.

Klinger, B. (1989) 'Digressions at the Cinema: Reception and Mass Culture', *Cinema Journal*, 28, 4, 3–19.

Krämer, P. (1998) 'Post-classical Hollywood', in J. Hill and P. Church Gibson (eds) *The Oxford Guide to Film Studies*. Oxford: Oxford University Press, 289–309.

Kücklich, J. (2003) 'Perspectives of Computer Game Philology', *Game Studies*, 3, 1. Available online: http://www.gamestudies.org/0301/kucklich.

Kuffner, A. (2001) 'Do The Right Thing: Be Wary of Movie Stereotypes, Spike Lee Says', *The Providence Journal*, B1.

Kuhn, A. (1990) 'Introduction: Cultural Theory and Science Fiction Cinema', in A. Kuhn (ed.) *Alien Zone: Cultural Theory and Contemporary Science Fiction Cinema*. London: Verso, 1–12.

Kuleshov, L. (1974 [1929]) 'Art of the Cinema', in R. Levaco (ed.) *Kuleshov on Film: Writings of Lev Kuleshov*. Trans. Ronald Levaco. Berkeley: University of California Press, 41–123.

Lamm, S. (2000) 'Foreword', in *The Art of The Matrix*. New York: Newmarket, 8.

____ (2003) 'Introduction,' in *The Matrix Comics*. New York: Burleyman Entertainment, 4.

Latour, B. (2003) 'Do You Believe in Reality? News from the Trenches of the Science Wars', in R. C. Scharff and V. Dusek (eds) *Philosophy of Technology: The Technological Condition*. Oxford: Blackwell, 126–37.

Lavery, D. (2001) 'Cinescape to Cyberspace: Zionists and Agents, Realists and Gamers in *The Matrix* and *eXistenZ*', *Journal of Popular Film and Television*, 28, 4, 150–7.

Lawrence, M. (2004) *Like a Splinter in Your Mind: The Philosophy Behind the Matrix Trilogy*. Oxford: Blackwell.

Lee, S. (2001) 'Thinking About the Power of Images: An Interview with Spike Lee', *Cineaste*, 26, 2, 4–9.

Levy, S. (1984) *Hackers: Heroes of the Computing Revolution*. New York: Dell Publishing.

Lindsay, J. (1985) *Turner: The Man and His Art*. London: Granada.

Lipp, M. (2004) 'Welcome to the Sexual Spectacle: The Female Heroes in the Franchise', in M. Kapell and W. G. Doty (eds) *Jacking in to the Matrix Franchise: Cultural Reception and Interpretation*. London: Continuum, 14–31.

Lipschutz, R. D. (2003) 'Aliens, Alien Nations, and Alienation in American Political Economy and Popular Culture', in J. Weldes (ed.) *To Seek Out New Worlds: Exploring Links Between Science Fiction and World Politics*. Basingstoke: Palgrave, 79–98.

Lupton, D. (2000 [1995]) 'The Embodied Computer/User', in D. Bell and B. M. Kennedy (eds) *The Cybercultures Reader*. London: Routledge, 477–88.

Luhmann, N. (1995) *Social Systems*. Stanford: Stanford University Press.

Madolan (1999) 'First Run'. Available online: http://www.fanfiction.net.

Mailer, N. (1957) *The White Negro*. San Francisco: City Lights.

Marinucci, M. (2003) 'Feminism and the Ethics of Violence: Why Buffy Kicks Ass', in J. B. South (ed.) *Buffy the Vampire Slayer and Philosophy*. Chicago: Open Court, 61–76.

Majors, R. and J. M. Billson (1992) *Cool Pose: The Dilemmas of Black Manhood in America*. New York: Lexington Books.

Manovich, L. (2001) *The Language of New Media*. Cambridge: MIT Press.

Marinetti, F. T. (1973 [1909]) 'Founding and Manifesto of Futurism 1909', in U. Apollonio (ed.) *Futurist Manifestos*. London: Thames and Hudson, 19–24.

Marriot, M. (2003) *The Matrix Cultural Revolutions: How Deep Does the Rabbit Hole Go?* New York: Thunder's Mouth Press.

Marx, K. (1992 [1843]) 'A Contribution to the Critique of Hegel's Philosophy of Right', in *Early Writings*. Trans. R. Livingstone and G. Benton. Harmondsworth: Penguin.

Marx, K. and F. Engels (1967 [1848]) *The Communist Manifesto*. Trans. S. Moore. Harmondsworth: Penguin.

*The Matrix Comics* (2003) New York: Burlyman Entertainment.

Maturana, H. and F. Varela (1980) *Autopoiesis and Cognition: The Realisation of the Living*. Dordrecht: Reidel.

McCaffery, L. (ed.) (1991) *Storming the Reality Studio: A Casebook of Cyberpunk and Postmodern Science Fiction*. Durham: Duke University Press.

McClintock, A. (2004) 'Maid to Order: Commercial S/M and Gender Power', in P. Church Gibson (ed.) *More Dirty Looks: Gender, Pornography and Power*. London: British Film Institute, 237–53.

McGinn, C. (2002) 'The Matrix of Dreams'. Available online: http://whatisthematrix.warnerbros.com.

McKeever, T. (2003) 'A Life Less Empty', in *The Matrix Comics*. New York: Burleyman Entertainment, 27–40.

McKenzie, J. (ed.) (1968) *The Anchor Bible: Second Isaiah*. New York: Doubleday.

McPherson, T. (2000) 'I'll Take My Stand in Dixie-Net', in B. Kolko, L. Nakamura and G. B. Rodman (eds) *Race and Cyberspace*. New York: Routledge, 117–31.

Mix, T. (1915) 'My Shadow and I: On and Off the Screen', in *Pictures and the Picturegoer*, 7, 56, 500.

Morrison, T. (1992) *Playing in the Dark: Blackness and the American Literary Imagination*. New York: Vintage.

Mugwum (2003) 'Review of *Enter the Matrix*'. Available online: http://www.eurogamer.net/article.php?article_id=52134.

Murray, J. H. (1997) *Hamlet on the Holodeck: The Future of Narrative in Cyberspace*. Cambridge: MIT Press.

Nakamura, L. (2002) *Cybertypes: Race, Ethnicity, and Identity on the Internet*. New York: Routledge.

Nathan, I. (2003) '*The Matrix*', in I. Freer (ed.) *The Ten Most Influential Sci-Fi Films of All Time*. London: *The Independent* and *Empire Magazine*, 12–13.

Neale, S. (2000) *Genre and Hollywood*. London: Routledge.

Nelson, A. (2002) 'Introduction: Future Texts', Special Issue: Afro-futurism. *Social Text*, 20, 2, 1–15.

Nietzsche, F. (1974 [1882]) *The Gay Science*. Trans. Walter Kaufmann. New York: Vintage.

O'Flaherty, W. D. (1980) 'Karma and Rebirth in the Vedas and Puranas', in W. D. O'Flaherty (ed.) *Karma and Rebirth in Classical Indian Traditions*. Berkeley: University of California Press, 3–37.

Oliver, P. (1990) *Blues Fell This Morning: Meaning in the Blues*. Cambridge: Cambridge University Press.

O'Toole, L. (1999) 'Interview with Keanu Reeves', *Time Out*, 14–15.

Parrenas, R. (2001) *Servants of Globalization: Women, Migration and Domestic Work*. Stanford: Stanford University Press.

Pearce, C. (2002) 'Towards a Game Theory of Game', in N. Wardrip-Fruin and P. Harrigan (eds) *First Person: New Media as Story, Performance, and Game*. Cambridge: MIT Press, 143–53.

Piercy, M. (1991) *Body of Glass*. London: Penguin.

Pierson, M. (2002) *Special Effects: Still in Search of Wonder*. New York: Columbia University Press.

Pirandello, L. (1985) *Six Characters in Search of an Author*. Trans. John Linstrum. London: Methuen.

Pisters, P. (2003) *The Matrix of Visual Culture: Working with Deleuze in Film Theory (Cultural Memory in the Present)*. Stanford: Stanford University Press.

Plato (1955) *Phaedo*. Trans. R. S. Bluck. London: Routledge & Kegan Paul.

_____ (1987) *The Republic*. Trans. Desmond Lee. Harmondsworth: Penguin.

Pountain, D. and D. Robins (2000) *Cool Rules: Anatomy of an Attitude*. London: Reaktion.

Prigogine, I. and I. Stengers (1984) *Order Out of Chaos: Man's New Dialogue with Nature*. London: Heinemann.

Prince, S. (1996) 'True Lies: Perceptual Realism, Digital Images and Film Theory', *Film Quarterly*, 49, 3, 27–37.

Rich, F. (2003) 'There's No Exit From the Matrix', *The New York Times*, Section 2, 1.

Romney, J. (2003) 'Everywhere and Nowhere', *Sight and Sound*, 13, 7, 24–7.

Ross, A. (1991) *Strange Weather: Culture, Science, and Technology in the Age of Limits*. New York: Verso.

Rovira, J. (2003) 'Subverting the Mechanisms of Control: Baudrillard and *The Matrix* Trilogy'. Available online: http://artisanitorium.thehydden.com/nonfiction/film/matrix.htm.

Rucker, R. (2004) *Frek and the Elixir*. New York: Tor Science Fiction.

Sajban, M. [aka 'Irish'] (2003) *Enter the Matrix FAQ/Walkthrough*. Available online: http://faqs.ign.com/articles/403/403763p1.html.

Said, E. (1978) *Orientalism*. London: Routledge.

Salen, K. and E. Zimmerman (2003) 'This Is Not A Game: Play In Cultural Environments', in M. Copier and J. Raessens (eds) *Level Up Digital Games Research*. Utrecht: Universiteit Utrecht Press, 14–29.

_____ (2004) *Rules of Play; Game Design Fundamentals*. Cambridge: MIT Press.

Sardar, Z. (2002) 'Introduction', in Z. Sardar and S. Cubitt (eds.) *Aliens R Us: The Other in Science Fiction Cinema*. London: Pluto Press, 1–17.

Sconce, J. (2000) *Haunted Media: Electronic Presence from Telegraphy to Television*. Durham: Duke University Press.

Scott, A. O. (2003) 'The Matrix: Revolutions', *The New York Times*. Available online: http://movies2.nytimes.com/gst/movies/movie.html?v_id=282917.

Scott, M. (1994) *Trouble and Her Friends*. New York: Tor Science Fiction.

Seay, C. and G. Garrett (2003) *The Gospel Reloaded: Exploring Spirituality and Faith in The Matrix*. Colorado Springs: Pinon.

Sellors, C. P. (2000) 'The Impossibility of Science Fiction: Against Buckland's Possible Worlds', *Screen*, 41, 2, 203–16.

Serres, M. (1995) *Angels: A Modern Myth*. Trans. F. Cowper. Paris: Flammarion.

Severini, G. (1973 [1913]) 'The Plastic Analogies of Dynamism – Futurist Manifesto 1913', in U. Apollonio (ed.) *Futurist Manifestos*. London: Thames and Hudson, 118–25.

Shaviro, S. (2003) *Connected: Living in a Networked Society*. Minneapolis: University of Minnesota Press.

Shelley, M. (1965 [1818]) *Frankenstein Or, The Modern Prometheus*. New York: New American Library.

Silver, D. (2002) 'theglobe.com: Image, Anti-image, and the Shifting Languages of New Media', Houston: Association of American Studies Annual Conference.

Snead, J. (1994) *White Screens, Black Images: Hollywood From the Dark Side*. New York: Routledge.

Sobchack, V. (2000 [1994]) 'New Age Mutant Ninja Hackers: Reading *Mondo 2000*', in D. Bell and B. Kennedy (eds) *The Cybercultures Reader*. London: Routledge, 138–48.

Solnit, R. (2003) *Motion Studies: Time, Space and Eadweard Muybridge*. London: Bloomsbury.

Spigel, L. (2001) *Welcome to the Dreamhouse: Popular Media and Postwar Suburbs*. Durham: Duke University Press.

Springer, C. (1999a) 'Psycho-cybernetics in Films of the 1990s', in A. Kuhn (ed.) *Alien Zone II: The Spaces of Science-Fiction Cinema*. London: Verso, 203–18.

_____ (1999b [1991]) 'The Pleasure of the Interface', in J. Wolmark (ed.) *Cybersexualities: A Reader on Feminist Theory, Cyborgs and Cyberspace*. Edinburgh: Edinburgh University Press, 34–54.

Staiger, J. (1999) 'Future Noir: Contemporary Representations of Visionary Cities', in A. Kuhn (ed.) *Alien Zone II: The Spaces of Science-Fiction Cinema*. London: Verso, 97–122.

Stam, R. (2000) 'Beyond Fidelity: The Dialogics of Adaptation', in J. Naremore (ed.) *Film Adaptation*. London: Athlone, 54–76.

Steele, V. (1996) *Fetish: Fashion, Sex and Power*. Oxford: Oxford University Press.

Stephenson, N. (1992) *Snow Crash*. New York: Bantam.

Sterling, B. (ed.) (1988) *Mirrorshades: The Cyberpunk Anthology*. London: Grafton.

_____ (2000) *Zeitgeist*. New York: Bantam.

Stoppard, T. (1966) *Rosencrantz and Guildenstern Are Dead*. London: Faber & Faber.

Street, S. (2001) *Costume and Cinema: Dress Codes in Popular Film*. London: Wallflower Press.

Stross, C. (2003a) 'Charles Stross: Exploring Distortions', *Locus: The Magazine of the Science Fiction & Fantasy Field*, 511, 84–6.

_____ (2003b) *Singularity Sky*. New York: Ace Books.

Tasker, Y. (1993) *Spectacular Bodies: Gender, Genre and the Action Cinema*. London: Routledge.

_____ (1998) *Working Girls: Gender and Sexuality in Popular Cinema.* London: Routledge.

Taylor, D. (1996) 'Virtual Camera Movement: The Way of the Future?', *American Cinematographer*, 77, 9, 93–100.

Telotte, J. P. (1989) *Voices in the Dark: The Narrative Patterns of Film Noir.* Urbana: Illinois University Press.

Terranova, T. (1996) 'The Posthuman Unbounded: Artificial Evolution and High-tech Subcultures', in G. Robertson (ed.) *Futurenatural: Nature, Science, Culture.* New York: Routledge, 165–80.

Turkle, S. (1995) *Life on the Screen: Identity in the Age of the Internet.* New York: Simon & Schuster.

Uhlmann, A. (1999) *Beckett and Poststructuralism.* Cambridge: Cambridge University Press.

UK Film Council (2003) *Film in the UK 2002: Statistical Yearbook.* London: UK Film Council.

Varley, J. (1978 [1976]) 'Overdrawn at the Memory Bank', in *The Persistence of Vision.* New York: Dial, 197–226.

*Video Game Review.* Available online: http://www.videogamereview.com.

Vinge, V. (1993) 'The Coming Technological Singularity: How to Survive in the Post-Human Era.' Available online: http://www-rohan.sdsu.edu/faculty/vinge/misc/singularity.html.

Wachowski, L. and A. (2000) '*The Matrix* Screenplay', in S. Lamm (ed.) *The Art of The Matrix.* London: Titan, 271–394.

Wegenstein, B. (2002) 'Shooting Up Heroines', in M. Flanagan and A. Booth (eds) *Reload: Rethinking Women and Cyberculture.* Cambridge: MIT, 332–54.

Wertheim, M. (2000) *The Pearly Gates of Cyberspace.* London: Virago.

West, C. (1994) *Race Matters.* New York: Vintage.

Wilde, O. (1986 [1889]) 'The Decay of Lying', in *De Profundis and Other Writings.* Harmondsworth: Penguin, 55–87.

Williams, L. (2001) *Playing the Race Card: Melodramas of Black and White from Uncle Tom to O. J. Simpson.* Princeton: Princeton University Press.

Williams, W. J. (2003) 'Yuen Woo-ping and the Art of Flying', in K. Haber (ed.) *Exploring the Matrix: Visions of the Cyber Present.* New York: Byron Preiss, 124–35.

Wolmark, J. (2002) 'Staying with the Body: Narratives of the Posthuman in Contemporary Science Fiction', in V. Hollinger and J. Gordon (eds) *Edging into the Future: Science Fiction and Contemporary Cultural Transformation.* Philadelphia: Pennsylvania University Press, 75–89.

Wood, A. (2002) 'The Timespaces of Spectacular Cinema: Crossing the Great Divide of Spectacle versus Narrative', *Screen*, 43, 4, 370–86.

_____ (2004) 'The Collapse of Reality and Illusion in *The Matrix*', in Y. Tasker (ed.) *Action and Adventure Cinema.* London: Routledge, 119–29.

Woolf, V. (1945 [1922]) *Jacob's Room.* London: Hogarth Press.

Wyatt, S. (2001) 'Growing Up in the Belly of the Beast', in F. Henwood, N. Miller and S. Wyatt (eds) *Cyborg Lives: Women's Technobiographies.* York: Raw Nerve, 77–90.

Yeffeth, G. (ed.) (2003) *Taking the Red Pill: Science, Philosophy and Religion in The Matrix.*

Chichester: Summersdale.

YukiYoshi (2004) *Zion Diaries*. Available online: http://www.fanfiction.net.

Žižek, S. (1993) '"The Thing that Thinks": The Kantian Subject of the Noir Subject', in J. Copjec (ed.) *Shades of Noir: A Reader*. London: Verso, 199–226.

_____ (1997) *The Plague of Fantasies*. New York: Verso.

_____ (2000) *The Art of the Ridiculous Sublime: On David Lynch's Lost Highway*. Seattle: Walter Chapin Simpson Center for the Humanities.

_____ (2001) *Enjoy your Symptom! Jacques Lacan in Hollywood and Out*, revised edition. London: Routledge.

_____ (2004) 'Reloaded Revolutions', *Purple*, 1,12, 328–34.

Zournazi, M. (2002) 'The Art of Living [Interview with Michel Serres]', in M. Zournazi (ed.) *Hope: New Philosophies for Change*. Sydney: Pluto Press, 192–208.

# FILMOGRAPHY

*2001: A Space Odyssey* (Stanley Kubrick, 1968, US)

*Alien* (Ridley Scott, 1979, US)

*The Animatrix* (2003, US)

    *A Detective Story* – dir. Shinichirô Watanbe

    *Beyond* – dir. Kôji Morimoto

    *Final Flight of Osiris* – dir. Andy Jones

    *Kid's Story* – dir. Shinichirô Watanbe

    *Matriculated* – dir. Peter Chung

    *Program* – dir. Yoshiaki Kawajiri

    *The Second Renaissance: Part I* – dir. Mahiro Maeda

    *The Second Renaissance: Part II* – dir. Mahiro Maeda

    *World Record* – dir. Takeshi Koike

*The Addams Family* (Barry Sonnenfeld, 1991, US)

*The Avengers* (ABC Weekend Television/Association British Picture Corporation, 1961–69, UK)

*Barb Wire* (David Hogan, 1996, US)

*Barton Fink* (Joel and Ethan Coen, 1991, US)

*Basic Instinct* (Paul Verhoeven, 1992, US)

*Batman* (Tim Burton, 1989, US)

*Being John Malkovich* (Spike Jonze, 2000, US)

*Blade Runner* (Ridley Scott, 1982, US)

*The Campanile Movie* (Paul Debevec, 1997, US)

*Charlie's Angels* (Joseph McGinty Nichol, 2000, US)

*The Cook, The Thief, His Wife and Her Lover* (Peter Greenaway, 1989, UK)

*Dandy Dust* (A. Hans Scheirl, 1998, UK/Austria)

*Disclosure* (Barry Levinson, 1994, US)

*Double Indemnity* (Billy Wilder, 1944, US)

*Enter the Dragon* (Robert Clouse, 1973, US)

*eXistenZ* (David Cronenburg, 1999, US)

*Final Fantasy: The Spirits Within* (Hironobu Sakaguchi and Moto Sakakibara, 2001, (US/Jap.)

*The Green Mile* (Frank Darabont,1999, US)

*GoldenEye* (Martin Campbell, 1995, UK/US)

*Ghost World* (Terry Zwigoff, 2000, US)

*Hardware* (Richard Stanley, 1990, UK/US)

*Hulk* (Ang Lee, 2003, US)

*The Hurricane* (Norman Jewison, 1999, US)

*The Invasion of the Body Snatchers* (Don Siegel, 1956, US)

*Johnny Mnemonic* (Robert Longo, 1995, US)

*Jubilee* (Derek Jarman, 1977, UK)

*Jui Kuen/Drunken Master* (Woo-ping Yuen, 1978, HK)

*Jurassic Park* (Steven Spielberg, 1993, US)

*Kill Bill: Volume 1* (Quentin Tarantino, 2003, US)

*Kill Bill: Volume II* (Quentin Tarantino, 2004, US)

*Kung Fu* (Warner Bros., 1972–75, US)

*Lara Croft: Tomb Raider* (Simon West, 2001, US)

*The Last Seduction* (John Dahl, 1994, US)

*Lawnmower Man* (Brett Leonard, 1992, US)

*Lawnmower Man 2* (Farhad Mann, 1996, US)

*The Lord of the Rings: The Fellowship of the Ring* (Peter Jackson, 2001, NZ/US)

*The Lord of the Rings: The Two Towers* (Peter Jackson, 2002, NZ/US)

*The Lord of the Rings: The Return of the King* (Peter Jackson, 2003, /NZ/US)

*The Maltese Falcon* (John Huston, 1941, UK)

*Making The Matrix* (Josh Oreck, 1999, US)

*The Mask* (Chuck Russell, 1994, US)

*The Matrix* (Andy and Larry Wachowski, 1999, US)

*The Matrix Reloaded* (Andy and Larry Wachowski, 2003, US)

*The Matrix Revisited* (Josh Oreck, 2001, US)

*The Matrix Revolutions* (Andy and Larry Wachowski, 2003, US)

*Metropolis* (Fritz Lang, 1926, Ger.)

*Minority Report* (Steven Spielberg, 2002, US)

*A Night to Remember* (Roy Ward Baker, 1958, UK)

*Olympiad* (Leni Riefenstahl, 1938, Ger.)

*Once Upon a Time in the West* (Sergio Leone, 1969, It./US)

*Point Break* (Kathryn Bigelow, 1991, US)

*The Postman Always Rings Twice* (Tay Garnett, 1946, US)

*The Remains of the Day* (James Ivory, 1993, UK)

*RoboCop* (Paul Verhoeven, 1987, US)

*Romeo and Juliet* (George Cukor, 1936, US)

*Romeo and Juliet* (Renato Castellani, 1954, It.)

*Romeo and Juliet* (Franco Zeffirelli, 1968, UK/It.)

*Romeo + Juliet* (Baz Luhrman, 1996, US)

*Scooby-Doo* (Raja Gosnell, 2002, US/Aus.)

*Seung fei/Princess D* (Sylvia Chang and Alan Yuen, 2002, Tai./HK)

*She xing diao shou/Snake in Eagle's Shadow* (Woo-ping Yuen, 1978, HK)

*Shurayukihime/Lady Snowblood: Lovesong of Vengeance* (Toshiya Fujita, 1973, Jap.)

*S1m0ne* (Andrew Niccol, 2002, US)

*Singin' in the Rain* (Stanley Donen and Gene Kelly, 1952, US)

*Space: 1999* (Group 3, 1975–77, US)

*Spider-Man* (Sam Raimi, 2002, US)

*Star Trek: The Next Generation* (Paramount Pictures, 1988–94, US)

*Star Wars: Episode I – The Phantom Menace* (George Lucas, 1999, US)

*Star Wars: Episode IV – A New Hope* (George Lucas, 1977, US)

*Star Wars: Episode V – The Empire Strikes Back* (Irvin Kerschner, 1980, US)

*Star Wars: Episode VI – The Return of the Jedi* (Richard Marquand, 1983, US)

*Starsky & Hutch* (Todd Phillips, 2004, US)

*The Stepford Wives* (Bryan Forbes, 1975, US)

*Strange Days* (Kathryn Bigelow, 1995, US)

*Super Mario Brothers* (Annabel Jankel and Rocky Morton, 1993, US)

*Superman* (Richard Donner, 1978, US)

*The Terminator* (James Cameron, 1984, US)

*Terminator 2: Judgement Day* (James Cameron, 1991, US)

*Terminator 3: The Rise of the Machines* (Jonathan Mostow, 2003, US)

*The Thirteenth Floor* (Josef Rusnak, 1999, Ger./US)

*Titanic* (James Cameron, 1997, US)

*TRON* (Steven Lisberger, 1982, US)

*Virtuosity* (Brett Leonard, 1995, US)

*WarGames* (John Badham, 1983, US)

*War of the Worlds* (Byron Haskin, 1953, US)

*West Side Story* (Jerome Robbins and Robert Wise, 1961, US)

*What is Bullet-Time?* (Josh Oreck, 1999, US)

*The Wizard of Oz* (Victor Fleming, 1939, US)

*Wonder Woman* (Warner Bros., 1976–79)

*X-Men* (Bryan Singer, 2000, US)

# GAMEOGRAPHY

*Baldur's Gate* (BioWare Corp., Pub. Black Isle Studios, 1998)
*Enter the Matrix* (Shiny Entertainment Inc., Pub. Atari Inc., 2003)
*Max Payne* (Rockstar Canada, Pub. Rockstar Games, 2001)
*Tomb Raider* (Core Design Ltd., Pub. Eidos Interactive, 1996)
*The Matrix On-Line* (Eon Digital Entertainment, Pub. Monolith Productions, 2004)

# INDEX

# LIQUID METAL
## The Science Fiction Film Reader
*Edited by Sean Redmond*

2004
366 pages
1-903364-87-6   £16.99 (pbk)
1-903364-88-4   £50.00 (hbk)

*Liquid Metal: The Science Fiction Film Reader* is the first extended collection of previously published essays on science fiction film and television. This Reader brings together a great number of seminal essays that have opened up the study of science fiction to serious critical interrogation. It is divided into eight distinct themed sections and includes important writings by Susan Sontag, Vivian Sobchack, Steve Neale, J. P. Telotte, Peter Biskind and Constance Penley amongst others, writing on films such as *Blade Runner, Alien, Star Wars, Total Recall, Them!* and *The Thing*.

Sean Redmond is Programme Director in Film, in the School of English, Film and Theatre at the Victoria University of Wellington, New Zealand. He is co-editor of *The Cinema of Kathryn Bigelow: Hollywood Transgressor* (2003) and contributor to *Contemporary North American Film Directors: A Wallflower Critical Guide* (2002).

> 'A significant collection of essays addressing the major themes that have informed the genre since it emerged on film and television screens in the 1950s ... it provides an invaluable – and singular – text for both students and scholars interested in surveying the key literature in the field and exploring a range of interpretive methods and critical practise.'
> *Prof. Vivian Sobchack, University of California, Los Angeles*

# THE BLADE RUNNER EXPERIENCE

The Legacy of a Science Fiction Classic

*Edited by Will Brooker*

2005
240 pages
1-904764-30-4   £15.99 (pbk)
1-904764-31-2   £45.00 (hbk)

Since its release in 1982, Ridley Scott's *Blade Runner*, based on Philip K. Dick's novel *Do Androids Dream of Electric Sheep?*, has remained a cult classic through its depiction of a futuristic Los Angeles, its complex, enigmatic plot and its underlying questions about the nature of human identity. *The Blade Runner Experience: The Legacy of a Science Fiction Classic* examines the film in a broad context, examining its relationship to the original novel, the PC game, the series of sequels, and the many films influenced by its style and themes. It investigates *Blade Runner* online fandom and asks how the film's future city compares to the present-day Los Angeles; and it revisits the film to pose surprising new questions about its characters and their world.

Contributors include Dominic Alessio, Barry Atkins, Aaron Barlow, Peter Brooker, Christy Collins, Jonathan Gray, Matt Hills, Deborah Jermyn, Judith Kerman, Nick Lacey, Sean Redmond, Stephen Rowley and Susana P. Tosca.

Will Brooker is Associate Professor in Communications at Richmond, the American International University in London. He is the author of *Batman Unmasked: Analyzing a Cultural Icon* (2000), *Using the Force: Creativity, Community and 'Star Wars' Fans* (2002) and *Alice's Adventures: Lewis Carroll in Pop* (2004) and co-editor of *The Audience Studies Reader* (2002).

35H

3541 200 3590 8548
0258407215?